"*The Anatomy of Organized Hate* high
the U.S. are actually outlawed at the s
report their experience to police, and
justice. The author explains why mc
that emerge from this cruel and deceptive gauntlet. Like the individuals profiled
here, one solution is for those who hate to reconsider their biases and rededicate
themselves to compassion."

MW00777064

Jason Marsden
Executive Director, Matthew Shepard Foundation

"There is both hope and despair found in the pages of *The Anatomy of Organized
Hate*. Hope in the stories of those who have left the world of hate and can now
reflect on their paths, despair because the problem is woven so deeply in our culture
and institutions. Fortunately, Lusardo's compelling narrative bridges those two
realities to give us a path out through strategies to reshape our relations to power.
In the end, we learn how to end hate from the hate mongers themselves."

Randy Blazak, Ph.D.
Chair, Oregon Coalition Against Hate Crimes
Former Sociology Professor, Portland State University

"Lonnie Lusardo has written the definitive exposé, including law enforcement's
abject failure to prevent, or even to report hate crimes. In this extraordinary new
book he tells the stories of former extremists convicted of malicious harassment, or
crimes committed because of the victim's actual or perceived race, color, religion,
ancestry, national origin, gender, sexual orientation, or mental, physical, or sensory
disabilities. Lusardo asks why a whopping 85 percent of police departments report,
year after year, zero hate crimes in their jurisdictions. Is there any wonder why
victims of bias crimes profoundly distrust or fear their local police? Read this book,
learn what you can do to turn this sad situation around."

Norm Stamper, Ph.D.
Seattle Chief of Police (Ret.)

The Anatomy of Organized Hate marks a monumental achievement that could very
well change the trajectory of how we combat hate in America. Lonnie Lusardo
has created a careful inventory of the types of hate crimes common in the U.S.
(from LGBT to those against people of color, those with disabilities or experiencing
homelessness, Muslims and Jews, and more) as well as the often myopic and
misinformed motivations behind them. The personal stories are particularly
compelling. But, the author explains, the onus for change is not on individuals
alone. Lusardo indicts the broader culture, the negative impact media mergers and
social media have had on journalistic standards, and the reality that many political
leaders today do more to stoke American extremism than stop it.

Diane Anderson-Minshall,
Editorial Director, The Advocate
Author, *Queerly Beloved: A Love Story Across Genders*

The
Anatomy
of
Organized
Hate

*Stories of Former
White Supremacists
and America's Struggle
to Understand
the Hate Movement*

Lonnie Lusardo

Anatomy of Organized Hate

Copyright © 2019 Lonnie Lusardo

For information, questions, or comments, contact:
www.diversitycollaborative.com or llusardo2@gmail.com

ISBN Paperback: 978-1-7331033-0-5
ISBN E-book: 978-1-7331033-1-2

Cover and interior design:
Illumination Graphics

For
LueRachelle Brim-Atkins
Colleague
Inspiration
"My Sister"

Table of Contents

Foreword

By Tim Wise

THIS YEAR IS AN ANNIVERSARY OF SORTS. And although the occasion hardly calls for celebration, it is worth noting nonetheless. This is especially true as the nation comes to grips with the rise of a reinvigorated white supremacist movement, an upsurge in overtly hateful violence, and a presidential administration that gives rhetorical aid and comfort to these same forces on a near weekly basis. Perhaps if we remember our not-so-distant past – maybe if we had paid more attention to it at the time and in its immediate aftermath – we could have seen this coming, after all.

As I write these words it has been exactly thirty years since David Duke – former head of the largest Ku Klux Klan group in the United States, and the nation's most prominent white supremacist – was elected to the Louisiana legislature. Victorious by a mere 227 votes, Duke rode a wave of white resentment towards welfare recipients, anger over affirmative action, and fear of "black crime" to political victory. He denied his ongoing connection to extremists and neo-Nazis of course. But even the most cursory of glances under the hood of his electoral machinery revealed the multitude of hateful sinews still attaching him to his past.

At the time of his election and for more than 18 months after it, Duke would continue to lead the National Association for the Advancement of White People (NAAWP). The group, which he founded upon leaving the Klan – but which observers had called "the Klan without robe or ritual" – had long advocated the breaking up of America into separate

1

racial sub-nations, the creation of a eugenic sterilization program for people of color (and government subsidies for the breeding of superior whites), and had sold books like The Hitler We Loved and Why from the back pages of its newsletter, among other Nazi-inflected tomes. But despite attempts to expose his ongoing affiliations with any number of hateful groups, individuals and ideologies, he had managed to win election anyway. Within ten months he would announce his plans to run for even higher office – this time the United States Senate – by throwing his hat in the ring against a sitting Democrat who would be up for re-election in 1990.

Though Duke would lose that race, and his next electoral attempt the following year for Governor, those of us who were centrally involved in the efforts to defeat him, had a saying about those elections. They had been referenda on hate, and hate had won. Oh sure, Duke had lost, but in both the Senate and Gubernatorial elections he had managed to capture between fifty-five and sixty percent of the white vote. Had it been up to white Louisianans, a Nazi – someone whom we learned had thrown literal birthday parties for Hitler and insisted the Holocaust of European Jewry had never happened – would have represented us in Washington or Baton Rouge. Only high turnout by black folks in the state had saved us.

In the wake of those elections more than a little ink was spilled by journalists and pundits trying to figure out what had happened. How had someone like Duke come so close to wielding real power? Although reactionary politicians had been dog-whistling to racists for years, from George Wallace to Richard Nixon to Ronald Reagan – the latter of whom told phony campaign stories about "strapping young bucks" buying steaks with food stamps and a "welfare queen" in Chicago who drove to pick up her checks in a Cadillac – Duke was hardly dog-whistling. Though he denied his allegiance to overt white supremacy, his campaigns were transparently rooted in a politic of white resentment and grievance. If he could come so close to winning, and indeed get most whites to support him, even without having to be subtle, what might that portend for the nation?

To some, of course, Duke was written off as a product of the peculiarities of Louisiana politics. We were just different, some tried to explain. After all, in the Governor's race, voters were ultimately asked to choose between Duke and former three-time Governor Edwin Edwards, known for his romantic exploits to say nothing of the kind of legal irregularities that would ultimately land him in prison several years after he completed his fourth term. Only in Louisiana, they insisted (perhaps in an attempt to convince themselves), could the Governor's race come down to a criminal and a Nazi, prompting the anti-Duke organization with which I worked to craft the campaign slogan, "Vote for the Crook – It's Important," as an attempt at both political persuasion and dark humor in dangerous times.

But Louisiana wasn't that different. A year after Duke lost the Governor's race, Pat Buchanan launched his campaign for President, in which he exploited the same race-based themes upon which Duke had focused. Buchanan even admitted he was stealing from Duke's playbook of "winning issues," in an attempt to build his political movement. Though his campaign fell short, he garnered millions of votes from angry whites, and gave a speech at the 1992 Republican National Convention that many likened to a Nuremberg rally, both for its themes of "us versus them," and for the orgiastic reaction it received from those assembled.

Even when Bill Clinton won the presidency that year, let us recall, he won while talking about "ending welfare as we know it," and campaigning on a "tough on crime" message, both of which harkened back to those racialized issues that had been so central to Duke's campaigns. And it was Clinton who signed a crime bill in 1994 that everyone knew would – and which ultimately did – disproportionately target black communities, especially for non-violent drug offenses. And it was Clinton who signed a welfare reform bill that everyone knew would – and which ultimately did – intensify hardship for millions (again, disproportionately people of color), once the 1990s economic boom evaporated and the nation entered recession in 2008.

No, Duke was not (is not) a product of Louisiana's swamps, either the literal ones or those of a political nature. Rather, he is a product of America. He is the product of a nation that for hundreds of years has failed to address its legacy of white domination and the subordination of black and brown peoples. That legacy has inculcated in far too many the notion that white prerogatives and advantages should remain unquestioned and intact, and that peoples of color are to remain in their place, and surely not in our neighborhoods or the schools our children attend. So that when the nation begins to change, however slowly it may seem at times, the shifts are seen as cataclysmic by millions. The election of Barack Obama, the meltdown of the economy – which confronted millions of whites with a type of economic insecurity unseen since the 1930s – a popular culture that is now thoroughly multicultural, and the demographic changes underway in the nation, all have conspired to create the perfect storm for white anxiety.

And into the breach of that storm, into that maelstrom, stepped Donald Trump, with his calls to "Make America Great Again." Though not an experienced and deeply ideological racist like Duke, Trump has proved himself to be a far better salesman of the product. His campaign began with bigoted harangues about Mexican rapists, drug dealers and murderers – and calls to build a wall between the U.S. and Mexico – and featured a non-stop litany of racial and religious grievance claims. Those people were taking your jobs. Those people were coming to kill you. Those people were terrorists. Those people needed to be profiled or stopped-and-frisked by police. Those people (Muslims) needed to be blocked from entering the country altogether. The politics of Dukism were not a one-off. And they weren't defeated. They metastasized and now, in only a slightly less obvious form, govern the nation we share.

All of which is a long-winded but necessary way to say that the book you have before you now could not come at a better time. In these pages Lonnie Lusardo has done us all a great service. First, by exploring the personal aspect of white supremacy, hatred and extremist ideology – encapsulated in the stories told by the former adherents to those ideologies he interviews – but even more so in the way he connects those stories to a larger and more collective narrative.

Too often we look at neo-Nazis, Klansmen, skinheads and other individuals in the hate movement as outliers. In fact, viewing them in this way provides the rest of us with a kind of comforting distance. It's a way of saying, "look at those horrible racist white people . . . over there. Gosh, I sure am glad I'm not one of them, and that I don't even know anyone like that." The problem, on this accounting, is someone else. Such a narrative allows us to preserve our own sense of innocence, and to ignore the ways that we all have been exposed to racist thinking, racial stereotypes about people of color, and a society in which racial inequities have been so normalized as to be taken for granted. Indeed, they are taken for granted by far more than just the types of people who burn crosses on lawns, paint swastikas into their skin, or carry torches around the University of Virginia before rallying in defense of white power and murdering an anti-racist protester, as happened in Charlottesville in 2017.

But what this volume shows us is that the thing we call extremism is just a more acute form of a chronic national disease – one especially blatant symptom of a virus that has been lurking in the cells of the nation from the beginning. What racist extremists represent is not a break with the national tradition, but a carrying out of that tradition to its logical, if terrifying conclusion. They are not separate and apart from us. They are part of us, and we are part of them, however much we might try and avoid acknowledging the harrowing truth. When a nation is founded as a white settler colony, with liberty and justice for some (putting aside the lofty rhetoric suggesting a universality of such things), it really ought not surprise us that some who see white hegemony threatened might turn to particularly hateful and even violent movements to reassert their dominance.

This is especially true if their own lives have turned out to be less than they expected and hoped for. After all, in a nation that promises success to anyone who makes the effort – that is our secular faith, the myth of rugged individualism – to see yourself as a failure requires of you either the internalization of self-hate or the projection of one's own inadequacies onto others. Or both. But in any event, the racism and the self-loathing are products of the American experiment. They are not mutations. They are examples of simple cell division.

Unlike so many other volumes on the subject, *The Anatomy of Organized Hate* seeks to connect the dots between the personal, the political and the structural. Lusardo notes the way that the targets of organized extremist groups are not randomly chosen, but mirror the same targets of systemic violence going back hundreds of years. The haters, it seems, have learned the lessons of their nation well. This book also makes clear how, even in the face of hateful and bigoted violence by so-called extremists, the system of law enforcement (and even the system of data collection to keep up with such actions) is wholly inadequate to the task. And what does this suggest, if not that to some degree we don't really value the lives of those targeted by hate any more than the haters themselves do?

Furthermore, Lusardo explains the way hate groups and their members make use of mainstream tools, first and foremost media, to spread their message. Indeed, white supremacists have proved far more adept at new media and web-based communication than most over the years, and it was Don Black of Stormfront who was setting up a network for such interaction in the earliest days of the internet, before most of us even had e-mail addresses. This is not your grandfather's hate movement, in other words.

The image of toothless, ignorant, uneducated rubes as the norm for white supremacists is not only false, it's dangerous. The people highlighted in this volume are not stupid. Nor are many of their contemporaries who have remained in the movement. They are well-versed in the politics of racism, and they often know American history better than the rest of us do. When Richard Spencer, one of the nation's leading white nationalists, says America was founded by and for white men, he's only being slightly hyperbolic. His version of the founding is quite a bit more accurate than the rosy, kumbaya version often peddled by textbooks and well-meaning but naïve chroniclers of the American experiment, still devoted to the melting pot narrative, as if that's really what slave-owners and Indian killers had had in mind.

But the fact that America was founded in white supremacy is not to say that it must remain as such. Past is not prologue unless we wish it so. We can create different futures. And just as those founders sowed the soil of our national biases and inequities, so too did they – and many freedom fighters since them – provide us with certain roadmaps out of white domination. The constitution, the notion of equal protection (however regularly disregarded it has been), the promise of equality, the examples of the abolitionists, the suffragettes, the civil rights movement, women's movement, LGBT liberation struggle and labor movements – all of these point to a different way.

And so too, the stories of the "defectors" or "formers" in this volume tell us something about alternative endings. They suggest that even the most broken of us is not beyond redemption. That even the sickest can get well. That we are not merely the worst things we have done, or said, or believed.

Let us hope that this truth, so masterfully demonstrated for the individuals highlighted in this important book, will also prove true for the nation as a whole, and for the world. Or rather, let us not hope for this. Let us work to make it so.

Introduction

AFTER 13 YEARS OF RESEARCH INTO THE BEHAVIORS of former white supremacists and the hate movement in general, I've discovered that what most Americans know or believe about hate groups and hate crimes is misleading, grossly incomplete, and often dead wrong. Our most trusted sources of information often do not include adequate information to draw reasonable conclusions.

This book is written in two parts: Part One is profiles of six individuals. I also talked to more than two dozen other defectors by phone and email and reviewed countless media reports and online biographies. Part One closes with an analysis of the characteristics defectors have in common and makes their stories so important for the rest of us.

Part Two extends beyond personal stories to reveal the underlying factors that cause the hate movement to persevere. Part Two builds on the premise that **The Father of All Hate Groups Is The United States Government** and reviews a historical pattern of exclusionary laws, Presidential orders and governmental policies designed to eliminate Constitutional rights to some Americans and block others from ever becoming U.S. citizens. Those policies disregarded or took freedoms away from the very same categories of people targeted by hate groups – "minorities" defined by their skin color, race, religion, sexual orientation, gender identity, disabilities – and other marginalized populations.

Most of the six women and men featured in Part One are pioneers who first shared their experiences at a time when other former extremists said nothing. From their pasts, in addition to research from experts across the U.S., we can understand how people fall under the spell of savvy recruiters and charismatic leaders. We can also be more cautious when our own emotions veer to extremes.

As these profiles attest, some defectors can – and do – abandon their former roles and risk serious consequences to publicize the circumstances of their conversion. They describe in vivid detail how they converted from white supremacist extremists to advocates *against* racism, homophobia, anti-Semitism, and other forms of hatred. Their candid disclosures help us learn what non-extremists – everyday bigots and bullies – can learn from their experience.

The narratives in these pages satisfy an overwhelming curiosity. How do ordinary people just like me get lured into organized hate groups and harm innocent bystanders? Once they embrace radical beliefs or distorted ideologies, what motivates them to abandon such a lifestyle?

I am a recovering racist. I grew up in a racist, anti-Semitic, and homophobic environment. The racial epithets and slurs I learned in my youth were routinely used in my childhood home, at school, and among my closest friends. Although no one I know has ever been part of an organized hate group, I was hard-wired to see myself as higher on some mysterious evolutionary scale than non-white people, oblivious to the privileges that came from my being a child of white parents.

That paradigm began to shift in the early 1960s when I started to question my own identity and realized my sexual orientation was not the norm. After four years in the U.S. Navy, I understood that, despite its drawbacks, being gay offered a different perspective on humanity. I saw that the lives of other marginalized people were so much easier to appreciate. Putting down others because of their race, religion, gender, or whatever difference, no longer made sense. *I was one of them.*

In 1981, I experienced the other side of hate, as the victim of a violent hate crime committed by four enraged Spanish-speaking men who saw me exit a popular gay bar in Key West, Florida. Throwing beer bottles at me from a moving vehicle as I mounted my bicycle, they shouted the contemptible terms gay men are forced to endure. Then the car stopped, they leaped out and started punching and kicking mercilessly, leaving me for dead on a quiet sidewalk.

Without those personal experiences, this book would have been impossible to assemble.

I interviewed more than two dozen defectors who served in leadership positions in one or more hate groups. Most had been convicted of hate crimes (also called bias crimes or malicious harassment) and served time in prison for their offenses. All are repentant, as measured by personal actions since they left the movement, some more so than others. They continue to reconcile the harm they caused to innocent people. Interviews focused on emotions, core values, and personal accounts, as well as family life, religious upbringing, and interactions with people from cultures unlike their own.

Leadership roles in the movement varied from organizer, newsletter editor, and recruiter to the founders of some of the most violent skinhead groups in the U.S. Some were involved in national organizations such as the National Alliance, Church of the Creator, and others. One was the religious director and number two leader of a Christian Identity group with more than 150 members, nestled in a rural compound shielded deep in the Ozarks. Others led smaller groups, like a handful of skinheads living conspicuously in a neighborhood along Main Street USA or invisibly in a tiny suburban town. The hate groups they were a part of have been identified and described by government agencies and major watchdog organizations, notably the Southern Poverty Law Center (SPLC) and the Anti-Defamation League (ADL), as well as by scholarly researchers at universities and think tanks.

The courageous individuals who tell their stories here experienced profound emotional shake-ups. They chose defection only after internalized moral and ethical struggles. They no longer share the values and beliefs inculcated by followers coerced into a lockstep fight for white superiority. Their conversions didn't come overnight and were neither easy nor simple. For them, unlearning is impossible and relearning never stops.

But, courageous does not mean heroic. Most of the subjects here committed multiple hate crimes and leave behind a trail of injuries and damaged lives in their path. It would be unfair to recognize only their courage without acknowledging a violent history.

The women and men profiled in these pages have followed an often-painful trajectory through a dramatic series of events that eventually brought them enlightenment. Their transformation includes lost friendships, a criminal record, and persistent memories they would much rather forget. Their path blends a formula of equal parts self-forgiveness, reconciliation, and atonement. Some manage their past quietly, while others have written autobiographies, appeared in films, launched websites and blogs, created radio programs, served as educators and advocates for civil rights and human rights groups, or entered the public speaking circuit.

Their stories reflect a composite of agonizing, multi-faceted events in the lives of ordinary people who joined, and now shun, neo-Nazi-styled and other white supremacist groups. The ability defectors use to explore their experiences with a liberated hindsight helps us examine what causes otherwise loving people to mimic a consciousness collectively referred to as the hate movement. Perhaps more important, their first-hand know-how helps us discern how to level the arc from irresponsibility to more balanced and life-affirming personal choices in the face of human differences. If these narratives open a dialogue about race alone, separate from all other human conflicts, perhaps homegrown American racism will become more apparent for those with the mistaken belief that we are living in a post-racist society.

Extensive help came from SPLC and ADL, two organizations without which the hate movement would be a much greater threat. I also interviewed university professors in the fields of psychology and sociology, criminology, communications, and technology, as well as police officers, prosecutors, and lawyers.

My research relied almost exclusively on the subjects themselves, with little opportunity to corroborate or verify information. Media reports were helpful, although exceedingly limited because of an abysmal lack of investigative reporting into the hate groups they represented. For those whose crimes were committed more than a decade prior to our interview, beyond the legal time limit police are required to store files, Freedom of Information requests had outlived their value. Based on anecdotal evidence, the narratives provide a flavor of each person's life before, during, and after their involvement in a hate group. Each profile describes the incidents that led to their decision to abandon the movement, or a single pivotal event that caused them to question why they were there.

Defectors agree that the most common pathway to accepting differences lies in finding common ground with people from groups they previously targeted for their assumed "inferiority." Some catalyst triggered an oddly unexpected relationship. In their past, talking with such a person was equal to consorting with the enemy – until they saw each other as equals.

New entrants to the hate movement relinquish their own values in order to assimilate a white supremacist ideology. By spending time with newly adopted comrades, they absorb a progression of hate that vilifies the most common targets of hate groups – people of color, members of non-Christian religions, people with disabilities, homeless and LGBTQ people, and others. As they become indoctrinated, they are rewarded for employing brutal tactics, such as defacing property, threats and intimidation, harassing people emotionally or physically, and in the most extreme situations, arson and murder. Advancements in the movement are honored by permission to show a new element that reflects the group's identity: a uniform, boots, shoe laces, or a distinctive patch, tattoos or other symbols that separate them from mainstream norms.

Examples of shifting values are apparent in every profile. Defectors say that only when they could no longer tolerate the trail of denials, hypocrisies, bizarre beliefs, or extreme behaviors of their group's leaders and members, were they able to start thinking about severing their ties. Only then could they plan an exit strategy, including how to manage the wrath of former colleagues and return to their personal values and integrity, if not their sanity.

I make no effort to apologize for the behaviors of former extremists or make them appear as something they are not. Those profiled in these pages are intensely aware of the devastating brutality they imposed on people and communities. In addition to hate crimes, some were also tried and convicted of assault, for building arsenals of illegal weapons, and other offenses.

Their crimes, some of which did not legally qualify as malicious harassment, also include battery, breaking and entering, burglary, manufacturing and storing illegal firearms, harboring known fugitives and other convicted criminals, obstruction of justice, attempted murder, and other felonies. Incidents not prosecuted as a hate crime were often committed in the context of hate. These offenses include robbery to fund the needs of a hate group, making weapons specifically to be used for hate crimes, and hiding known killers with histories of offenses against marginalized people. One defector told me about having a role in an unsolved murder.

Part Two uncovers the background of federal laws and policies that served as a mold for organized hate groups to emulate. These chapters disclose how a growing number of hate groups put more pressure on law enforcement. Among the biggest challenges facing police today is the evolution of lone wolf zealots acting on the ideology or doctrine of a group to which they have no known connection. In addition, a growing number of "whites-only" websites unite hundreds of thousands of American domestic terrorists behind an undercover online presence. While such sites identify themselves as "whites-only," they are accessible by anyone who cares to read their content.

Social media capitalize on First Amendment rights. That includes a Constitutional protection of statements saying all members of a protected category should be murdered.

Technology has driven one-time clandestine operations even deeper underground so that extreme right wing operatives are now able to function below law enforcement radar. The political power of the radical right also creates a sweeping influence of exclusion and outright hatred from within the highest of political offices, an effort further fueled by the resources of highly financed lobbying groups that aim to destroy any organization or political candidate proclaiming to share progressive values.

Part Two describes how technology and social media have changed how hate groups operate and examines the extent to which American institutions have contributed to cultural norms that tolerate hate rather than calling for its end. It also investigates the role the government has had in fostering a social environment that protects the majority over marginalized people.

This book is not intended to serve as a resource for legal guidance. Should questions arise about laws in your state, contact your state's Attorney General's office or the state's and regional Human Rights Commission, Equal Employment Opportunity Commission. Regional chapters of the SPLC, ADL, ACLU, and local legal services organizations can also be helpful, as well as many nonprofit legal services that may be able to provide legal representation at little or no cost to victims of a hate crime. Various community organizations created to help citizens in protected categories are also able to offer support and guidance.

Throughout the text, hate crimes are also referred to interchangeably as bias crimes, bias-oriented crimes, or acts of malicious harassment, all with the same meaning.

Note: I chose to put the word "minorities" in quotes for three reasons: one, the term minority suggests "lesser than," putting so-called "minorities" at a psychological disadvantage rather than being recognized as equals; two, on a global scale, ethnic "minorities" and people of color vastly outnumber white people; and three, census data show that by 2043 most populations currently considered "minorities" will be the majority.

PART ONE

From Hate to Compassion/
Defectors' Stories

*"I imagine one of the reasons people cling to hate
so stubbornly is because they sense once hate is gone,
they will be forced to deal with their pain."*

James Baldwin, *The Fire Next Time*

PART ONE

Kerry Noble:

The Rise and Fall of CSA

CSA Rising

KERRY NOBLE HAD THE ENTIRE CONGREGATION at the Kansas City, Missouri, Metropolitan Community Church in the palm of his hand, and the former Baptist preacher wasn't even in the pulpit.

On a sunny day in June 1984, Kerry climbed the steps to the one-time Baptist stronghold at the corner of East 40th Street and Harrison, entering a house of worship primarily for lesbians and gay Christians who had abandoned more traditional denominations. Kerry wore his Sunday best. He glided through the doors with a friend at his side, expressly to leave with a new and unique bond between them. For a man who had been ridiculed by elementary school classmates because a health condition forced him to take gym classes with girls, the moment was a monumental achievement for him and a huge step for his community.

Uniting with the congregation that morning, at the age of 32, ended a series of decisions Kerry and his companion had worked through before they got there. They hoped their latest decision, a big one for both, would create controversial headlines in newspapers across the United States and beyond. They were ready.

The two were not about to advance a shift in national thinking on same-sex marriage 15 years before any state in the U.S. had adopted

---

The author has received permission from Kerry Noble to use excerpts from his two books, *Tabernacle of Hate: Why They Bombed Oklahoma City* and *Saved By My Enemies*.

marriage equality. Nor were they about to join together in holy matri-
mony before God and the roughly 60 to 70 congregants seated in the
pews. They had a different plan and they were in it together. For better
or for worse.

Greeted warmly and escorted solemnly to their seats, the two edged
nervously into a pew toward the rear of the sanctuary. They tried their
best to blend seamlessly into the assembly. Kerry was a little fidgety.
Both devout Christians, this was the first time either man had attended
a gay service.

Neither man was gay. Yet aside from a friendship united over years,
they had something between them others in the church did not. In his
hand, Kerry clutched the handle of a briefcase, gently placing it at his
feet. Tucked inside were enough Composite C4 military explosives and
dynamite to blow the church into the heavens and kill everyone in it.
Their plan was mass destruction. They wanted people to die, specifically
lesbian, gay, bisexual, transgender, and gender non-conforming people.

They also wanted the world to know the dead deserved a violent
death. As if murder were not an adequate toll, the amount of firepower
in the briefcase would have leveled the historic building to a heap of
charred rubble, human remains co-mingled with the remnants of every
other building standing on the entire city block. Instead, on a whim,
the plan was aborted.

Kerry, who helped to conceive the bombing plot, got help from
colleagues at a group called The Covenant, The Sword, and The Arm
of the Lord (CSA). CSA was part of a Christian-oriented network
known as Christian Identity (CI). Despite adopting elements from
the Old Testament, CI groups have no relationship to Christian theology. CI is part of the nationwide hate movement. Adherents, often
extreme fundamentalists and anti-Semites, believe non-Christians and
non-Caucasians have no soul and that members of other races can never
earn God's favor.

In 2014, 19 CI groups in the U.S. were identified as hate groups
by the Southern Poverty Law Center (SPLC). As second in command
at CSA, one of the largest CI groups at the time, Kerry had persuaded
other CSA leaders to leverage the Kansas City plan as a pathway to
international recognition. But the bombing didn't go as planned. In his

words, and confirmed in FBI reports, had the bombing been carried out, Kerry would have masterminded and executed the largest domestic terrorist act in U.S. history.

Before he and his CSA colleague entered the Kansas City church, Kerry had traversed an extraordinary path that, at the outset, would never have included deliberate death and destruction. It was partially because of his belief in CSA founder James (Jim) Ellison and the progression of hate within the CSA camp, a development that he knew did not sit well with his wife, Kay, that when he drove north that day, Kerry had been careful not to share his intentions with his loving spouse.

Decades after the ominous Kansas City trip, Kerry cut to the quick. "All we had to do was flip one switch to set the timer." He went over every detail of the plan. Sitting in his office, surrounded by plaques and awards from Toastmasters International and in recognition of speaking engagements, Kerry described how the plot was solidified only after two failed attempts the night before he and his accomplice entered the church. The called-off bombing ended a series of potentially deadly events at three separate venues, each endeavor foiled by quirky circumstances. Minus the threatening stakes, the decision to halt the bomb plot involved a chain of events that borders on slapstick.

The idea to bomb the church had not been part of the original plan. Before the bombing plot was hatched, a Plan A blueprint called for murdering gays by gunfire. After hearing rumors about widespread public sex between men that made a popular Kansas City park sound to Kerry like some modern-day Sodom and Gomorrah, he and his colleague armed themselves with a .22 pistol and silencer. They were fully intent on cold-bloodedly killing as many gay men as possible in the act of unrestrained sex. They discovered they themselves were the only men cruising through the trees that night.

After the murders in the park failed to materialize and still hot on killing gays, Kerry and his accomplice devised Plan B. Because Ellison hated porn shops, they searched for just such an establishment. It didn't take long for the two to find a small X-rated storefront. From the door, Kerry could see peepshow booths in the back. The plan was to find a quiet corner inside, set the timer, plant the briefcase, and bolt before the cataclysm reduced the building and its customers to a pile of smoking debris. After the fruitless park scene, Kerry and friend were nearly giddy with visions of detonating the bomb and, from a distance, watching the building disintegrate.

When they entered the porn shop, the cashier and sole employee invited them to use the facilities as they pleased. The man then politely said to Kerry, "You can set the briefcase here until you're ready to leave." They froze. The two quietly left the store, bomb in hand. Another tragedy averted. Discouraged and disappointed, Kerry and his CSA colleague decided to spend the night at a hotel in Kansas City and see if a new plan would arise the next day. In telling the story, Kerry steadfastly declined to reveal the name of the man who accompanied him on the trip.

Plan C came from heaven. In their room that night, as the two rested after their escapades in the park and the porn shop, Kerry's accomplice regaled him with stories about growing up in Kansas City. In fact, the man fumed, the very same Baptist church where he used to worship as a child was now a gay church.

Bingo.

Kerry interpreted the coincidence of his friend's childhood church converting to a gay place of worship as an unambiguous sign from God. He was convinced the church was supposed to be their target from the start. After a night of rest, they arose early to set Plan C in motion.

Sitting in sunlight cast through a stained glass window, Kerry's plot took an unexpected twist. Minutes before activating the detonator, he was swept by an epiphany that would neutralize the plan and change his life forever.

After all the planning and the visions of physical and human destruction, Kerry made a spontaneous and impulsive decision to spare lives and advance his own redemption. Rather than activate the timer and coolly exit the church in time to witness the carnage from a distance, he convinced his colleague to sit tight through the service.

Why the sudden reversal to a detailed strategy that required scheduling, coordination, weapons, and driving over 250 miles with the sole intent of wreaking untold havoc on unsuspecting women and men? Contrary to what he envisioned, Kerry was surprised to see the

worshipping sinners the same as any other Christian assembly. "The
people were not horrible looking," Kerry recalls thinking at the time.
"They didn't look like the devil. They were not stereotypical. They were
fully dressed. They were not openly flaunting homosexuality. They were
not what I expected." The only difference was that men sat on one
side of the aisle and women on the other. Pressed to describe what he
had expected to encounter, Kerry acknowledged, "I wouldn't have been
surprised to see orgies in the aisles of that church."

"Overall," Kerry told me, "what I saw was different from a traditional church. We observed many parishioners holding hands, arms
around each other, giving a peck on the cheek." These were expressions
of love Kerry had never seen between same-sex partners. The image was,
evidently, not quite as offensive as he'd anticipated.

The lack of immediate disgust as he saw LGBTQ people on their
own turf suggests Kerry had entered territory that followers of hate
groups avoid at all cost – relating to the victim. "I immediately realized
on a subconscious level that I was starting to put a face on the enemy,"
he said. "These were no longer blanket-label homosexuals. They were
not the standard stereotype. They were people, just as human as me."

For Kerry, the turning point was cemented when Pastor John
Barbone led the congregation in song. "They were singing the same
hymns I'd sung as a child; the same hymns we sing in our own church.
They were praising my God," he lamented. "I had a big conflict on my
hands." This was not supposed to happen. Rational thinking was not
part of the design.

Kerry remembers a flood of questions clogging his mind while he
sat quietly in the pew: If we do this, what's going to happen? Would this
start a revolution in America? Would this be another event to pit the left
wing against the right, liberals against conservatives?

He knew the bomb was powerful enough to kill parishioners,
level buildings, and injure innocent people. "Many families would be
grieving," he thought. "What would happen to me?" he asked himself.
"Would I go to prison?"

After an eternity that lasted mere nanoseconds, Kerry ended the
dilemma. He remembers thinking *I cannot kill people in the act of praising
my God.* As the congregation rose to sing, he saw the commonality between

them and himself. The separation ceased to exist. In his words: "I saw women and men raise their hands to God. To my God." Kerry had spent his entire life surrounded by religious music. To him, when the worshippers began to sing, the notion of superiority and supremacy disappeared. He was on the very same playing field as the group he had intended to obliterate.

He leaned to his friend and whispered, "We're leaving." At the end of the service the two calmly walked out of the church surrounded by a crowd of LGBTQ Christians and returned to the CSA compound in northern Arkansas.

Kerry knew that Ellison, the leader of CSA, was going to be unhappy about the aborted bomb plot. Indeed, when he returned to the compound, Ellison was quick to express his disappointment. "You didn't do what God wanted you to do," Ellison spat. He called Kerry weak and a coward for his failure to act. Discouraged and hurt, Kerry began to silently question Ellison's increasingly hateful motives.

Kerry says the questions and whirling thoughts that fogged his brain that morning represented a huge mental battle for him. He had already begun the difficult process that would eventually cause him to leave CSA and the hate movement entirely. The incident at the church was one more significant emotional event to put his escape plan on a fast track. But before he would leave the movement for good, other incidents intervened which had more menacing results.

At CSA's highest point of development, more than 60 families lived on the 224-acre site, following Jim Ellison's every word. Eventually Ellison bought the Christian Identity dogma, Eurocentric to the core, and condemning Jews as illegitimate Israelites who are reviled by God. He delivered the CI theology to his followers.

Before it adopted CI beliefs, CSA maintained what would appear to be an Earth-loving conservationism: no electricity, no indoor plumbing, and gardens to grow most of their own foods. While environmental concerns may have been a key value at the outset, as their numbers grew and religious values shifted, their lifestyle changed just as dramatically as their views of humanity.

In the early 1970s, beyond the confines of CSA, an undercurrent of young Christians fashioned their own special offshoot of hippiedom, fostering an international groundswell of adherents and ministries occasionally referred to as "Jesus Freaks." CSA members did not specifically consider themselves part of that movement, nor did they openly engage in hippy habits like smoking dope. However, the group allowed another facet of Christian-oriented consciousness to permeate its otherwise guarded universe.

"Among Jesus Freaks," Kerry notes, "the belief evolved that in order to purify yourself from a society that wasn't following God, you had to move away from that society." The ideals of Christian hippies living in a shared community merged into a new kind of groupthink crafted through Ellison's rapidly changing vision.

As CSA's morals morphed, conservation and self-sufficiency led to an atmosphere of survival and strict self-preservation. The group built food reserves and its own water supply. Preservation turned into protection. Over time, the protection grew to where men purchased and modified weapons and practiced military-style defensiveness. The protective mentality stretched to an outright social offensive against anyone deemed different than the traditional, Christian, white, male norm.

It didn't take long for the trends of creeping consumerism, urban sprawl, a national abuse of natural resources, and changing American demographics to threaten the CSA bubble. Common signs of regional growth were characterized as "wicked" or "sinful" by fundamentalist sects like CSA. Kerry's CI group eventually became hell-bent on shielding their ranks behind a veil of paramilitary armor and white power. The group started planning ways to cope with an onslaught of social changes.

Before the site Kerry still calls "the farm" transformed into what the FBI would eventually call a "compound," most of the families who moved there were devout Christians who relocated from other Christian communities. Seeing one another as peaceful and loving, CSA members seemed oblivious to a similarity that bonded them together. In addition to the Christian core, it was no accident the members of the group were all white, all perceived to be heterosexual, and with no major disabilities among them. They dressed alike, ate alike, worshipped alike, and thought alike. They were distinctly unified. One.

Fiercely committed to their own God-given freedoms, these were not modern-day peaceniks staging a Broadway revival of *Hair* or freedom riders marching through Selma arm-in-arm in honor of civil rights. Over time, they became fully intent not only on protecting their sameness, but also on deliberately and meaningfully causing harm to those who threatened the sanctity of their restrictive oneness.

As with other anti-Semitic, neo-Nazi, white supremacist, and anti-immigrant extremists, one of the most despised enemies at CSA was the perceived intrusive and omnipresent power of the Zionist Occupational Government (ZOG).

A Zionist is someone who supports a Jewish state in Israel. The term ZOG is part of a conspiracy theory that believes Jews secretly control countries and that the formal government in each nation is merely a puppet regime. Anti-Semitic groups, including Holocaust revisionists in the U.S. and Europe, ultra-nationalists in Russia, and right-wing groups in Poland often use the fear of ZOG to provoke violence. Anti-government groups turn the fear of ZOG into a fine art.

Among groups like CSA, laissez-faire doctrine is taken to the outermost limits. An overriding belief behind such a conviction is that government has no right to interfere with business and economic affairs. To followers of such groups, government is both unnecessary and destructive. As the ideology of white supremacist extremism took hold among CSA families, a militant archetype was growing within its ranks. At least once a week troopers-in-training at the CSA compound dressed in camouflage fatigues and fired automatic submachine guns into the hearts and heads of paper cutouts representing government agents. The CSA weapons were illegally modified to fire automatically. They were also fitted with specially made silencers, each one an illicit device.

The CSA women, fully aware of the military surge, dutifully maintained the households, and taught and nurtured the children. They were fiercely loyal and traditional in every way. They were the backbone of support and equally responsible for sustaining the group's existence on the same par as their male counterparts who worked logging jobs during the day and engaged in target practice after work.

The group that would eventually become CSA started in 1972, when James Ellison moved his family and six others from San Antonio, Texas, to Missouri. In Kerry's words the move came "after God ordered

Ellison to do so." The group later moved to the northern Arkansas site that would eventually become CSA's base.

A few years after Ellison began to bring families together, a main motivator for Kerry and Kay to move there, was to join another family they had befriended at Christ for the Nations, a Christian group with no known connection to Christian Identity or white supremacist beliefs. By the time Kerry and Kay arrived with their two small children, the community was established and growing. Kerry fondly remembers the men who lived there helping him build his own home in a quiet valley on the grounds, where four more Noble children would later be born.

Today, Kerry and Kay Noble live in a 2,400 square foot doublewide mobile home on a three-acre parcel outside Dallas next to a field of tall grass where the air is as quiet as it is dry. With the decadent exception of a 61–inch television, the home is comfortable, yet humble. Over three days of in-person interviews at the modest home, Kerry went over every detail of the aborted bomb incident and other issues that led to his exit from the hate movement. Affable and unpretentious, Kerry responded to all questions with traditional Southern courtesy, always inserting a polite, "Yes, sir."

Before the bombing plot, Kerry told me his only contact with a person he perceived to be gay was during his senior year of high school. He had strolled into a convenience store and asked to see magazines. The cashier led the young Kerry to the back of the store, a move that he interpreted as a sexually aggressive overture. The gesture upset him and triggered a deep-seated fear that would last for decades. He ran from the store as soon as he put the pieces together. When he went to the gay church in Kansas City, his only concept of gay people had been reinforced by media images from Gay Pride events. He said the hate movement teaches followers to believe gays are out to destroy civilization.

Throughout his life, Kerry has been driven by divine service. For six years before moving his family to Arkansas, he had served as preacher at a Southern Baptist church in Lubbock Texas. In May 1977, shortly before his 25th birthday, he and Kay moved to the farm. Aside from the group's Christian foundation, another reason Kerry joined the budding collective was to escape the drug scene in Lubbock. He had experimented with pot and psilocybin (mushrooms) in his younger years, but wasn't interested in going down that path. He also wanted to live in a small Christian community. He believed God was largely responsible for finding a new home where he and Kay could raise their children surrounded by loving friends.

He says God was behind most of the decisions at CSA, including his own one-time interest to kill. It was less than a decade after God led him to CSA that Kerry found himself sitting through a Christian service, about to carry out a deadly plot he firmly believed was charted with God's blessing.

Kerry looks back at the gay church incident in a very straightforward way. "[At the time], I would not kill gays because they were gay." Instead, he explained, reflecting Christian Identity thinking, "I would have killed gays *because God wanted me to kill them.* I didn't want to do something God didn't want me to do." According to CI reasoning, he clarified, "The gay lifestyle is under judgment for what a gay person has *chosen* to do, so my action would be a righteous act."

CSA Late 1970s to Early 1980s

Kerry says his first thoughts about leaving CSA were conceived *after* the plot to kill LGBTQ people. He believed that by killing gays, he would regain Ellison's respect following a string of disagreements between them. One major falling out evolved after Kerry objected to Ellison naming Wayne Snell an honorary member of CSA. At the time, Snell was wanted by the FBI for shooting a state trooper in Arkansas. Ellison allowed Snell to take refuge at the compound. Another dispute Kerry had with Ellison involved a growing number of CSA members who were jailed or in prison for a series of crimes. Law-breaking of any kind was in sharp contrast from his Baptist upbringing, and the crimes committed by CSA members heightened his anxiety.

In the days leading up to his plans in Kansas City, Kerry felt he was losing a moral conflict with Ellison. The leader he revered and was committed to support had shifted his own impression of Christian Identity. Noble began to see the CI orthodoxy as diametrically opposed to what he believed bonded CSA families together. As Ellison's chief lieutenant, he was frustrated in his inability to influence Ellison away from crime and back to the standards of "the farm." He was also feeling responsible for the criminal element.

At that point, he was shattered and at his lowest spiritual point ever. He felt he had betrayed Ellison, Kay, himself, and God. He felt worthless and wanted to leave CSA. But he and Kay didn't have the means to leave. He also felt that God didn't want them to leave.

It was at that emotional nadir that Kerry took the low road. He chose Ellison over his God. Torn and conflicted, he ignored criminal consequences when he packed a .22 caliber gun and silencer with the intent to kill innocent people.

Many defectors say the concept of "killing others to save our own" is a particularly motivating trend among extremists, a belief that causes them to act in ways that contradict their own core values and extend beyond the realm of rational logic.

Kerry thought that the destruction of a gay church would be a sign to the rest of the hate movement that the race war had started. He said, "We called it a race war even if it didn't include race and included other target groups, like gays. We knew when the war got started the right wing would start shooting anybody who wasn't white."

After roughly 14 years at CSA, Kerry realized that Ellison didn't care about the people, and that for Ellison, it was just a power trip. His new direction was self-serving and not based on a faith in God.

Changes Ellison instituted at CSA in the early 1980s included near-constant military training and accumulating enough weapons to arm a minor military deployment. By the early 1980s Ellison had fostered alliances with some of the most notorious hate groups in America. CSA would serve as a haven for murderers and arsonists on the FBI's Most Wanted List. Ellison's vision also seemed to include CSA's virtual isolation.

As Kerry recalls, before CSA had a name and an identity, Ellison held his community in a tight charismatic grip, with few objections from his loyal followers. Ellison was solely responsible for attracting the small group of Christian families who came together around the northern Arkansas site. At the outset, CSA was more like a Christian-oriented cult occupying an idyllic oasis in the Ozarks. By the early 1980s it was a full-blown religious hate group.

Over the eight years Kerry's family lived there, Ellison guided CSA through an evolution leading to extreme hate. As the chief visionary for the group, Ellison could not have done it without Kerry's help. Kerry's planned foray into Kansas City was just one of many events devised at CSA to harm or destroy one of three fundamental target groups in the crosshairs of Christian Identity at the time – Jews, blacks, and gays.

The church incident, Kerry says, "was, for me, a slap in the face of reality. It opened my eyes to a lot of stuff." Soon after returning to CSA from Kansas City, Kerry had his first conversation with Kay about the possibility of leaving the hate movement altogether. But he didn't tell her about his murder plot until months later.

"Besides myself," he said, "only three others knew about the bomb: the man who made it, the man who drove with me to Kansas City, and Jim Ellison. I didn't tell Kay so she wouldn't worry. She would have freaked out." When he eventually told Kay, she was largely unaware of the illegal activities at CSA and continued to rely on the tightly knit group for fellowship. When Kerry first expressed his reservations over CSA's involvement with recognized hate groups, Kay was conflicted, feeling a connection to the families and the once quiet, secluded environment of the farm. Unaware of what could lie ahead, she encouraged him to stay. Even though he was unhappy with the life there, Kerry acceded to his wife's plea.

Kerry Noble was born in 1952 in Abilene, Texas. His mother was a powerful and influential force in his life. Her steadfast adherence to the Golden Rule and strict "don't fight back" philosophy helped him understand how and when his personal path deviated from the values of his youth.

Chronic bronchitis at age six robbed him of the boundless energy and daredevil resilience other kids his age enjoyed. In first grade, a persistent cough and continually strained breathing made normally rambunctious child behaviors so difficult that his doctor ordered him to take Physical Education in the girl's gym. At that age, for a boy to be *seen* playing sports with girls was equal to having a permanent "Kick Me" sign taped to his back. At home, he was encouraged to rise above the near-constant name-calling and abuse and, instead, "trust God's loving hand." The bullying was relentless. "Based on my mother's philosophy, I felt unable to defend myself," Kerry says. "This was a huge conflict for me."

Kerry acknowledges that bullying begets bullying. By being subjected to taunts at school, he subconsciously cultivated an acute sense of how to bully as an adult. A history of childhood abuse is a conspicuous trend among many members of hate groups.

From age three when his parents got divorced, to age 10 when his mother remarried, Kerry's life was nearly devoid of male role models. He believes the presence of a dad could have balanced his mother's strong guidance to not fight back or turn the other check. His relationship with his stepfather got off to a bumpy start because by then, he really didn't want a role model. His stepfather moved the family to a rural area where farming chores connected Kerry to nature, a move he looks back on with fond memories.

Throughout his K-12 education, Kerry was a scholastic overachiever, partially due to bronchitis limiting his physical options. However, he felt like an underachiever in manliness. He speculates that being bullied as a child had an effect on his self-confidence, causing him to be more withdrawn that other kids his age. He turned his attention to books.

Through middle school and high school, as an outlet for his academic excellence, Kerry pushed himself to get involved in extracurricular work. He assumed leadership positions as president of his school's Math Club, Future Teachers of America, and Future Farmers of America.

After graduating high school, Kerry was called to the ministry. The call came in the form of a dream-like image of Kerry standing at a podium, turning pages in a big book. The vision included God telling him, "This is what I prepared you for – to preach." In 1971, still disillusioned over not being able to pursue college, he didn't know what to make of the dream. He went to a Baptist church down the street. The minister told him the apparition was a call to the ministry. Not understanding what the minster truly meant, he construed the dream to mean God was referring to his scholastic achievements as homework for the ministry. Over the next year he became a preacher in a Baptist church, a role in which he felt at home.

His post-high school years included an array of highs and lows. One low was being turned down by the military for health reasons. The high was meeting and marrying Kay. After their wedding in

1974, a short stint in college became stressful, mostly due to adjusting to married life, financial challenges, and ongoing conflicts between his mother and stepfather. Unable to afford college and ineligible for scholarships due to his stepfather's relocating the family too frequently, he dropped college entirely.

Kerry Noble is an outlier from other hate movement defectors. Unlike others, he never intended to join a hate group. Instead, the hate movement came to him. Yet, under his guidance as its number two leader, he and CSA went through a metamorphosis before reaching a point equal to the notoriety of older and larger hate groups.

Kerry's perspectives on Christian Identity and his candor about his own transformations from childhood to today make his story significant. His reflections on the emotional challenges he endured before, during, and after his time at CSA can help others comprehend the psychology of how extremists get hijacked into the organizational mechanics and structural foundations of hate. His background offers a unique view of the political and personal dynamics of the movement. It also poses important questions: Does one consciously turn to hate or is hate thrust upon them? Does being a part of the movement transform the individual? Since Ellison led CSA from a peaceful commune to an extremist group, it is reasonable to deduce that hate was not part of what attracted the Nobles to the original group.

As he tells his story, when Kerry moved his family to join the shared environment that eventually became CSA, the collective was united first and foremost around Christian values. Members also maintained a self-sustainable support network. The place appeared as a loving, family-oriented, child-friendly, natural environment where many parents would want to raise their children.

The original group had been operating nearly four years before the Nobles arrived. Over the span of a dozen years at the site, the wooded haven nestled in the Ozarks descended from Kerry's vision of a commune-like family with Christian overtones to become The Covenant, the Sword, and the Arm of the Lord, a borderline heartless military compound with a dubious title. Kerry recounts that CSA emerged out of the free spirit mold of the 1960s. To hear him describe the farm gives the impression of a tranquil sanctuary where hippies run naked through open meadows and peace-loving flower children slip daisies down the gun barrels of Army riflemen.

In reality, not all who lived there were as wholesome and loving as others. Kerry knew some were aligned with organizations known to be hostile to "minorities." The farm slowly vanished as the group started to amass illegal weapons, conducted daily paramilitary training, and prepared for a racial holy war.

CSA's conversion to a hate group started in 1970 when Ellison was employed as an ironworker building missile silos in Missouri. There he obtained an audiotaped message by Dan Gayman, a former high school principal and then-pastor of the Church of Israel in Schell City, Missouri, a group known for espousing right wing extremist values. The tape was recorded during a non-traditional Christian service featuring patriotic American songs rather than standard hymns.

According to the Anti-Defamation League (ADL), Gayman is widely regarded as one of the theological leaders of the Christian Identity movement. ADL notes that Gayman popularized the "two seedline theory," widely accepted among CI adherents. The theory, also known as the "serpent's seed doctrine," purports that Jews descend from a sexual union between Eve and Satan and that only white Christians descend from Adam and Eve.

Ellison was hooked. He wanted Gayman's message to become a part of his developing group's foundation. He hand-picked Kerry as his Bible teacher. Assuming the role, Kerry was responsible for inculcating religious messages, including Gayman's philosophy, to all of Ellison's followers. It was Kerry's first step into the CI world.

Starkly deviating from any Christian norm, Gayman preached about the "true Israel," claiming that Anglo-Saxons had forgotten who they were *racially*. Gayman ranted about the Declaration of Independence and the U.S. Constitution being inspired documents of God and claimed that the founding of America was based on Christian principles. His talk was interspersed with a congregation singing God Bless America and My Country 'Tis of Thee.

As it grew, CSA armed itself with more hardware. Members also developed the technology to convert high powered rifles into automatic weapons, an illegal process. As CSA evolved, Kerry evolved with it.

Over the years, the group became one of the most radical CI groups in the U.S. The mild mannered, peaceful preacher from Lubbock converted into a shell of his former self, willing to detonate a bomb-filled suitcase and destroy a church and its congregation, all in the name of Ellison's mission.

Based on his tenure as the organization's spiritual guide, Kerry was unquestionably a key CSA operative. By default or by intent, he was connected to an assortment of hate-related crimes. In his autobiography, *Tabernacle of Hate: Why They Bombed Oklahoma City*[1], he noted that the FBI eventually branded him "the number two leader of the second most dangerous domestic terrorist organization in the United States."

By 1976, prior to the advent of CSA as its official title, Ellison originally named the community Zaraphath-Horeb. The name derived from Zaraphath, "a purging place" where the Bible's Elijah was fed in a famine, and Horeb, an ancient name for Mount Sinai, where Moses received the Ten Commandments. The environment that became CSA was steeped in Christian symbolism. Kerry said this was a place for families to purge the sins of the flesh. The new organization started as a group of Christian families who had migrated together to a patch of bucolic Americana tucked in the Arkansas Ozarks, just south of the Missouri state line. Building on a Christian foundation, the land was purchased from its former owner, Campus Crusade for Christ.

In 1979, Ellison was preaching to Zaraphath-Horeb in words very similar to those expressed by Dan Gayman. According to Kerry, Ellison had already made the leap to Christian Identity. Ellison was thumping an unmistakably anti-Semitic tune, this time with a racist chorus. His once peace-loving flock followed dutifully.

Kerry paraphrased one of Ellison's diatribes in the following excerpt from Kerry's online book, *Saved By My Enemies*[2]. This disturbing passage summarizes the depth of CSA's fear and its chilling commitment to white supremacy. As Ellison spoke, CSA men clothed in camouflage and armed with rifles and pistols, rose and saluted a Nazi-like salute. Standing before them, Ellison held a copy of the Declaration of Independence and the Constitution of the United States in one hand, and his Bible in the other, as he pontificated:

"This Jewish-controlled government is killing our white babies through abortion. It is destroying white minds with its humanistic teachings of evolution. I tell you this . . . Niggers may be descended from apes, but my ancestors never swung on trees by their tails! In order to preserve our Christian heritage and race, it is our right, our patriotic duty, to overthrow this Antichrist government. Standing by and doing nothing against the tyranny of this government is open rebellion to God! Prepare war, O Israel! Wake up the mighty men! Let all the men of war come near. Beat your plowshares into swords and your pruning hooks into spears! Let the weak say, I am strong!"

So much for the groovy love-in.

By then, images of peacenik children faded into a well-oiled machine brandishing rapid-fire machine guns, grenades, and cyanide. Ellison's message confirmed all the underpinnings of racism, anti-Semitism, homophobia and anti-government hate. Among its many enemies, ZOG – the Antichrist – was everywhere. This view united CSA with the ideologies of much larger nationally recognized hate groups, including Aryan Nations, one of the biggest.

In his monumental book *Blood and Politics: The History of the White Nationalist Movement From the Margins to the Mainstream*[3], Leonard Zeskind, researcher into extreme right, racist, and anti-Semitic organizations, writes about CSA:

"Unlike the Klan, which still kept one foot in the suburban town square, groups such as CSA lived separately from the rest of society. As they grew, these groups created their own system of institutions and allegiances, becoming, in effect, a white nationalist enclave at war with the multiracial state they called ZOG. If the CSA proved to be the most militarized of these outposts, then Aryan Nations served as its central political address."

In the spring of 1980, the more ominous credo was starting to direct the Zaraphath-Horeb sensibility. Ellison had effectively guided the group through a path of distorted beliefs, still unified under the broad umbrella of Christianity. Throughout the twists and turns, Kerry, an elder of the "congregation" since 1977, became the organization's main Bible teacher preaching his and Ellison's beliefs to the families that lived there.

By 1982 Zaraphath-Horeb was aligned with the Ku Klux Klan, neo-Nazis, and other extreme factions of right-wing thinking. As the philosophy matured into CSA tenets, the group placed higher values on white supremacy and white survivalist thinking than on mainstream Christian ideals. It was no accident that the group's name posed an acronym that mirrored the Confederate States of America. Like its namesake, CSA maintained an anti-government, secessionist thinking similar to that expressed by slave states at the start of the American Civil War.

According to Kerry, one element that differentiated CSA from traditional Christian beliefs, as well as from the theologies of other CI groups, was how he and Ellison influenced the group's beliefs around two fundamental references in the Bible's *Book of Revelation*: the Rapture and the Tribulation. Understanding these concepts from the perspective of the two top CSA leaders helps to untangle what motivated Kerry at the time and how he guided his flock. From childhood, Kerry's deeply ingrained Christian beliefs and values presented a biblical filter through which he observed the world. Within the context of the Rapture and the Tribulation, he explained his thought process about what was happening at CSA in the late-1970s and early- to mid-1980s.

As we talked in his at-home office, Kerry explained the connections between CSA's theological underpinnings and its need to stockpile weapons. CSA interpreted everything the government did as preparation for the last days, the biblical Tribulation, a time when the Antichrist arrives on Earth with the theoretical goal of maintaining a one religion/one-world government over the whole planet. *"That's why we made the weapons* – because everything the government did was leading to the Tribulation."

Kerry described the CSA mindset as believing "We [CSA] were the *true* Israel." At the time, Kerry told CSA followers, "The bad guys would be non-Christians and non-whites. Jews were counterfeit people." This basic principle follows a pattern in which humans have perpetrated extremely violent actions in the name Christianity, Islam, Judaism, and other religions throughout history.

CSA's own interpretation of heaven and Earth was a critical part of its orthodoxy. With his gift of verbal acuity as preacher, organizational leader, and CSA's Bible teacher, Kerry defined who went to heaven and who did not. He said CSA families were a bit radical in that they would practice Christianity 24/7 together as one big family, separate from those who lived outside the CSA community.

By the time the group assumed its formidable name, followers had been steeped in both survivalist thinking and a militia mentality. Also, having amassed a food supply and a stash of illicit automatic weapons, families were prepared to protect themselves from any non-CSA person who would even think about challenging their existence. Whatever religious, social, or geopolitical conflicts were happening in real time, CSA believers were a stand-alone army against all forces biblical and domestic, committed to survive the end of the world. The group's existence depended on what its adherents believed, or more accurately, what they *were told to* believe.

Kerry briefly explained the heart of Christian Identity values: "According to CI beliefs, Jews could *never* believe in Jesus. They don't have the capacity to believe in Jesus because they are children of the devil." Unravelling his own understanding of the Biblical differences between deception and reality was a monumental breakthrough that helped Kerry conclude that he didn't believe the CSA/CI theology anymore.

The paradigm embraced by autocratic leaders and totalitarian regimes serves as a role model for hate groups and loner extremists. Those predisposed to such thinking are often influenced by their own unique interpretations of the Bible, the Koran, the Torah, or any other codified set of religious tenets. CSA's actions in the early 1980s drove Kerry's reality.

By the late 1970s, in an effort to protect itself against the dreaded ZOG, Ellison and Kerry started to form alliances with larger, nationally recognized white supremacist organizations. The other groups were attracted to CSA primarily because of the group's impressive armament.

In return, CSA got national recognition.

Hate groups often function in defiance of anything resembling common sense. CSA was no exception. In addition to his unique point of view, what makes Kerry's clarification of the CSA philosophy so meaningful is that he describes how shifting conditions caused individuals and this entire community to become detached from reality and attached to weapons.

In the early 1980s, Kerry's effort to share his insights with Ellison did not go as planned. "When Ellison asked, 'What do you want to do?' I said, 'Let's get rid of the weapons. Rather than being opposed to the government, we should be supportive. We need to start blessing people instead of cursing people. After all, that is how we started out, as good citizens and helpful in the community." Clearly, it was a tough sell. Ellison accused Kerry of fearmongering.

Kerry's recommendation for Ellison to ditch the weapons and make peace with the government came two years before CSA faced its biggest crisis. Over the next two years, the group's worst fears would become reality as government agents started to narrow their focus on the CSA compound.

While CSA rhetoric shifted into anti-Semitic, racist, and homophobic overdrive, its ideology did not go unnoticed nationally. By the late 1970s, the Southern Poverty Law Center (SPLC) had identified CSA as a hate group. CSA was also being scrupulously and stealthily monitored by a host of government agencies as one of the most notorious CI groups in America.

By way of an aside, during our interviews, Kerry's patient attempts to help me understand the CI concept overall and his own theological thinking during his time at CSA became more challenging to comprehend. To decipher and explain a vexing circle of theories helps others understand what drives groups like CSA. Feeling foolish for not being able to grasp the fundamental roots of CI logic after Kerry's step-by-step explanation, I met with Rabbi Anson Laytner, who was then Program Manager of the Interreligious Initiative at the Seattle University School of Theology & Ministry, and former Executive Director of the local chapter of the American Jewish Committee.

At one point during our talk, Rabbi Layner saw the struggle on my face. Flummoxed, I told him it was all going over my head. He paused to make a simple, yet profoundly helpful statement that has guided me through all of my interviews with former extremists. In a calm and direct tone, he told me the key reason so few are able to understand how or why *any* hate group does what it does. He said in words close to these: "You may not be *able* to understand it. You're looking at these groups from the mind of a rational, reasonable person who thinks logically. That's not how Christian Identity thinks."

Indeed, that's not how *any* hate group thinks.

Over the decade after CSA's decision to become part of the CI network, the compound had grown in size and stature to become an internationally recognized hate group. By 1981, CSA attracted increasing interest from other racist and neo-Nazi groups. At the same time, the level of paranoia inside the CSA compound amounted to a constant post-9/11-style Red Alert.

As a measure of safety to assure trust within its ranks, all new members who came to CSA were given a Voice Stress Analyzer (VSA) Test[4]. The VSA is a kind of lie detector that, to some degree, mimics the unreliably of "scientific" equipment the Nazis developed during the Holocaust to distinguish Jews from non-Jews.

In early 1982, CSA boasted a membership of 152 women and men, including 32 families and several unmarried members. That year, Kerry convinced the CSA leadership to organize a National Convocation, a meeting of other hate groups, with the primary intent of forming a coalition of like-minded organizations. "Our goal is simple," Kerry told the others as he pitched the concept. Kerry's goal was to unify splintered groups and autonomous extremists into one national organization.

A covert goal CSA had for the conference was to seat Jim Ellison as the leader of a new mega-group. Little arm-twisting was necessary to earn nearly unanimous support in the compound. Ellison could practically taste the power of leading the entire hate movement.

In October 1982, the National Convocation drew more than 100 men, women, and children from across the U.S. to the CSA compound, more than Kerry had expected. Conferees observed weapons, attended workshops, learned about survivalism, and heard speakers degrade Jewish-controlled media and banks, and denounce "BATFAGS," slang for agents of the Bureau of Alcohol, Tobacco, Firearms and Explosives (ATF). In attendance was a company of nationally recognized hate gurus, including Richard Butler of Aryan Nations, Tom Robb of the Ku Klux Klan (KKK), Colonel Jack Mohr of the Christian-Patriots Defense League (CPDL), and members of Posse Comitatus, a far right anti-government and anti-Semitic group.

CSA had by then achieved a reputation for its paramilitary focus and munitions. The event took place in a newly constructed forty-foot by fifty-foot structure on the CSA property. Built largely for the convocation, the edifice would later serve as a sanctuary and meeting space, with the second floor designated to become a library and school. The new building had thick concrete walls with a veneer of heavy stone. The narrow downstairs windows doubled as gun ports for taking aim at future uninvited guests. The building also served as a ZOG-proof fortress. Lest the multiple uses cause one to forget, the building was also a place of worship, even if CSA's brotherly love was unyieldingly selective.

While planning and coordinating the Convocation, internal conflicts between his own core values and Ellison's power play caused Kerry to more seriously question his involvement in a hate group. He recalls asking a prospective CSA member at the time why he wanted to move there. The man answered enthusiastically, "It's the guns, man. The guns," he told Kerry. "You guys are the best paramilitary group in the country. Hell, everybody talks about CSA. You guys are like gods. Everybody expects you to start the war." Kerry remembers thinking, "Guns? What about God, Jesus, the Bible? What about love of our brethren?"

Nah.

By the end of the Convocation, the goal to name Ellison the leader failed to materialize, although he became more widely recognized. Each group left with its own master feeling further exalted. Although no single group leader was designated to head the newly baptized, yet very loosely knit coalition of hate groups, CSA was elevated to center stage in the international white supremacy movement.

Around the time of the Convocation, Ellison did receive a new distinction. He was anointed "King James of the Ozarks" by Robert Millar, spiritual leader of Elohim City, an Oklahoma based Christian

Identity group with strong ties to Aryan Nations. The title stuck and later appeared in numerous print and online references.

As his hope of ascendancy to the throne of the modern white supremacist movement waned, Ellison tended to forget one small irony, a former selling point with early settlers at the farm. In the pre-CSA days, Ellison boasted about being one eighth Cherokee. Evidently, in the 1970s, multicultural heritage was an asset to Ellison. By the 1980s, a case of selective amnesia kicked in and Ellison's invisible non-white ancestry became an unreferenced footnote. The truth of Ellison's arguably non-white bloodline was not one of the louder messages heralded at the whites-only Convocation.

Kerry recalled that after the Convocation he weighed his own vision of a loving Christian life in contrast with Ellison's public hate-mongering, a classic struggle between internally opposing values. He remembers praying, "Is this what you want from me, God? In my quest to do what God wants, are my struggles because I am not seeing God, but seeing the contradictions? Or is it because I'm losing faith in God?" Ultimately, he reasoned, "Even if I didn't like what was going on [at CSA], if it is God's will, I should be doing it anyway."

Ellison's spiritual grip was so compelling that Kerry was largely incapable of thinking for himself. As CSA's number one leader, Ellison had expropriated the entire group's ability to think and act independently.

Plans began for another National Convocation in 1983. Ellison and Kerry were at cross purposes for the second assembly. This time, Ellison's vision was to attract attendees with business dollars who could support CSA financially and build the group's numbers. Kerry was more intent on returning to CSA's one-time focus on Christian values.

A divisive kink in the already contentious CSA unfolded in 1982 when Ellison announced at a prayer service that he had received another message from the Almighty. God told him to take a second wife.

Ellison asked the CSA elders for their blessing on wife number two. He said without their unanimous support, he would not pursue the calling. Kerry and another CSA elder supported Ellison's new direction. All others disapproved. The idea did not end there.

This was not the first time the subject of multiple marriages had arisen at CSA. A senior CSA member had recently left his wife and child behind when he decided to enter a polygamous relationship. This time, the idea came from the CSA leader, with a sordid twist involving the previous polygamist. After Ellison's oath to take his second wife, he expressed his interest to pursue the former wife of the CSA member who had left to live with a second spouse. Ellison again claimed divine intervention when he told CSA elders, "She is the one God has chosen."

Kerry saw his own support of Ellison's polygamy as one way to once again express a true loyalty to the leader he worshipped. Kerry also believed he could use his supportive position to nudge Ellison back to a more spiritual direction and away from CSA's paramilitary direction. Ellison had also told him something no other CSA member knew. Long before God made the match, Ellison had already had sexual relations with his soon-to-be-second wife.

As he and I spoke, Kerry revealed another secret, one that would be the source of personal anxiety for many years afterwards. Throughout the debate among CSA elders over Ellison's polygamy, Kerry harbored polygamous desires of his own. As a torn look crossed his face, he reasoned his own justification for the fascination. "If it were time for Ellison to take a second wife, and since God had given him the revelation, wouldn't it make sense that I would, too? Also, siding with Jim showed my strong allegiance to him. Wouldn't that help to elevate my position in our group?"

"The polygamy deal was challenging for me," Kerry asserts with a pained expression. "Ellison wasn't being truthful with me and the other elders about his motives. Yet, I wasn't completely convinced I was right." The issue of legitimizing polygamy at CSA became deeply divisive among the families. The paramilitary members strenuously opposed it. A dividing line emerged in the ranks. Ellison's domination over CSA was beginning to fall apart.

That Kerry would even *entertain* the thought of a polygamous relationship demonstrates the depths to which a member of an organized group can stoop in order to remain within the good graces of its leader. It also shows just how deeply the grip of illogical reasoning from a charismatic guide motivates admirers to follow. Such a rationale, plus the notion of consecration by the Creator, is a hallmark of the Christian Identity creed.

By late 1982, Kerry began to see discrepancies. He realized Ellison was no longer perfect. This was problematic because of his early childhood messages to always respect your elders.

Because many CSA followers believed "Thou shalt not covet thy neighbor's wife" with no waver from its literal interpretation, more than a few CSA followers were troubled by polygamy being modeled and promoted by their leader. Within a three-month period in late 1982 and early 1983, two-thirds of CSA members left the group, reducing the overall membership to fifty men, women, and children.

The year 1983 marked a major schism at CSA. That year, Kerry sensed the group was heading away from the right wing movement. After the polygamy squabble, he said, "There were fewer of us. We had lost two thirds of our members." Ever the believer, Kerry wondered if the changes meant a return to the group's religious roots. He asked himself, "Is God correcting our path and guiding us in a more spiritual direction?"

Kerry remembers that after many long-term members exited, leaving CSA with only a few worshipers, it felt like they were all going through a divorce. "The world was crashing around us. We were without direction, numb, as if family members had died. The pain was excruciating. After the shift toward polygamy, the whole atmosphere changed. My bible studies slowed down. We didn't have military day on Sunday anymore. We no longer had military tactics meetings and we voluntarily stopped wearing military gear during the day. Appearances changed, the mood of our meetings changed. In a split with former policy, newer members could drink alcohol and smoke in their homes."

The polygamy issue was never truly resolved beyond being scorned by CSA members.

Another development in 1982 caused more friction in CSA. The compound had quietly welcomed and embraced a number of hardcore felons. Members of other groups with whom CSA had very close ties were getting arrested for violent crimes including murder, arson, and armed robbery. While proceeds from robberies were used to fund the operations of other hate groups, their offenses against "minorities" were inspired by pure hatred. Love thy neighbor as thyself had apparently faded into a sick cartoon. The one-time farm was now manufacturing illegal weapons and harboring hardcore criminals.

For some, Kerry among them, the profile of gun-wielding CSA members had created added tensions. "Newer people coming in had heard about us from other white supremacist groups. They wanted to be a part of God's Army," Kerry said. "People were there for guns." God was quickly becoming a distant memory.

In the summer of 1983, the violent death of Gordon Kahl, the 63-year-old leader of North Dakota's Posse Comitatus, brought a new concern to the floundering CSA. Posse Comitatus is a far-right populist social movement started in the late 1960s. Many Posse members embrace CI's anti-Semitic and white supremacist beliefs.

Kahl, a tax-protesting vigilante, died in a gun battle with federal marshals. Buzz about his death spread quickly through CSA, especially after members learned Kahl was hiding at the farm of a former CSA colleague.

Even the advent of Kahl's instant martyrdom failed to mend deep cracks in CSA's previously watertight discipline. By the fall of 1984, just months after the aborted Kansas City bombing mission, Kerry didn't like where the farm was going. "Too much hypocrisy. Members of The Order [a violent anti-Semitic group] were getting busted and some of our members were getting busted, too. No longer was I seeing God blessing the movement." The Order was identified by the FBI at the time as the most organized group of terrorist-type people to have ever operated in the United States. The Order was aligned with other nationwide white supremacist groups, including the KKK and Posse Comitatus, and strongly populated by members of Aryan Nations. The organization was destroyed in late 1984, when its leader, Bob Mathews, was killed during a shootout with some 75 federal law enforcement agents who surrounded his house on Whidbey Island, Washington.

By the winter of 1984, CSA was in mammoth disarray. The rift was evidenced by a significant reduction in members, the influx of criminals on the FBI's most-wanted list, dissension between remaining members, and negative dynamics over changing values, not the least of which was the swing to multiple spouses.

The turmoil did not shake CSA's focus from its ideology of an eventual God-ordered separation from mainstream America. Resentment and outright hate toward government and anyone deemed different from its straight, white, American-born, Christian clan helped coalesce the group's loyalists behind the distorted belief that their group could still outwit, outgun, and outmaneuver their one most elusive enemy – the Zionist Occupational Government. ZOG.

Going into 1985, CSA was still torn by divisive and discordant spats. Conflicting attitudes foreshadowed an inevitable catastrophe. How CSA navigated the obstacles that threatened its people, its buildings, and the forested cocoon of the compound sheds a light on how easily logic and reason become the first casualties of an ever-escalating fear. Throughout its rocky history, the CI dogma again held CSA together, notwithstanding its philosophical departure from more traditional Christian values and the restrictions of government.

Through its lifecycle and with God's blessing in the form of Jim Ellison, the farm had mutated into a violent anti-government militia motivated by blind racism, Christian fanaticism, ignorance, and fear.

In following CI principles, including messages directly from God, Ellison divined another message from heaven, this time to conceal its arsenal of illegal weapons. Law-breaking actions, like the CSA members' production and distribution of illegally automated weaponry to other hate groups, led the FBI to name CSA one of the biggest terrorist groups in the U.S.

Little did Ellison and Kerry know that at the very same time CSA was beginning to regroup, refocus, and bury its firearms in shallow graves, every detail about its operation was under close scrutiny by a vast consortium of local, regional, and national government forces.

In the spring of 1985, the CSA compound was being methodically watched, counted, measured, assessed, and catalogued by a team of highly trained professionals. The analysis accounted for every visible gun, bomb and instrument of death on the CSA grounds, along with every individual who entered or left its carefully guarded premises. Without its knowledge, CSA had become host for a big, hairy, uninvited guest.

The group would soon come face to face with ZOG.

The Rise and Fall of CSA

The Fall

In the early months of 1985, CSA was more than a minor blip on the FBI's radar screen. After a series of coldblooded murders committed by members of the most notorious hate groups in America, including Aryan Nations and The Order, a federal investigation scrutinized CSA members who were allegedly involved in a number of federal crimes.

That spring, as a result of the FBI's assessment of CSA as a terrorist organization and a grand jury indictment, the FBI ordered a siege of the compound. Largely undetected by their Arkansas neighbors, the flagrantly abusive exploits and weapons build-up at CSA had not gone unnoticed by its biggest opponent, the federal government.

No one at CSA was aware of how seriously the group's actions were being examined, least of all Kerry Noble. In 1984, behind-the-scenes events at CSA merged into a blur of rapid-fire sub-plots and character twists, each one causing Kerry to assess his options for getting out while the getting was good. With each passing day, Kerry was more committed to separate from the group and return to a self-sufficient lifestyle with Kay and their children. Yet, a daily barrage of internal CSA challenges caused him to focus on supporting Ellison and the dwindling number of CSA families. Two of Kerry's biggest problems were Bill Thomas and David Tate.

In April 1984, four months before Kerry's scheme of a mass murder in Kansas City, CSA member Bill Thomas, along with two accomplices, was arrested for stealing a flatbed trailer. The truck was stopped by police, who found Thomas in the vehicle with a machine gun and silencer at his side. Because he was affiliated with CSA, Thomas was offered a plea bargain as part of his prosecution. Rather than getting 10 years for carrying the weapon and silencer, the prosecutor said he would recommend five years, that is, if Thomas would plead guilty, and turn state's evidence against Ellison.

Not surprisingly, Ellison pressured Thomas to reject the offer. He told Thomas to tell the judge that a black man sold them the trailer with the guns inside. He assured Thomas that racist locals who would likely make up any jury would refuse to convict him. Further, he assured Thomas that even if that scheme failed, Thomas would never spend a day in jail because Ellison and CSA would break him out. Ellison also advised Thomas that any plea bargaining would be compromising with the government and that if he didn't plea bargain, God would release him.

Ellison's bizarre and misguided advice may have played a role in Thomas' getting the maximum penalty.

Showing an uncharacteristic lapse of reserve while describing Ellison's legal advice to Thomas, the consummately mild-mannered Kerry huffed, "That really pissed me off. Pardon my language." Kerry described how Ellison was out of touch with reality for leading Thomas to believe that: one, copping a plea was a bad idea; two, CSA would break him out of prison; and three, if CSA wouldn't do it, God would.

After the Bill Thomas incident put CSA in the news, word circulated around the compound that an invasion by government agents was imminent. Kerry knew that CSA's cache of illegal weapons alone was adequate reason for government intervention. The armament was physical evidence to substantiate charges against both Ellison and other CSA members. Kerry had already influenced Ellison to bury the guns in the thicket of the camp or in Bull Shoals Lake, the water body that lapped along the shores of the family's homes.

Ellison was defiant. He reasoned with other CSA leaders, that if the government comes in, it won't look good *for them*. According to Kerry, Ellison envisioned keeping and using the weapons for CSA's own defense during any showdown with government agents. The ever-feisty Ellison told the elders he was convinced CSA could win. He assured his followers that the likelihood of such a raid was part of the reason they had amassed weapons in the first place and had been conducting paramilitary training for years.

On April 15, 1985, roughly a year after Bill Thomas's arrest, a situation occurred near the CSA compound that would throw CSA into a tailspin. That day, two Missouri troopers stopped a van in Harrison, Arkansas, for a routine traffic check. The vehicle was driven by David Charles Tate, a 22-year-old neo-Nazi extremist with no direct connection to CSA. A shootout ensued at the scene, during which Tate fatally shot Jimmie Linegar, a 31-year-old police officer, with an automatic submachine gun quieted by an illegal silencer, a weapon similar to those manufactured inside the CSA compound. Another trooper, Allen Hines, was wounded. Tate fled the scene unharmed.

Well aware of CSA's arsenal of unlawful weapons, the FBI suspected Tate would take refuge at the CSA compound, which was located less than 25 miles from the scene of the crime. The FBI considered Ellison, mastermind of CSA's weapons stockpile, as the number one suspect to support Tate's asylum.

Tate was named in a federal indictment, which also implicated 23 purported members of The Order. The indictment accused Tate of murdering officer Linegar and alleged that specific members of The Order had committed some 50 crimes, including murder, attempted murder, arson, possession of illegal weapons, counterfeiting, and armed robberies totaling over four million dollars.

As it turned out, Tate was not hiding out at CSA or being harbored by members of The Order. Five days after Linegar was killed, Tate was taken into custody in a public park where, according to police reports, he was found hiding under a bush not far from a machine gun believed to be the weapon that killed Linegar. Tate went to trial in November 1985, was found guilty of assault and murder, and was sentenced to life without parole in a Missouri state prison.

While the Tate incident came alive through Arkansas news media, The Order was also under the FBI microscope. Kerry, not being completely up-front at the time, told reporters that no members of The Order who were staying at CSA were fugitives from the law. Not so. Kerry knew, but did not disclose to media or to police, that CSA was indeed protecting members of The Order who were wanted by the FBI for violent felonies including murder and bank robbery.

Kerry believed certain government action against CSA was inevitable. In addition to concerns about his own family, Kerry had an escalating fear that a wholesale shootout between law enforcement agencies and CSA would devastate the few remaining families who lived there, obliterate the households of loyal followers, annihilate shrewdly constructed support buildings, and turn every sacred meeting place on the compound into a muddy trash heap. He had good reason to be afraid.

Convinced of pending action, Kerry made a hard decision to do whatever he could to avert a disaster. Without the knowledge of anyone at CSA, particularly Ellison, he visited a trusted officer in the Arkansas State Police Department (ASPD) whom he had befriended in his capacity as CSA spokesperson. When they met at the ASPD, Kerry begged the officer to please come to him *first* if any issues arose against Ellison.

After his surreptitious chat with Arkansas police, Kerry wanted out of CSA and out of the movement. Begging for God's understanding. he prayed, "Lord, I don't care if you're giving me permission to change, I'm out of here." Before informing his wife and family of his intentions, Kerry decided they would leave the compound on May 15, 1985, the anniversary of his eighth year with the group. He didn't tell a soul. "To tell anyone would have made life worse," he explained. "I was nonetheless torn with my own betrayal." This is a concern that all defectors from the hate movement can appreciate.

He didn't have the chance to escape.

In early April 1985, the CSA compound was being slowly and systematically surrounded by its biggest enemy. Lurking undetected around every inch of the CSA perimeter, the mythical ZOG had stealthily arrived in resplendent military style. FBI agent Danny Coulson had already reviewed enough photos from surveillance cameras to authorize tactical maneuvers.

On April 19, 1985, a multi-jurisdictional force under agent Coulson's command encircled the CSA stronghold. Aside from their quest to seize illegal weapons, police had an arrest warrant for Ellison charging him with ordering his followers to manufacture illegal machine guns and firearm silencers. Jim Ellison and Kerry became aware of the troops when members first detected a division of military-clad personnel around the perimeter.

In Kerry's books and another written by Coulson[5], the two men carefully dissect what happened over the days of the CSA siege. Each describes, from contrasting perspectives, how everyone at the compound, inside and out, was hunkered down.

Unknown by CSA members and possibly by the FBI, the few remaining CSA families were seriously outnumbered in every conceivable way. Until troops were detected on the CSA grounds, members were unaware that, for days, a unified regiment guided with unyielding precision had meticulously observed every move they made. Coulson's team included 200 law enforcement officers in fatigues and camouflaged faces[6]. The operation included an amphibious unit on Bull Shoals Lake (cleverly disguised in rented fishing boats); a silent FBI-piloted surveillance helicopter; a perimeter of FBI agents situated within arm's-length of one another; anti-terrorist technology provided by the FBI, CIA, and ATF; and police units from city, county, state, and federal agencies.

To anyone unaware of how hate groups operate, the use of combined forces and that much government firepower may sound like overkill. To Coulson, an expert in the psychology of gangs, cults and domestic terrorists, nothing was taken for granted. An accomplished FBI tactician, Coulson, is a former Deputy Assistant Director of the FBI. In his thirty-year tenure at the Bureau, Coulson created and commanded the FBI's Hostage Rescue Team and commanded four field divisions.

Stationed on-site in the Ozarks, Coulson already knew CSA was armed with heavy artillery. He could not underestimate the convictions, strength, and firepower hidden behind the thick, reinforced walls around which his troops maintained a tense and careful watch. CSA's rigid, illogical focus and cultish mentality, augured by a string of directives from God's lips to Ellison's ears, made the group's intent difficult to fathom, much less control. Coulson had the group figured out. While his plan was largely tactical, his principal weapon was psychology.

One thing Coulson neither knew nor expected was that his ability to assess the group's weapons and capacity would be rivaled by Kerry's emotional intelligence and intuitive perception.

To Kerry, the siege unfolded as more of an exercise in diplomacy than an invasion by government agents. His strength to use his own capabilities, in concert with a finely-honed negotiating skill, put Kerry in the burdensome position of being the *only* person capable of striking a deal with Coulson. Subconsciously, Kerry knew any agreement he could conceive would rest solely on *his own* core values, principles he was no longer willing to deceive in the name of CSA or his esteemed mentor, Ellison. He was on his own.

As Kerry's thinking churned, Ellison's men waited behind barricades inside the compound. It takes a superhuman ego to believe a ragtag group of loyalists can break through a coordinated firing line of America's finest combat-trained forces on a mission. Ellison's line of defense was driven by a heaven-sent supply of macho. The men of CSA were stoked.

For three days after he and Ellison learned they were enclosed behind a heavy brigade of law enforcement agents, Kerry met with Coulson at least once a day to negotiate some miraculous Hail Mary pass that would avoid the loss of lives. Throughout their meetings, Kerry felt the responsibility of balancing his own moral imperative against Ellison, a leader he loved but recognized as unable to apply reasonable judgment. He believed in his heart CSA had fallen far astray from its loving, self-sustaining values. He had fully supported Ellison's righteousness until he came face to face with the recognition that he, Kerry, had a major role in creating an uncontrollable beast.

Kerry says his talks with Coulson led him to weigh everything important in his life, all of which he knew could be destroyed by simply standing on CSA's moral footing while the FBI rifled through homes in the compound with devastating consequences to Kay and their family, their home, their friends, and the community they had worked so hard to build.

After a process that had taken Kerry and Coulson nearly 36 hours to finesse, the siege officially ended when, on behalf of CSA, Kerry agreed to a settlement in which he and Ellison would surrender to federal authorities.

For much of its existence, CSA had been preparing, training, and practicing for just such a face-off. Attuned to a possible showdown, all CSA men were dressed in full paramilitary uniforms whenever they were on the grounds. Bullet-pocked cardboard cutouts of cops proved to Ellison his men were ready.

Coulson knew his team was up against more than a Boy Scout troop with spitballs and peashooters. Since many followers had recently fled CSA, the government forces silently surrounding the compound outnumbered the remaining inhabitants more than three to one.

Kerry writes in his books about a laundry list of weapons concealed on the CSA compound before the siege. The cache included handguns, shotguns, illegal automatic rifles with silencers, assault weapons, an illegal submachine gun, hand grenades, an M-72 anti-tank rocket, a WWII-era anti-aircraft machine gun, a makeshift heavy armored tank, and 15,000 rounds of assorted ammunition.

Kerry said CSA also stocked 86 packs of binary explosives[7], three half-pound blocks of military C-4 Plastic explosives[8], 270 blasting caps, and 2,000 feet of detonation cord. The compound housed a 30-gallon drum of cyanide, destined to poison the water supply of an unidentified American city. Also hidden on the premises were gold coins and Krugerrands, the currency of the apartheid regime in South Africa, valued at $40,000.

After the siege, Ellison and Kerry were immediately taken into custody. The FBI also apprehended two members of The Order who were being protected inside the CSA compound, Randall Evans and Thomas Bentley. In 1984, Evans was allegedly involved in the holdup of a Brinks armored car in California, taking $3.6 million with the help of submachine guns suspected to have come from CSA. Bentley and four other members of The Order were charged with killing a person they considered a "race traitor" by beating him with a hammer, then shooting him. Two other members of The Order also surrendered during the CSA siege, Jefferson Wayne Butler, and James Wallington. According to the FBI, evidence seized during their investigation directly linked CSA with members of The Order.

In the wake of the siege, Kerry told a reporter from the *New York Times* that the main reason the showdown ended peacefully was because, "God said this was not the time to take the direction of violence." He told me his thinking at the time also included, "If God says to shoot it out, we shoot it out. If we die, we die."

The FBI believed that over a period of up to four years CSA had been making wholesale conversions of otherwise legal firearms into outlawed MAC-10 (automatic) submachine guns. The uniquely crafted weapons uncovered by the ATF at the compound were distinctly similar to the weapon used by Charles Tate to kill officer Linegar. The ATF believed the weapons were also similar to the one used to kill Alan Berg, a popular Jewish Denver-based liberal radio host. Berg had been murdered at his home on June 18, 1984, a year before the CSA siege. The actual weapon used to kill Berg, a MAC-11 submachine gun fitted with a silencer, a trademark signature of the CSA weapons outfitters, was later found in possession of a member of The Order. The weapon used to murder Berg and those on the CSA property provided forensic evidence to further cement connections between the two groups.

The date of the CSA siege is meaningful to neo-Nazis. History books identify April 20, 1889 as Adolf Hitler's birth date. The Department of Justice (DOJ) also notes April 19 is crucial to self-styled patriots in militia movements as the anniversary of the 1775 battles between British soldiers and American Minutemen at Lexington and Concord. April 19 is worrisome enough that, every year, DOJ officers alert federal, state and local law enforcement agencies around the country to heighten their security awareness.

On April 19, 1993, more than 75 men, women, and children committed suicide at the Branch Davidian Compound in Waco, Texas, rather than cede to FBI agents and other federal officials trying to capture their leader, David Koresh. It is believed some were shot by other Davidians against their will by setting their own homes on fire. Four government agents and six Branch Davidians were killed in a gun battle during the 51-day standoff.

It is also no coincidence that exactly two years after the Waco siege, on April 19, 1995, Timothy McVeigh bombed the Murrah Federal Building, killing 168, the largest pre-9/11 terrorist act on American soil. Reports suggest McVeigh planned and timed the bombing to coincide with the second anniversary of the Waco fire.

Kerry was charged with 19 counts of possession of illegal weapons, one count of receiving stolen property, and one count of conspiracy to possess unlawful weapons. He says he never liked having automatic weapons at CSA and that he shot an automatic weapon only once.

Prosecutors offered Kerry a plea bargain in hopes of having him turn state's evidence against Ellison, the main target of their investigation. In Kerry's words: "If I would roll on Ellison, the government would drop all charges against me, with the exception of the conspiracy charge, and guarantee no prison time for me. I said no. I refused to testify against Ellison. I would not betray him."

Still caught in Ellison's demoralizing power hold, Kerry told me years later, "Ellison had done more for me than any man alive." As a testament to his commitment to the CSA leader, when he was booked into the Arkansas jail, he requested to be put in the same cell as Ellison.

During the month prior to grand jury proceedings to investigate potential criminal conduct at the CSA compound, Kerry told Kay everything that had gone on previously without her knowledge, including the incident at the gay church.

After meeting Kerry in his home, I asked if he knew what was going on for Kay at the time of the siege. He invited me to ask her myself and called her to join us in his office. Kay spoke fondly about the families and warm fellowship at CSA. As she began to describe the final few years at the farm, she suddenly drew her hands to her face and sobbed. Even without her knowledge that criminal actions were happening behind the scenes, the ever-obedient wife and caring mother told me she still feels responsible for influencing her husband's decision to continue as the group's Bible teacher after he first talked to her about bailing out.

As Kerry was being booked and jailed, he envisioned CSA buildings and homes being hopelessly destroyed by ruthless FBI agents on a search for evidence. When the ordeal was over, he was stunned to learn that not a single shot was fired and not a single CSA man, woman, or child was injured. According to Kerry, Coulson's team, the very embodiment of the once-dreaded ZOG, had left the camp in better condition than they found it.

Kerry's ability to negotiate a peaceful settlement and Coulson's order to conduct the operation as harmlessly as possible led to an enduring friendship between the two, long after his release from prison. Their families remain closely in touch.

The CSA siege and the cost to American taxpayers to finance it took a phenomenal amount of coordination, time, and resources to be successful. Other defectors from the hate movement point out that, were the government not to respond to the actions of such groups, the cost would be much greater. They say that hate crimes, many of which news consumers seldom see reported in detail, threaten the Constitutional promises of life, liberty and the pursuit of happiness. Allowing hate groups to terrorize citizens, defectors say, also threatens to denude liberty and justice for all as more of a bankrupt promise than a plausible standard of national policy.

In contrast with the dramatic events in Waco and Oklahoma City, most Americans are unaware of the FBI siege on the CSA compound. The siege was covered by some major metropolitan dailies and broadcast stations; however, its overall media impact on a national scale was minimal. When he was writing *Tabernacle of Hate*, Kerry asked reporters who covered the event why the unfolding drama got so little ink. The answer: "Nobody died."

The key lessons Kerry learned from his experience at CSA and his time in prison are about people who are different from him and the importance of maintaining an internal grasp of his own core values. Today, he is the same remarkably sensitive man, genuinely interested in people of all backgrounds.

Through days of grueling in-person questions and many follow-up phone interviews, Kerry exhibited an unfalteringly warm and courteous manner. He is an attentive listener who allows a speaker to complete every thought before offering his own. He is candid about what he now sees as the misjudgments and mistakes of his past.

Since the fall of CSA and after his release from prison, Kerry helps the FBI and other law enforcement organizations and civil rights groups. He occasionally speaks to high school audiences. His presentations provide a compelling way for young people to understand prison life. "First," he said, "I line out the confines of a jail cell on the classroom floor. Then," he continued, he tells his young listeners, "This is the space you have in prison. You experience no silence. You have no one to share anything with. No personal items. If you're lucky, you will see family once a week through a little frame of glass. Everything that is important to you is gone. Self-worth and ambitions? Gone. Goals and aspirations?

Gone. You will not trust anyone. You will be labeled a convict. You can never erase that feeling. You can't do enough good, can't shower long enough to get clean of this." By way of advice, he closes his in-school talks by saying, "You have one decision to make: Follow the path to this outcome or follow a different path."

At the close of our in-person interviews, Kerry told me about a significant change he made after the fall of CSA, a contradiction from the mild-mannered former Baptist preacher who later led a violent Christian Identity group. "I don't believe in teaching religion in schools. Instead, he said, his preference is to "teach Ethics to all children in K-12 schools, without exception."

Although CSA was officially dismantled and abandoned after the siege, when families first arrived on the land, they tried their best to carve a peaceful niche out of the Arkansas hills and lead a quiet and loving life, free of government intervention and away from negative elements that could corrupt their children and their personal values. Hate was not in the equation.

Kerry's memory of CSA – before, during and after its brush with government forces – offers an uncommonly unabashed view into the mindset of a hate group, its followers, and how they think and live. Kerry's post-hate wisdom, crafted to a great extent during his time in federal prison, sheds a clear light on how many defectors evolve.

Kerry Noble is not the first to be squeezed in a philosophical vice between hate and compassion. Nevertheless, he used his intellect, emotions, and love for humanity to avert a disaster. His logic overpowered madness. Danny Coulson, the FBI commander, told me he is convinced that without Kerry, the operation in Arkansas would have presaged the siege in Waco with a comparably fiery and deadly end.

After coming within a hair's width of decimating a church full of mostly gay parishioners, today he shares his wisdom with the Human Rights Campaign, the largest and most politically powerful LGBTQ group in the U.S. He now spends his days as a sales representative for a company near his home.

Bryon Widner
Julie Miller

IT STARTED WITH A THREE-YEAR-OLD TUGGING on the T-shirt of a man whose tattooed face would freak out most adults. The child's mother interpreted her daughter's baby-gibberish to mean, "Isabella wants a photo with you." Bryon Widner obliged, and an unconventional romance was born.

The backdrop for the snapshot was Nordic Fest 2005, a family-oriented Memorial Day event held over three days in a remote corner of Kentucky. There, crowds listened to internationally recognized speakers interspersed with the music of world-renowned bands. One online promotion forecasted, " . . . the great time children will have in our new playground." The playing field was part of a compound that the Imperial Klans of America (IKA)[9] called home.

Unlike what most Americans visualize for a family experience, this three-day festival was promoted online for its unmistakable purpose: "To insure the survival of the white race." The Internet's first major racial hate website, Stormfront.org[10], asked followers, "Where else can you go and not have to worry about your children's safety and just be with your own kind in unity . . . "

An annual to-do, this Nordic Fest was heralded throughout the white supremacy world as "the biggest 'whites-only' social event of 2005". The program was hosted jointly by the Klan and Blood &

Honour USA[11].   Hate rock bands from all over the world, such as Faceless Enemy, Patriots Call, and Teardown appeared on the main stage. The crowd also heard rousing speeches from Rev. Brian J. Moudry of the Creativity Movement[12], Commander Jeff Schoep of the National Socialist Movement, Jason Tankersley[13] of the Eastern Front, and Steven Boswell, a member of the Missouri branch of the neo-Nazi National Socialist Movement (NSM)[14], a white nationalist party operating in the United States and internationally.

When Bryon hunched over his knee to pose with the girl, his gesture impressed the child's single mother, Julie, as especially genuine and sincere. The two spoke briefly before Bryon, one of the event organizers, was pulled away. Through the entire three-day event, Bryon and Julie had only minutes of conversation. The conversation was consequential enough to spark an eight-month long distance romance and a marriage.

In Julie's words: "The thing about Isabella yanking on Bryon's T-shirt, that was 100% Isabella. I didn't put her up to it. I don't remember what he and I talked about, but I do remember that something was there. He was so intellectual, articulate. I liked that. I thought he was cute, but I wasn't looking for a man. I had just booted out a younger man I had been living with for a couple months. Isabella wanted a photo with him. I appreciated that he stopped for her."

I visited Bryon and Julie over three days in August 2014. They had been married for eight years and were temporarily staying at the home of Bryon's sister, Sara, in the New Mexico suburb where Sara lives with her husband and three children. Bryon and Julie made time to talk during a move from Sara's house to a nearby rental. We met three years after the release of the 2011 documentary, *Erasing Hate*[15] a two-hour film that highlights the laser surgery process Bryon went through over 24 extremely painful procedures to remove tattoos from his face, neck, and hands. The film references their decision to leave the hate movement, focusing on the impact Bryon's tattoos had on his post-hate job search.

In the documentary and in person Bryon and Julie were at ease sharing their experiences before, during, and after their time in the hate movement. To Bryon, each tattoo represented years of involvement in various hate groups, including those identified by name on his body, along with a near life-size image of Bryon's "weapon of choice," a straight edge razor, imprinted along his jawline – with red blood dripping from the blade.

Through our first in-person interview, Bryon was edgy and apprehensive. He fidgeted and gave quick responses. I asked if he felt comfortable. He raised a can of Red Bull in a mock toast, exclaiming, "My third today."

Julie was more relaxed when she and I met, unshaken by a steady stream of interruptions from children in the house – hers, Bryon's sister's, and kids from the neighborhood. As a family unit, Bryon and Julie showed an exceptionally high level of care for the children around them.

When Bryon met Julie, his most distinguishing feature was the unmistakably neo-Nazi and racist tattoos on exposed parts of his skin. When he took off his shirt, his chest, stomach, and back revealed more menacing images. Each tattoo communicated its own meaning. Since he left the movement, Bryon has had much of his ink removed, altered, or covered with new images.

After they met, Bryon's perceptions of people, as well as his social interactions, changed in dramatic ways. One of the biggest changes is how he related to former colleagues and people considered different, particularly non-whites. Yet, no matter what changes were brewing in his mind and spirit, his exterior until 2010 still screamed an inky neo-Nazi threat.

When they had their first conversation at Nordic Fest, Bryon was at the pinnacle of his trajectory in the hate movement. He was involved in four skinhead crews prior to forming a new Hammerskins offshoot called Vinlanders Social Club. Hammerskins are among the most violent faction of skinheads. Crew is another word for a skinhead group.

By then, Bryon had already served time in two county jails: one on a misdemeanor battery conviction for beating up a Mexican in Noblesville (Hamilton County), Indiana; the other for a murder charge for beating up a non-racist white man. The murder charge was later reduced to a lower offense.

When Julie met Bryon, she had recently left the National Alliance (NA) after four years with the neo-Nazi group. When I

asked about her possible role in any bias-related crimes, Julie specified, "I was not involved in any hate crime activity during my
time in the movement." She had joined NA with an ex-husband
and served in a supportive role as a recruiter and an NA loyalist.
Like other women in the movement, Julie's role generally included
caring for families and children, especially those moving into a
new location. While they may not be directly involved in a crime,
women inside the movement often cover for crimes committed by
skinhead men, including misleading police and other law enforcement investigators. Julie was no exception.

When she snapped that first photo of Bryon with her daughter, the
two bonded in part through the language of the tattoo, the markings
that covered much of Bryon's exposed skin at the time and some of
her own. Their tattoos formed a common language – words, symbols,
icons, and images – some specifically designed to trigger a reaction.
Both had a rich history behind every marking on their body.

A punk rocker at heart, 14-year-old Bryon got his first tattoo, the
letters "TR" for The Rejected, a plotline element in the 1984 cult classic
Suburbia, a film about the Los Angeles punk rock scene in the 1980s.
"The tattoo was hand-picked into my arm," he said, referring to the
non-electric method of a freestyle needle-and-ink tattoo. Next up were
the letters H-A-T-E across his right knuckles, also hand-picked. Julie's
tattoos, although numerous, are not nearly as threatening as Bryon's.
After Bryon's laser surgery to remove his ink, he and Julie modified
their remaining tattoos that are visible to bystanders so as to mask the
original image.

When they met, Julie brandished her own neo-Nazi symbols on
her hands, arms and chest: a swastika, German war eagle, Totenkopf
skull, the German Mother's Cross, and the words "Sieg Heil" on her
right thigh. All of her hate-related tattoos have since been obliterated,
covered with more innocuous images. Julie belies the tone of her former
body art, always beaming a broad smile and an engaging personality.

For many men at Nordic Fest, overlooking Julie would have been
improbable. A hearty laugh defies a lifetime of tough encounters and
hard knocks. Her blue eyes are striking and made even more so by a

steel barbell pierced through the far end of her right eyebrow. After putting on pounds after six pregnancies and 13 surgeries, Julie jokes, "I'm a lot more to love than I used to be." With her own children almost always by her side, as well as the children of friends and family, Julie stands out as an exceptionally caring mom, ready to listen and defer her own needs to those of a child.

By virtue of her innate good looks, Julie's every move was watched at Nordic Fest. Bryon is quick to point out, "These shows are usually male dominant. Women are with their husbands." Since men used their inborn senses to detect that Julie was single and available, a rare combination at such an event, the competition for her interest was fierce. In Bryon's own words, "Every male was hitting on Julie – or wanted to."

Julie recalled one situation that sheds a light on the gender dynamics that are often typical at a white-only event like Nordic Fest. As she was strolling through tables and exhibits, a skinhead from California approached Julie with a request. "He told me that a fellow skinhead's girlfriend had him 'pussywhipped.' He asked if he could take a picture of me kissing his buddy." Julie obliged. "I didn't know anything about the guys. It took about 30 seconds and it was over." Doing things like that, she shrugged, were all part of loyalty to the movement. Loyal or not, the half-minute sparked an annoying regret from Julie, who was quickly growing tired of being objectified wherever she turned.

Because of his role as a sponsor and organizer for the event, Bryon was distracted through most of Nordic Fest. After the photo with Isabella, he tried to talk to Julie one more time. They carved out another few minutes for the second chat before going their separate ways at the end of the festival. Lacking time to enter a deep philosophical dialogue, the centerpiece of their first conversation was tattoos. Each made an impression on the other.

Bryon saw more than ink. "Aside from the obvious physical attraction, she was cool. Okay, she was hot. Her blue eyes did it. She also has a great body – and a brain. We talked for maybe 30 minutes." At the end of the show, when the stage was collapsed, tents folded, and beer bottles swept into a pile, Bryon headed off to his apartment in Ohio and Julie drove back to her home in Michigan without as much as exchanging phone numbers.

After Nordic Fest, Julie maintained a phone friendship with the girlfriend of a "brother" in one of Bryon's skinhead crews. More than a month after the festival, Bryon's name came up in a phone conversation with her friend. Julie remembered Bryon well. Bryon remembered Julie in minute detail.

One night in October 2005, a full five months after the bands and the speeches in Kentucky, Bryon returned with friends to his apartment in the wake of a beer binge. He said, "My friend's girlfriend was talking to a woman on the phone." He overheard the name Julie. In a nanosecond, Bryon pieced together that the woman was talking to the Julie he met at Nordic Fest. He "hijacked" the phone call.

Intoxicated by booze and a burning libido, their first phone chat was, well, uncommon – in a psycho-erotic kind of way. Bryon told me that at one point during the call, with just enough spin, "I told Julie I was gonna' rape her and cut her with a razor blade." Marking her territory as a master of repartee, Julie's comeback was just as shaded and provocative. "Can we use my razor?" Julie said it was partially through their kinky talk that Bryon's "warped sense of humor" became an unforgettable attraction. With a devilish grin, Julie told me, "It was all in love. For him to start off that way, instead of me, showed we have the same kind of humor. Twisted."

Their conversations bloomed into a romance that belies the fierce righteousness of white supremacy. With their tattoos and sharp-tongued humor, their romance was easily outside the limits of conventional courting rituals. Over the next two months, Bryon and Julie talked daily in conversations lasting hours, each call probing deeper into the other's thoughts, dreams, and aspirations.

Julie was the first to break the traditional barriers that hate group members tend to build around independent thinking. "I brought up my disenfranchisement with the movement." She told Bryon how she felt after witnessing a number of troubling incidents at Nordic Fest, each confirming to her that the environment she experienced in the movement was no longer acceptable. The fallacies voiced from the stage at Nordic Fest confirmed to her that being around hate groups was no place for a family.

Julie told Bryon that she could no longer conceal the disgust she felt. One incident she witnessed at the event stood out as the ultimate contradiction at a family festival. She was standing near one of the many tents housing families and skinhead groups over the weekend when a man emerged. She had seen another man enter and leave the same tent earlier. The second man "walked out and unashamedly announced, 'I just fucked her! Who's next?'"

Maternal instinct led Julie to intervene. She entered the tent to find an underage girl naked, now covering herself with a blanket. Julie said the girl "was still lying there after the second guy. I wanted to get in her face." Julie sat down on the young woman so she couldn't escape. "I told her to have some self-respect."

When he heard Julie's experience, Bryon related another tent scenario from Nordic Fest, one in which a woman in her 20s was similarly shuffling men one at a time. Hearing Julie's observation, in contrast with his own example of the same abuse, was a contradiction too big for Bryon to ignore. Together, their stories cracked a code on the fundamental fallacy behind hate group ideology, that is, the righteous thinking that their principles are ironclad and followers act according to God-given beliefs: family, patriotism, freedom.

Through Julie's insights, and for the first time through his history in the movement, Bryon saw that the values and philosophy represented by the groups to which he had committed his life might actually be a delusion. For Bryon, a leader still responsible for inspiring some of the most violent men in the movement, the revelation forced him to question his own truth.

After less than two weeks into their phone dialogues, Bryon took a risk. "I knew I could confide in Julie without fear." He sensed he could be honest, that his words wouldn't show up on the Internet or in some conversation with another skinhead. After exchanging their mutual misgivings about the hate movement in general, Bryon took an even bigger leap of faith. "I told her I was tired of it; sick of the politics." Philosophically, they were aligned. But Bryon was still a leader of the Vinlanders. His neo-Nazi crews depended on him as their role model and motivator.

As their phone conversations progressed into November of 2005 Bryon was able to talk more and more candidly about personal things, issues important to him, yet generally out of bounds between skinheads.

With Julie, he no longer felt restricted to veil his true emotions behind the rigid bravado of white supremacist ideology. What Julie found most compelling was Bryon's intelligence. Even more than his brainpower, she admired his personal goals. "He wanted a family, a wife, and children." She saw Bryon as a suitable father for her children from a one-time fiancé and an ex-husband.

While most relationships rely on flowers, chocolates, and wining and dining to show the romance is building, Bryon and Julie developed their courtship on shared beliefs and values they cherished and a commitment to live their lives according to their own thinking. After months of telephone dating they started to realize they could grow new interests together, as a couple, away from the strict confines of hate.

Julie had learned from past experiences that men require a certain savvy to guide them toward mutual goals. She also learned a critical element about Bryon's behaviors at the time: He consumed massive quantities of beer every day. After two relationships in which alcohol abuse led to physical abuse, Julie considered Bryon's drinking to be a problem.

Bryon's past taught him that few humans are worthy of trust. In Julie, he found a rare combination: a good listener with a first-hand understanding of his past. He also recognized a kindred spirit who treated the people around her less judgmentally than he.

One night in early December 2005, seven months after he met Julie, Bryon returned to his apartment, in his word, "shitfaced." Following what had become a nightly ritual, he picked up the phone. With no particular fanfare after talking for nearly eight-hours, Bryon suddenly asked Julie to marry him.

Fully aware of his condition, Julie wasn't sure how to react. A bit cautiously, she said yes. The next day, while Bryon was getting settled at the tattoo shop where he worked, Julie called from Michigan. Feeling uncertain, she asked if he remembered the conversation. "Do you mean the part where I asked you marry me? Yeah."

Within days of the proposal, Julie gathered her daughters Isabella and Destiny for the eight-hour drive from their home in Michigan to Bryon's apartment in Ohio, her other children stayed at home. After a week at Bryon's place they drove back to Julie's house to start a new life together.

For Bryon, marriage was uncharted territory. While his previous relationships were measured in weeks, Julie, who is five years his senior, was not a first-time bride. Her courtship with Bryon was a vivid departure from the caustic pattern that defined her two previous long-term relationships.

For starters, Julie and Bryon didn't really date before their engagement, other than brief conversations at Nordic Fest followed by nightly phone calls. Julie *knew* their love was real. One big aspect of their romance made it strikingly different from Julie's relationships with the last two men in her life. Bryon had not threatened to kill her.

For Julie, capitalizing on Bryon's trusting nature and willingness to talk meant she had to find the means to alter his hate group behaviors in a way that was more consistent with their mutual values. Her ability to interpret what people were thinking based on word choices, intonation, and other verbal cues paid off. Not only could she tell when Bryon had been drinking, even over the phone she knew how to use his alcohol consumption to her own advantage: "Get a man drunk and he'll just roll," she chuckled. The two were meant for one another.

Having cemented a mutual trust within months after they met, Bryon and Julie started focusing their talks on a taboo issue: hypocrisy in the ranks of the hate movement.

At Nordic Fest they heard acclaimed leaders talk about the importance of family. At the same time, some of the honored speakers were widely known for their abuse of women, including their own girlfriends and wives. Their regard for children was no less phony. Seven years before speaking at Nordic Fest, Jeff Schoep, one of the keynote speakers and a pillar of the National Socialist Movement, pleaded guilty to aiding and abetting a burglary while his girlfriend's children waited in a getaway car. It was no secret that Schoep had a reputation for recruiting children into the hate movement, specifically 14- to 17-year-olds. According to the Southern Poverty Law Center (SPLC)[11], Schoep taught military skills and how to become a "more effective warrior" in NSM's Viking Youth Corps.

James Moudry, another Nordic Fest keynoter, exercised a selective definition of family during the years he was involved with World

Church of the Creator. In 2007, two years after Nordic Fest, Moudry allegedly burned down the home of a black family in his Chicago neighborhood. In June 2013, he received a 10-year prison sentence for the crime.

Bryon was born in Albuquerque, New Mexico, in April 1977. At age three, he and his infant sister moved to Corrales, an artsy, upper middle class New Mexico suburb, some 15 miles away. They were raised by their maternal grandmother in a three-bedroom house with a garage converted into a fourth. Even though the neighbors "had money," Bryon remembers growing up close to poverty.

"In our house, we were raised to be non-racist," Bryon told me during our first telephone interview. But, he said, the social environment around where he grew up could be bigoted. He said, "Some people of color lived there, mostly Mexicans and Native Americans." He recalled hearing racist jokes at school, with friends, and in social settings. But, he said, such language never tainted his childhood home and there was no Klan presence in the community.

Through his early years, Bryon was more attached to his mother than his father, who was largely absent. Much of Bryon's childhood included "the weekend dad thing . . ." He felt tormented wherever he turned, with no role models or adults with whom he could talk about his emotions. In their absence, he forged his own way of meeting life's day-to-day challenges. "Life doesn't come with an instruction manual," he lamented.

As his own inner unrest grew, Bryon was also dealing with childhood bullies. He said he was ridiculed at school because his parents were divorced, because he lived with his grandmother, and because of the family's substandard economic status. Depressed and dispirited, he lashed out at the people around him. When he was 12 years old, his father returned to the family. Although they lacked a tight father-child bond, Bryon gained an abiding respect for his dad's intelligence as an entomologist and university professor.

Bryon went through his entire K-12 education in Albuquerque public schools. Feeling bullied and uninspired, he funneled his rage into reading. "I spent time in libraries." By the time I was ten I had read the encyclopedia."

Clubs and extracurricular programs were even less inspiring than course work. He told me, "I didn't hang out a whole lot. I was more of a loner. I didn't know how to talk to people very well." During that awkward time, he was restricted from physical confrontations by his grandmother's rule to avoid fights. "I learned to defend myself from the people around me."

Bryon's family went to a Baptist church until he turned ten. Although he "got tired of fire and brimstone," he said he's still religious. During his time in the movement Bryon became an Odinist[16], a type of Germanic neo-pagan religion common among other skinheads. In his words, "[Odinism], plus the skinhead ideology is a formula to be the biggest asshole you can be. It's a medieval religion, irrelevant to this day."

After he left the hate movement, Bryon returned to Christianity. "I still have a relationship with God, but [I'm] not part of a denomination." He said religious fanaticism is widespread in the hate movement. One example of Christian dogma Bryon cited as a contradiction in his post-hate-movement thinking is "all homosexuals are going to hell." As soon as the words left his mouth, he sniffed sarcastically, "I missed that part in the Bible . . ."

Not long after his 14h birthday, Bryon's sense of self-determination was thrown off kilter. By the time he entered high school, he was demonstrating all of the parameters of an ideal recruit for a hate group: disassociation from family, social isolation, uncontrolled rage and a need for someone else to blame for not having everything he wanted.

Until he enrolled in a community college in the fall of 2014, Bryon says he was self-educated. "My dad and brother are certified geniuses. From experience, I look at things differently." Although his mother died at the start of his teenage years and he was separated from his father for most of his life, he developed a positive appreciation of the English language through his dad's intellect and reasoning. He attributes his rational, independent thinking to his father – or at least his *return* to rational thinking.

That year, Bryon lost a key part of his roots. After his mother died, he found himself at another crossroads. At age 14, he was surrounded by disillusionment and despair. Disengaged from others his age, he didn't know where to turn for help. By then his brother and sister had already been active in neo-Nazi groups. It didn't take much convincing for Bryon to be swayed in the same direction. Skinhead logic and rhetoric from those closest to him spurred the teenaged Bryon to blame his own woes on others.

Before he turned 15, Bryon assumed a rougher image and started calling himself a skinhead. At 16, he dropped out of high school, worked full time, and started living independently. "The year I became a skinhead, I became a really bad kid. My soul was destroyed. I was a chronic runaway. I went to the streets. I was confused."

During that time in his life, Bryon was intrigued by tattoos. By the time he turned 20 he was working as a piercing expert in the tattoo industry. He learned how tattoos provide a way for hate groups to recognize one another.

Once he started to meet more skinheads and leaders of larger and more violent hate groups, Bryon fell into the progression of hate that entices countless other novices to take out their aggressions on anyone they believe is inferior, undeserving, immoral, or not entitled to the American dream.

His goal was to look as threatening as possible. By working in the tattoo trade, Bryon was in constant touch with the latest images and their meaning inside the movement. "As I progressed in the white power movement," he told me, "tattoos reflected a more and more monstrous form." With each new tattoo, Bryon was assuming a more freakish identity.

By the time he reached his mid-twenties, he lost count of the number of tattoos on his face, head, neck, hands, arms, legs, chest, and back. Many of his markings represented a popular meaning in the hate movement; others were words and symbols significant only to Bryon, his followers, and those who know him. Combined with a powerful build, gritty facial expression, and a booming voice, Bryon's body presented a formidable exterior that matched the ire buried inside.

One of the most recognized tattoos among skinheads and Hammerskins is the Nazi SS bolts, a graphic blend of stylized letters that have the appearance of lightning strikes. The SS symbol is an insignia used by the German Schutzstaffel (SS) between the 1920s and 1945 to signify Nazi ideology and Germanic mysticism.

Bryon told me that when he was 16, he faced a test for his own SS bolts. Repeating what other defectors have said, he told me that before a group member is allowed to wear SS bolts on their skin, they are required to "commit a violent act on a minority." Bryon passed the test when a Native American man crossed his path. Avoiding graphic details, yet describing the scene as "bloody," Bryon assured me he earned the right to wear his SS bolts as a badge of honor.

In 2003, at the peak of his career in the hate movement, Bryon and his colleagues formed a Hammerskins group, Vinlanders Social Club. Their goal, he said, was "to take over the North American white power scene." To that end, he was recruiting heavily in Indiana, particularly Muncie and Newcastle. "I was travelling as part of my job in the tattoo industry. We wanted numbers." He knew precisely how to snag newcomers.

When we met, Bryon told me his step-by-step psychology for recruiting mostly younger men into a hate group. "First, you go to parties and concerts. You look for the guy sitting alone. He'll do anything to say he now has a friend. Then, you talk about values. You convince him that any problems he has are not his fault and not his responsibility. You tell him the fault is the Jews who own the media . . . " From there, Bryon's formula progresses to a blame game that spirals down to include anyone who doesn't measure up to the standard white supremacist profile. Whether he realized it or not, Bryon described the exact conditions he and Julie were a part of before getting hooked on the movement.

Once a prospective recruit agrees to hang out with a group, Bryon continued, that person is manipulated into a pattern of heavy drinking, tough language, disparaging talk about Jews, blacks, gays, immigrants or anybody who doesn't look like them. Before they know it, the new crew member is in the middle of a fight in which proving loyalty to the group is imperative. Throw in a pair of Doc Martin boots and a Nazi salute and voilà, you're a skinhead. Bryon employed his recruiter role with precision.

As he climbed the rungs of neo-Nazi leadership, Bryon conveyed more ominous messages with his body. They were not idle threats. As he explains in *Erasing Hate*, the intended message was: "Don't mess with me or you WILL get hurt."

Part of Bryon's notoriety as an exceptionally savage skinhead came from what he describes as his "weapon of choice," a straight edge razor. During his years as a crew leader, he had a razor in his pocket at all times "just in case." In our first phone interview I asked what he did with the blade. His words cut to the core. "Well, I wasn't shaving with it. I was using it to hurt people."

He described one example in which an argument in a bar led to Bryon being confronted by six men in an alley. "All six started hitting me at once. I had to do something. I stabbed one of them in the belly. There was a lot of blood, a lot of it got on me. I have no idea of the damages." Bryon later briefed me on another incident involving his razor. At the end of that story, he sniffed, "Let's just say I didn't stop to check pulses . . . " Bryon walked away from both incidents with no arrest.

The more Julie and Bryon talked, the more it became clear that as their relationship grew, the constant call to conform with the hate movement's rigid extremist beliefs was fading. The values that had drawn them to the groups they were affiliated with didn't outweigh what drew them together.

A commitment to family, independent thinking, and authenticity surfaced as key elements that united them. With the memory of a recent disastrous marriage behind her and their love for one another clear, Julie put all of her energy into building an enduring relationship. Bryon, a latecomer to the concept of settling down, was unabashed in expressing his love for Julie and his interest in having a family of his own.

Julie was born in Detroit in the fall of 1971, at a time Detroit's neighborhoods were being revitalized. In many ways, Motor City's urban renewal was an apt metaphor for Julie's own development. Race issues were apparent in her hometown and in her family. "My dad's racism was focused on blacks," she said. In his later years, Julie's father became more sensitive to human differences, found religion (Christianity), and gave up alcohol. Family talk about Latinos was less harsh, mostly due to having a Guatemalan uncle.

Julie grew up in a family dynamic she said was marked by strife, neglect, and abuse. Without dwelling on her family history, she characterizes her early childhood with parents who were less than ideal.

Through her early teens her mother and stepfather were heavy drink-ers. "My dad was a drunk. He abused my mom." Following a pattern that mirrors that of other defectors, Julie's early childhood included abandonment, loneliness, parental hostilities, trauma, and occasional self-abuse. "I was molested by the oldest son of a neighbor at a home where we camped. He was in his late teens. The way he got me to not tell was by [telling me], 'You know what your dad is like, so don't tell.'" She didn't.

Julie's parents divorced in 1979 when she was about eight years old. Shortly after the breakup she lived with her mother, surrounded by a new family. The arrangement included frequent visits to her birth father. "My mom moved herself to Arizona [after] dad threatened her life." It was at that time when Julie first started acting out her family issues through tobacco, alcohol, and pot. By the time she reached age 10, she went to live with her mother in Arizona.

During the years after she moved to Arizona, Julie also started to show signs of self-abuse. "I was a cutter," she said. In addition to slicing into her skin, she found solace by punching walls and jumping from buildings – "for fun." Her family and school administrators advised counseling. "It failed. I saw through the [therapist's] manipulation. I felt everyone was against me. Bryon tells me I'm always looking for a conspiracy."

The drama at school and at home affected Julie's education. "In the seventh grade I was on the honor roll. In eighth grade, I was doing badly [academically]." She was sent to a school counselor for troubled kids. "That's the time I decided I was living to die." A future was not part of her vision.

In 1984, when she turned 13, Julie was living with her mother and stepdad in Scottsdale, Arizona, a suburb with no resemblance to her native Detroit. "I was going to parties with strangers; adults who would buy alcohol for minors." Around that time, "My mom and stepdad started drinking more heavily."

That year she got an itch to defy conventionalism and express her penchant for political disorder and extremist thinking. "I cut my hair almost all the way down. On one side, I shaved an anarchy sign, on the other a swastika. I did it myself. That was before [Scottsdale] was as chic as today. Then, it was just Scottsdale."

In 1985, as her self-destructive behaviors grew more serious, she recalled, "My mom and stepdad didn't know what I was doing." I asked her if she felt loved by her parents. She responded without hesitation, "Not really." Asked if she felt loved by *anyone* at that time, she recalled, "My aunt, my mom's sister loved me." But, she added, "I never felt like I deserved to be happy."

At 14, refusing to be restricted, Julie ran away from home to live on the streets. "That's when I started using acid, coke, meth, and a few other random drugs." Worried about Julie's rebellious behaviors, her aunt, mother and brother, searched for her, eventually finding Julie in the regional airport. "They dragged me to the hospital. They tried to put me in the loony bin." When they arrived, she told me, "I knew what to say and what not to say." She dodged being admitted by pouring on "mock tears and complaints about harsh treatment at home."

While Julie was 15 and still living on the streets around Phoenix, she was raped. Without shedding light on the details, she said, "[For] my whole life, I wanted to sabotage whenever I was happy. Because of my past, I felt like I never deserved to be happy." Her self-perception deteriorated. "I just didn't care anymore."

In addition to psychological trauma, Julie survived a number of health crises at an early age, including a childhood accident which, decades later, was discovered to have caused a fractured pelvis. Her shifted pelvis is the reason for five C-section births. The babies, she said, couldn't fit through her birth canal.

Julie's first experience with a live-in lover was tainted by intense and abusive fights. She tolerated a three-year on-again/off-again affair from 1989 to 1994 with Dave, the man who fathered her first two children. Although they were engaged for three years, they never married.

They met in the spring of 1989 when Julie was 17 and living near Detroit. She described Dave as "a tall, skinny skinhead," a raucous biker prone to heavy drug use and dealing, and violent outbursts. After a couple months, the bond kicked up a notch when Julie became pregnant. Dave's pressure to get an abortion didn't fly. She opposed the procedure because "too many friends had bad experiences during or after abortions." After her first son was born [he asked not to be identified by name], Julie became pregnant with her daughter Sadie, who was born in 1991. Later that year she was engaged to marry Dave.

One day in 1994, Dave was at home in an agitated mood. He told Julie he was going out on a drug run. By then, Julie was fed up with his drug dealing. "I told him I was done." Not long after he left, Julie got a call from a friend who tipped her off about her fiancé's real intentions. "My friend told me to get out of the house. Dave's going to kill you." Knowing he kept his own stash of guns and other weapons, Julie packed her things, sat two of her three children, ages three and four, in her car and drove to Scottsdale. Dave was history.

As a single mom in 1996, Julie maintained her family and household by working at a hospital in Phoenix. She later lost the job and her apartment after being diagnosed with manic depression. Her morale declined, along with her will to live. At age 25 she was back to living on the streets. The world became a joyless journey. When disability payments from her hospital job ended, Julie was dealing meth. After a while, she said, "I had seen so much drug, alcohol, sexual abuse, and divorce – I just wanted to die. I contemplated suicide every day. I was depressed. I *lived* to die."

It is experiences like Julie describes that make down-and-out young people susceptible to the allure and the false sense of belonging that enables the hate movement to grow and endure.

After one attempt to take her life, Julie was couch surfing with skinhead friends at a meth house in Phoenix. She had opened up about feeling suicidal when a male friend told her, "Suicide is not the answer."

Later that night she was sitting quietly at the kitchen table when she heard a single gunshot ring out from an upstairs bedroom. When she ran to the room, she found the man who had given her that sage advice now lying on the floor in a widening pool of blood from a self-inflicted gunshot wound. The event was a terrifying reality check. She decided she wanted to live.

Not long after that experience Julie fell into a state of deep melancholy. In addition to the daily challenges of being a single parent, the haunting experience of her friend's suicide led to her feeling unable to move forward. She was diagnosed as manic depressive. For survival, she relied on her children. "The kids gave me a reason to live." She may not have known it at the time, but Julie's attention to family unity would become an essential part of her time in the hate movement. Nevertheless, being recognized as a kind of domestic do-gooder is an inconsistent description for someone committed to the anti-Semitic intentions of the National Alliance.

In 2001, around her 30th birthday, Julie met the man who would be her first husband in a hook-up that starts out sounding like a joke. A traveling meat salesman made a random call at her house in Phoenix. After hearing his front door pitch, Julie told him, "I don't have money for meat. I'm a single parent with three children." The man returned to his truck and left.

The next day the meat vendor was back at her door. Unsure of his real intentions, Julie, an adventurous and trusting soul, invited him inside. "He casually mentioned he was a skinhead." The reference was not particularly alarming to a woman whose background included passing friendships with white supremacists. After chatting briefly, the two exchanged phone numbers. She agreed to meet again.

During his third visit to Julie's house, the meat peddler brought along his roommate. Distracted by her dog, the roommate, whom she later referred to as Elias, sat silently in her living room. His silence intrigued Julie, even more than his tall, physically fit frame and rugged good looks. "I like the challenge of the quiet men, the ones that ignore me." She struck up a conversation with Elias, who eventually invited her to the apartment where the two men lived.

Without her immediate awareness, Julie was Elias's latest lust interest and an unsuspecting pawn in a game to draw one more player into the hate group he was aligned with, the National Alliance (NA). Julie fit the ideal profile of a hate group recruit: white, single, socially detached, hard-strapped for cash, depressed, and angry. She was being skillfully seduced into the neo-Nazi web.

When she got to Elias's apartment . . . "I saw Nazi flags. But, I didn't freak. Seeing the flags wasn't a shocker. In my early 20s I had dated a supremacist who had 'WHITE POWER' tattooed on the back of his legs." Julie learned that Elias became a skinhead in prison. He had recently been released after serving a four-year sentence for aggravated assault.

Over the next few weeks, the relationship with the meat merchant's roommate went from a slow roast to a searing broil. Reflecting on the torrid affair, Julie's eyes narrow. "We didn't date very long. We were intimate one time." Once was enough to get Julie pregnant. "That," she said, was "the only reason I married him." A year and a half later, when she got the news yet another child was on the way, the family was barely making ends meet. It was the fourth child for Julie, her second with Elias. With their second pregnancy, circumstances got more complicated and less enjoyable.

After a hastily planned wedding in April 2002, Elias continued to push Julie into the hate movement. He talked about taking baby steps. But soon after they were married, he pressed Julie to become an NA volunteer. When she told her children about her decision to join the NA, Julie's four-year-old daughter, Sadie, told her that God told her, "Everything is going to be okay." When her ten-year-old son learned she was getting involved with a hate group, he tried to talk her out of it. Feeling conflicted, she called the local NA chapter. "They saw us and introduced us to other NA skinheads," she said.

Although NA shares the same basic supremacist ideology as many other neo-Nazi groups, its members often appear less *visibly* threatening. Julie saw NA men as more clean cut than other white power groups. "They're the suits part of the movement," she said. NA men are often neatly dressed in clothing that, from a distance, can pass as a military uniform.

An incident changed the situation with Eliias after the family relocated from Phoenix to Owensboro, Kentucky. Nine months after the move, Julie's oldest son, then 10 years old, got beat up by some kid around the same age. The two boys agreed to fight for their dignity in a dual at a local park.

Elias decided to escort her son to the park. Julie stayed at home. Elias later told Julie he watched from a hidden vantage point to ensure the fight was fair. The arrangement to support their son might have worked better if his sense of justice didn't follow the dark and distorted thinking of a neo-Nazi extremist. He told Julie that when he saw their son was on the losing end of the battle, he jumped out and beat the boy's opponent with the same vicious fury he reserved for hate crime victims.

Without knowing the extent of the child's injuries, Elias left the boy lying helpless in the park. He assumed the injuries were serious enough that he asked friends to drive him out of town. He was already dodging an outstanding warrant issued after he violated parole from his time in prison for aggravated assault. He told Julie his friends would drive him to Indiana. "He left me to deal with the cops coming to our house every day," she said.

After pummeling the child in the park and in fear of facing another prison term, Julie's husband connected with a skinhead couple through the National Socialist Movement (NSM), a white nationalist group. Julie and Elias moved the family from Kentucky to St. Paul, Minnesota, to stay with NSM members. Once in the Twin Cities area, she said, her husband would go on "bum rolls in the parks," a term he used for beating up gays and homeless men.

Months later, the family moved to Mercer, Wisconsin. "We stayed with a KKK guy in a place with no electricity." While they were there, Elias showed scant initiative to get a job or help support the family. Julie described the scenario: "The word 'SKINHEAD' was prominently tattooed across his shaved head. He was out of work. I would ask him, 'Who's going to hire you?' He refused to cover the tattoo with hair or even a hat."

With little prospect of work and no other income options, Julie went to the local Department of Social Services for help. At a time when Elias was beating up children, gays, and homeless men, and brutalizing "minorities" he assumed to be getting ahead on the public dole, his family was surviving through the generosity of U.S. taxpayers. Being oblivious to such contradictions is a hallmark of white supremacist thinking.

Julie plunged into NA with what became her own trademark way of helping mothers find homes and provide for their children. Her role, she explained, was "to mother." But her involvement in NA was not enough to sustain the original spark that united Julie and Elias. With the same speed that took them from first date to marriage, the steamy honeymoon soon grew icy. Adding a drug habit to his intimate knowledge of prison culture, Elias started treating Julie like a cellmate. They were married just over a year before her husband started to become more physically and verbally abusive to her and her children.

As we talked, Julie continued to draw a more frightening picture. She knew Elias's threats were not to be taken lightly. For one thing, she said, "He wore red laces." Within the hate movement, red laces generally signify the wearer has committed a very serious hate crime, often murder. She added simply, "I didn't know the details and I didn't want to know."

From St. Paul, Julie and Elias moved to a home in Bessemer, Michigan, in 2003. Julie started a new job as a bank teller in the small town. As sole wage earner, she was feeding two adults and three children plus preparing for a fourth. Not able to survive on her bank check alone, she started a newspaper route for extra cash. The pressure on Julie was at a high point – and was about to get much higher.

The bank enrolled Julie in a training program at a venue roughly two and a half hours by car from their home, where she stayed at a hotel. On a day Julie was in class, she received an emergency phone call from skinhead friends in Arizona. They told her Elias had called and told them he was going to commit suicide. She arranged for a ride back home.

That July day, Julie entered a crucible from which she was unable to escape. A trio of earth-shattering family crises that unfolded back-to-back over a period of six painful and unforgettable weeks.

The first horror hit one night after Julie got home from work. Elias appeared physically healthy and cogent. With little more warning than saying, "I need to tell you something," Julie said he blurted out, "I molested your daughter." Horrified, she remembered Elias had told her about his own run-in with a child molester when he was a boy. Yet, knowing his life history gave little comfort to a mom who just learned her husband had molested her 12-year-old daughter, his stepdaughter.

Doing her best to manage a boiling anger, Julie escorted her child outside to talk in private. "I asked her if she wanted me to go to the police. She said no for fear the story would show up in the local news-paper where every crime was reported. She didn't want her friends to know what happened."

When Julie walked back into the house, her husband warned, "If you go to the police, I'll kill you and the children." Convinced Elias had already committed at least one murder and showing all the drunken signs he was completely detached from reality, Julie locked herself in a room with her children. "I had to think . . . "

With tensions on the home front now potentially deadly, Julie was immobilized. "I was five months pregnant. I was showing and I could feel the baby kicking." Against her better judgment, she decided to stay with her abusive husband.

Two weeks later, Julie went to a routine visit with her OB/GYN. Tests indicated that her baby's heartbeat was good and other vital signs were positive. The physician detected a possible infection and recommended Julie return the next day for an ultrasound. "I left the visit feeling upbeat and positive."

The second of three rapid fire crises came that evening after Julie returned home from the visit to her doctor. Julie and her husband got into a nasty verbal fight. As she described the struggle and what followed, she spoke solemnly through a cold stare, looking into the distance as if watching the scene replay on an IMAX screen, speaking in a monotone.

Elias's next move happened so fast Julie was totally unprepared. "He pushed me down, then he kicked me in the stomach. The next day, I went in for the ultrasound." After a straight-faced doctor repeatedly slid his ultrasound device over a glob of gel on Julie's stomach, he suddenly stopped and set the instrument aside to deliver a message that, for Julie, would never end.

"The doctor told me there was no heartbeat. The baby was dead." Because the baby's heart was beating just one day earlier and was now inactive, it was evident to her that Elias's kick killed the baby. The doctor closed the visit by telling Julie that because of health concerns from previous births and possible complications from this birth, the fetus had to be surgically extracted.

Days later, when she arrived for the surgery, Julie made one special request. "I asked for my baby's body [when the procedure was done]. I didn't want my child used as a science project." As she was being prepped in the operating room, the last thing on her mind was the swastika, war eagle, skull, and German Mother's Cross on her arms and chest, and the "Sieg Heil" on her leg.

When the procedure was done, Julie walked away from the outpatient surgery dazed, weak, and doing her best to cope with overwhelming grief. She said "As I was leaving, a nurse came into the hallway and handed me a paper bag." She received no comforting words, no counseling, no emotional support.

When Julie eventually braced herself enough to remove a glass receptacle from the sack, she collapsed. An over-sized Petri dish about six inches in diameter and two inches high, held the remains of her baby. In the container she saw a tiny mutilated body only marginally distinguishable as human, its gender beyond recognition. "I cried and cried and cried. It was horrible." She is convinced the nurse's unprofessional bedside manner was because of her tattoos.

Julie's disdain for the treatment she received that day was insignificant in contrast with her disgust for the man she had married 16 months earlier. In the wake of Elias's horrendous treatment, plus the way she was treated during her most recent medical procedure, it took Julie all the emotional energy she could muster to get her feet back on the ground so she could have her baby cremated – and move on.

The third crisis broke two weeks after the death of her unborn baby when her husband came home, drunk and disheveled, after a bar fight. "He told me he stabbed a man." Without knowing the extent of the victim's injuries, Julie sensed the worst. "He ordered me to get in the car and drive him out of town. He wanted to hop a train. I kissed the kids goodbye, not knowing if I'd ever see them again." She was fully aware of how irrational her husband could be. By the time he slid into the vehicle, Elias was barely conscious. What happened from there Julie recalls through a blur of spontaneous events, each more grisly than the one before it.

Her husband was in the passenger seat, clutching the knife he had used earlier in the evening to stab a man. "He was wasted from drinking. He forced me to drive and threatened to kill me. Then he passed out. I wanted him out of the car." Julie could take no more of his endless abuse. She stopped the car and ordered him to get out. When he left, weaving as he walked down the street, Julie drove off, eager to return to her children.

Five hours after getting home, Julie received a call from the local hospital. She learned from the police that Elias had stolen a car and was killed in an accident. The terrorizing events of 2003 were over.

Julie was tasked with taking care of the details for her husband's funeral, a chore she felt was more an obligation than a step to emotional closure. She extended little more courtesy to him than he had shown for her through their short and miserable marriage. For her, the torment was over. Whatever Julie wore that day, she said, was not black. "There was no funeral. The kids went to school the day he was buried." In hopes of healing the wounds created over the gloomy weeks before her husband's death, Julie took a family leave of absence from her job at the bank. "I needed time to recover."

By then, she had been involved with the National Alliance for over a decade. She had grown disillusioned with the hate movement after watching her husband's life unravel. After being sensitized to a marked difference between what hate groups say they do and what they actually do, she was even more dispirited. The hypocrisy and a lack of integrity she saw inside the movement began to gnaw at her nerves.

A decade later, I asked Julie how she now felt about Elias's death. She summarized her emotions with a snort and two words: "Thank God." I later realized that at no time while she told me about her life with her ex-husband had she once referred to him by name. In a follow-up phone interview, I asked for his name. She paused . . . "You can call him Elias. That's his middle name. Whenever I see his first name in print I get sick. It's just too painful."

In 2005, some 21 months after Julie became a widow, her cheeky three-year-old asked to be photographed with a stranger whose face was dappled in tattoos. By the time Julie met Bryon, the hypocrisy that irritated her about her late husband was all too fresh on her mind. What she witnessed at Nordic Fest was just one more tier of double standards and two-faced deceit all melded together as a defining point for the entire hate movement. She knew her NA days were numbered.

As Julie and I talked before closing her account of the agonizing weeks leading up to Elias's death, contempt returned to her voice. She recalled that just days before her husband killed their unborn child, stabbed a man in cold blood, and threatened to kill her, "He was talking about murdering pedophiles. My skinhead husband. Mr. Gay Basher. Mr. Beat-up-Homeless-Guys-But-Don't-Look-for-a-Job. Mr. Righteousness. He molested my daughter."

On Christmas Eve, 2005, after seven months of phone calls and an 11-hour drive from her home in Michigan, Julie arrived outside Bryon's apartment building in Sydney, Ohio, with her daughters Destiny (eight) and Isabella (three). As a light snow animated the holiday sky, Julie gazed up at Bryon beaming down from his window – and froze. "Oh my God, I was soooo nervous." Suddenly it hit her: "I thought, I'm engaged to a man I haven't even kissed." When they met inside, Julie remembers being awestruck as she walked into Bryon's apartment. "It was so cute." Bryon had gifts wrapped for Julie and her daughters and silver bands for their wedding. They stayed at Bryon's place from Christmas Eve until New Year's Eve.

They kicked off 2006 with the drive back to Michigan. When they walked into the house, Julie's oldest son had prepared an unforgettable welcome. "The sink was stacked with dirty dishes. Dog accidents spotted the carpet. The place smelled. I was soooo embarrassed." Her son's bursting enthusiasm came in the form of a casual . . . "I didn't think you'd really do it."

Not quite two weeks later, on a frigid Friday the 13th in January, Bryon and Julie exchanged their vows before a Justice of the Peace, the hate group iconoclast and a NA mother in the process of separating from the hate movement. Julie describes their wedding as anything but traditional. "We were all wearing black. The Justice of the Peace put us in a side room. The tattooed freaks."

As a first-time groom, Byron knew his vows brought new responsibilities, which he was eager to accept. He was confident that centering his attention on his family would give him a revitalized, positive purpose that the hate movement was unable to offer. When the ceremony was over, Bryon left the court a new person. In Julie's words, "His goal of having a family literally came to fruition overnight. He was instantly the father of four."

Shortly after the wedding, Bryon and Julie talked about having a family together. "Physically, I was exhausted. I told Bryon, if you want a baby, we need to do it now." A long line of injuries had already weakened Julie's body. She often experienced excruciating pain from being run over at age seven, the accident that caused her pelvis to shift. Two months after tying the knot, Julie's maternal mode burst into high gear. Instinctively, she knew Bryon's dream of being a dad was about to come true. She was right. As the news sunk in, the thought of a fifth pregnancy created its own concerns for Julie, especially when the heartbreak of her last pregnancy was still fresh on her mind. Not to be halted by a history of physical and emotional setbacks, Julie was eager to be the mother of Bryon's child.

The pregnancy was not free of challenges for Bryon. In addition to grappling with his new role as husband and step-father, Bryon was still considering when and how to leave the Vinlanders, the Hammerskins group he helped to create less than three years before he met Julie. Plus, for the children, accepting a new dad turned out to be bumpier than expected.

Julie was also juggling a handful of heady personal dilemmas. When she met Bryon, the last thing on her mind was a long-term relationship. She attended Nordic Fest because she was still involved with the National Alliance, albeit with serious doubts about how much longer she could hang onto the ideology. She was certainly not expecting to raise questions in the mind of a Nordic Fest organizer, much less expose him to conflicts she saw in the leadership of the hate movement. Julie viewed the groups she knew intimately as out of sync with reality. As their relationship grew, one phone call at a time, Bryon allowed Julie to reveal her true emotions about the groups they were both involved in. Their private conversations gave them license to explore what love could be like when they were free of the hate movement.

Now they were soon to be parents.

As part of planning their future as a family, Bryon confirmed the decision they knew would affect their safety and the safety of their children. He was determined to sever all ties with the Vinlanders and begin a whole new independent life as a husband and father. Until the connections were cut, Bryon's intention to defect was private and intensely protected. They both knew that any inkling of Bryon's pending farewell from his crew would result in threats to the family – or worse.

From the day he moved in with Julie, Bryon's commitment to separate from the Vinlanders grew more intense and more impossible to conceal. Each hour Bryon spent with his family was one less hour with his crew. He knew it. They knew it.

Julie had already convinced Bryon of the false pretenses they had both endured through their time in the movement. They knew what happened under the tents at Nordic Fest and the lies from leaders they once respected. As the deceit came clearer, their respective groups continued to toe the rhetorical line of white supremacist values: family, unity, the continuity of the white race. Between Nordic Fest and their wedding, Julie made the commitment to disconnect her the NA ties.

Once they realized just how shallow and contradictory the hate movement rhetoric could be, Bryon's allegiance to the Vinlanders dimmed more by the day. In turn, his crew was getting edgy over what was happening to their chief organizer. They could sense Bryon falling away with each beer they chugged without him, every epithet they spat in his absence, and whenever his razor wasn't there to sharpen their odds in a fight on some unsuspecting victim.

With gut-level perseverance, Julie's focus shifted from her nurturing work with NA families, to keeping her own family safe. Although less confrontational in her skinhead days than Bryon ever was, Julie knew every person in the NA operation was critical to the overall impact on the cause of white supremacy. She didn't want deception to pollute the love in her own family.

Between marriage, parenthood, and his soon-to-be break from the Vinlanders, the changes in Bryon's life reached a crescendo. With one part clarity and two parts humor, Bryon said, "I misconstrued how much time family takes away from drinking." As a husband and parent, it was difficult for him to maintain his daily intake of a case of beer "and sometimes a bottle of Jack Daniels as a chaser."

Complicating the emotional flux was Bryon's increasing belief that Julie's two oldest daughters didn't want him. In addition to the demands of a new family, he was trying to balance his drinking and what to tell the Vinlanders. He had yet to learn how taxing it could be to walk away from the group he was instrumental in creating.

The more time Bryon carved out for family, the more time the Vinlanders demanded from him. He recalled how the group became mired in "jealousy, gossip, and drama – grown thugs acting like a sewing circle. I couldn't center myself." The conflict turned into a catastrophe.

Julie described a superficial spat that happened on an otherwise uneventful day in 2006. Bryon's tone made it apparent the issue was bigger than bickering over toast crumbs in the butter dish. Trying to manage the buildup of increasingly weighty issues affected every aspect of his life. She sensed the pressure he was under was sending him into a free fall.

As he explained the incident, Bryon said, "We got into a big fight. Julie was hormonal and I was dealing with club bullshit. I snapped. I pushed Julie and Isabella out of the room, barricaded myself, swallowed a bottle of pills and blacked out. I wanted sleepy time. I just couldn't find peace anywhere."

As depicted in the *Erasing Hate* documentary, Julie calmly verbalizes what went through her mind when she realized what was happening to her husband. She had been through the same ordeal when she tried to take her own life. In the documentary, she calmly expresses her thoughts at the time to Bryon: "I'm pregnant. Don't leave me with all this stuff going on. I love you. I finally found someone who relates to me, who knows me, and [to whom] I could be myself with heart and soul." In an intensely sobering one-liner to Bill Brummel, the producer of the film, Julie poured the full extent of her emotion, "I didn't want to lose him."

Bryon regained consciousness in a hospital room. As he was being treated by a roomful of emergency caregivers he "heard a snap." Through a haze, Bryon became aware that a nurse broke his nose trying to get a tube inside of him. "I started vomiting blood." Bryon insists her moves were more personal and deliberate. Mindful of the neo-Nazi symbols on his face, he believed, "She was trying to kill me. I went into Viking mode – and started swinging." Traumatized and hysterical, he struck out at the entire medical team. Police were called and Bryon was restrained. "I was basically comatose in the hospital for three days. I woke up where they take suicide victims." Through the entire ordeal, Julie and her then five-year-old daughter Isabella were beside him.

After the breakdown, Julie demanded Bryon see a doctor. He visited a family physician who, Bryon was pleased to learn, was versed in Celtic mythology and knew the meaning of the runes and symbols tattooed on his body. Feeling confident he now had a provider who could even remotely appreciate his background, Bryon opened up. The physician prescribed an anti-anxiety medication.

In addition to a broken nose, Bryon was diagnosed with Post-Traumatic Stress Disorder and borderline personality disorders. He was eventually prescribed an antipsychotic drug so he could sleep at night. After a year of medication and feeling like a "mad scientist," the prognosis was positive. Bryon lost the kneejerk urge "that made me want to kill people." He later learned that during his treatment, "They wanted to commit me."

One of the questions Bryon was asked during a psychological assessment was, "Do you feel like you're going to hurt people?" Under the circumstances at the time, medical applicability notwithstanding, the question was beyond ironic. Although the physician was talking to a man whose body was covered with unambiguously hateful tattoos and with a known history as a razor-slashing skinhead and the leader of one of the most violent hate groups in the U.S., Bryon's interests were now focused on his family.

Even though the meds were working as planned, Byron complained the medication he was taking, "made one beer feel like three." As his mental state was being tended to, Bryon set another monumental goal for himself. "I made the decision to get my head back together and quit drinking." He said going cold turkey from a case-a-day addiction was incredibly hard."

As leader of the Vinlanders, Bryon was expected to be with his crew, setting a tone and inflaming the fear of every victim they targeted. His national reputation as both a vicious warrior and a hard-driving organizational leader was difficult to duplicate. The Vinlanders believed the impact of losing its top lieutenant, a star fighter known for his motivational skill and exceptionally violent actions, would leave them heading to a slow demise. As the chasm between Bryon and his crew widened, a cold ultimatum came from his anxious colleagues: Us or your family – which is it?

Although Julie held onto organizational secrets from her white nationalist years as part of the NA, Bryon's behind-the-scenes stories from Vinlanders, if they were ever made public, could imprison some members, possibly for life.

Not long after learning of his impending fatherhood, Bryon took an audacious step when he publicly renounced his neo-Nazi views and left the Vinlanders to their own devices. It also left them feeling vulnerable to the secrets Bryon carried with him. He knew his former comrades would see him as no more than a race traitor. The consequences for making a pubic split from his crew were swift and strong.

After his breakaway, phone threats from Bryon's former crew-members mounted. Calls came to their home at all hours of the day and night, threatening Byron, Julie, and their children. Julie explained the fallout that follows defectors: "They take everything you entrusted with them and they throw it right at you." After Bryon's split from the Vinlanders, danger was omnipresent. He and Julie were on guard 24/7.

In an odd way, Bryon's mental breakdown helped him understand the magnitude of the changes involved in his transition from a skinhead juggernaut to parent and provider. He had made two of the most difficult decisions: to leave the hate movement and to manage his alcohol addiction. He took on both fights with the determination of a warrior on a mission.

His resolve became all the more dogged on a clear day in 2006 when Julie went into labor.

Tyrson Edward James Widner was born in November of that year in Ironwood Michigan, Julie's fifth Caesarian delivery. His middle names honor Julie's father and Bryon's brother, respectively. In the *Erasing Hate* documentary Bryon talks about Tyrson's birth as if it were a religious experience. It may have been. "When I saw Tyrson born, I saw God. That was one of the strangest, greatest feelings, one that I'll probably never feel again. The first time you hold a baby, that kind of love is truly amazing. Every breath I take is for him. I just want to do everything for him, give him everything I never had."

For Bryon, everything changed the day Tyrson was born. It was 18 months after Nordic Fest and 11 months after he married Julie. The emotional distance Bryon traveled over that time was more than many experience in a lifetime. From hate to love in a year and a half.

When we met in person, Bryon compared himself with a Vinlander colleague, saying his friend "has never been in a good place." Without pause, he continued, "I don't think I'd ever been in a good place before I met Julie. I never thought I deserved more than a roof over my head, coffee in the morning, rent paid . . . These are all small victories. I never aspired to be happier. With her, I'm already a better dad than my dad ever was."

Through his years in the movement, Bryon's tattoos were an imposing threat. Now that he was out and looking for work, they had the same effect. Imagine going to an employment interview when your face reads like a billboard blaring, I AM A RAZOR-WIELDING NEO-NAZI RACIST READY TO CUT YOU UP.

One night when he was discouraged by a series of job rejections, Bryon was online searching for a solution. Julie found him surfing eBay for a do-it-yourself acid treatment to remove his tattoos at home. Soon after that experience, she contacted the Southern Poverty Law Center for help. After a team from SPLC found their story to be authentic, the Center located a laser surgeon and, with funding from an anonymous donor, Bryon began the first of a dozen excruciatingly painful procedures. *Erasing Hate* presents the entire painful ordeal to remove the tattoos on Byron's face, neck, and hands.

The way Bryon and Julie deferred hard questions to one another during our in-person interviews showed a mutual regard for one another and a deep respect for their relationship. They spent time reflecting on their romance, each telling how they met, sharing their individual conflicts with the movement, and describing the pattern of how their love grew.

Until it didn't.

Within weeks after our in-person interviews, communicating with Bryon and Julie by phone, email, or text became more and more difficult. After months of unanswered attempts, I was able to connect with Julie via Skype. Bryon was in the room. During the conversation, Bryon relayed his response to a question I asked Julie, but he did not speak directly to me. This seemed odd after both had been so unabashedly candid in person, exhibiting unambiguous trust. The dots didn't connect.

Two months after my visit, I sent an email virtually begging Julie to call. In return, an ominous three-word email arrived that left me puzzled and disheartened: "We have split." Four months later, Julie answered one of my random mid-afternoon phone calls. At first, what she told me seemed inconsistent with what I observed from three days of warm, loving conversation between them during our in-person interviews. In a brief conversation, she intimated an incident had occurred in which Bryon had "molested" one of her daughters, adding no details. The incident moved her to file a protection order against him. She and her children later moved to another state. She and Bryon were in the throes of an unpleasant divorce.

More than a year later, Julie again responded to my request for an update. She got agitated and angry when she talked about Bryon; her comments disjointed and accusatory. I asked if they were both faking it when we met. "No. I felt I was in the marriage forever. We had a great friendship, but the love isn't there anymore." I wondered aloud how their marriage could come to such a bitter end after what appeared to be a made-for-TV romance. Now seemingly contradicting herself, Julie added, "The past nine years were a lie."

When she told me about the incident between Bryon and her daughter, I commented, "You seem to have a bad history with men." Julie snickered, "Ya' think?" Pausing to breathe, she added, "You know, I don't think I can do men anymore." Since she and I had established an abiding trust and had both talked about our personal lives, I couldn't resist the next question: "Do you think you can do women?" Her answer: "If I ever have a relationship again, it's not a matter of color or sex. I want someone to share my history without a grudge." For a former neo-Nazi, that's growth.

With little expectation of getting a return call from her now-estranged husband, I asked Julie, "Do you think Bryon would ever go back to the movement?" Without hesitation she said, "They wouldn't take him," adding, "He's always needed someone to tell him what to do, to guide him. If he could do it on his own," she mused, "he would." Her comment may apply to many, if not all, of the defectors I interviewed, including herself, at least during their time in the movement.

To a fair extent, what happened to Bryon and Julie's marriage is a product of the hateful environment in which they both spent the most formative years of their lives. When I told a friend about Bryon and Julie's background, our interviews, and the abrupt end to their marriage, he asked a poignant and appropriate question: "Do you think people in the hate movement are *able* to love?"

What defectors often imply, but seldom say directly, is that hate groups overpower their deepest emotions, especially love, the anthesis of an extremist's stock-in-trade, hatred. In the movement, relationships are often secondary to ideology. This is part of the reason many extremists stay in the movement long after their connection to a group or a website has outlived its usefulness to them on any personal level.

When we last spoke in 2018, Julie told me she spends much of her time caring for Tyrson and Isabella.

Since 2014, Bryon has not responded to repeated attempts to reach him.

Bryon's and Julie's Tattoos

Bryon's Tattoos

Aside from the eerie messages of hate and malicious intent, each tattoo on Bryon's body had a special significance, many relating to Nazi symbolism. As a part of working in the tattoo industry, Bryon spent time researching the meaning behind tattoos chosen by neo-Nazis, as well as symbols selected by other clients. Many have a meaning unique to Bryon. Many were surgically removed after he left the movement. The months-long, multiple procedure laser process is detailed in the 2011 documentary *Erasing Hate* (Bill Brummel Productions). This list does not include all of Bryon's tattoos. Many of these tattoos are common among neo-Nazis in the U.S. and across Europe.

"**ThugReich**" – This image appears in heavy three-inch high letters sprawled across Bryon's stomach. "ThugReich" is a term Bryon coined to merge the role of thug with the Third Reich.

"**Blood & Honour**" – These words are in thick letters below Bryon's neck and top of his chest. Blood & Honour is the name of a skinhead group Bryon was a part of in the 1970s early 1980s.*

Arrow – A thickly marked arrow (roughly .75" wide shaft, topped by a 4 – 5 inches high, 3" wide arrowhead) extended from below Bryon's right eye to roughly 2.5" above his right eyebrow. The arrow signifies being a killer. Bryon's arrow was emblematic of the Tiawaz, a rune or character used in Norse religion. Tiawaz signifies the Rune of Justice or the Rune of the Warrior. In most white power skinheads, it also represents the willingness to kill for your race. "I was willing to kill for the white race."

"**Vinlanders SC**" – Vinlanders Social Club is a skinhead group (club) of which Bryon is a founding father.

The word "**H-A-T-E**" appeared in thin letters across the knuckles on Bryon's right hand ("This was the first tattoo I ever got. I thought the word hate was real cool at the time . . . ")

Swastika – Several swastika tattoos appear on Bryon's body in various sizes and forms. Not all were removed during the laser surgery to eliminate tattoos on his face, neck, and hands.

Iron Cross – Several iron crosses mark Bryon's body, each stylized differently. The iron cross relates to Nazis awarded the Iron Cross Medal as a military decoration during the Third Reich. The iron cross symbol, visually similar to the Maltese Cross, had been in use as a military decoration for more than a century before WWII.

SS Bolts – Bryon: "You can't be a Nazi without a pair of SS bolts on ya' . . . " In many hate groups throughout the early 1990s, the right to wear the SS bolts tattoo was earned by committing a hate crime. In Bryon's words: "I earned mine years ago by attacking and beating down a minority."

Straight Razor – A tattoo similar to this image appeared on the right side of Bryon's face, fully extended with the added details of red blood droplets dripping from the blade. During his days in the movement, a straight edge razor was Bryon's "weapon of choice."

* Blood & Honour later split into two factions: Blood & Honour International and Blood & Honour Combat 18 [Bryon belonged to Combat 18]. The number 18 is code used to represent Adolf Hitler's initials: 1 for the letter A, 8 for the letter H. The original Blood & Honour group was created by Ian Stewart Donaldson, a British punk rocker with a white power band. Donaldson was killed in a car accident in September 1993.

Julie's Tattoos

Julie brandished her own neo-Nazi ink on her hands, arms and chest: a swastika, German war eagle, skull, the German Mother's Cross, and the words "Sieg Heil" on her right thigh. Many of Julie's tattoos have been covered, some with an overlay of up to three new tattoos over an older image. This list does not include all of Julie's tattoos.

 German War Eagle – This image originated as the coat of arms for Germany. Many neo-Nazi followers use the symbol in loyalty to Hitler and the Third Reich. Several versions of the image show the eagle with minor differences, although all follow the same basic theme of the coat of arms surrounded by an eagle facing left.

 Totenkopf skull– This skull and cross bones image is associated with the German military during the 19th- and 20th-century and is often used today as a sign of political extremism. The symbol was used by Nazi SS forces during World War II as German death squads undertook the Holocaust.

 German Mother's Cross – Also called the Cross of Honour of the German Mother, this image was a state decoration and civil order of merit conferred by the government of the German Reich to honor German mothers for exceptional merit to the German nation.

Angela King

ANGELA KING MESHED WITH OTHERS LIKE a leftover part from an Ikea bookcase. She didn't fit. Not with her childhood peers; not with her school classmates; not even in the palm-lined boulevards and sandy beaches of her family's home in Broward County, Florida.

Having grown up in a predominantly white neighborhood, she describes her family environment as prejudiced. Parental messages were powerful to a cantankerous young woman constantly out of sorts and trying desperately to adjust to her surroundings. As she matured, Angela didn't always feel supported in whatever she wanted to do. In looking back, she remembers a single profound and weighty caution, one that would stick with her for life: "You can do anything, just don't come home with a black man or a woman."

Family discord and racial ambivalence helped to shape a tangled understanding of how people in her life were connected or disconnected. "Before I got involved in the movement, blacks were in a separate category than other people of color." As one example, she notes the irony of growing up close to her paternal aunts; one Korean, one Ecuadorian, and one Jewish – and even closer to her bi-racial cousins. "I didn't consider my cousins as minorities because they were essentially raised with the same racial prejudice that I was raised with. I didn't see a difference between my aunts and myself," Angela recalls, adding with caution, "But that would most likely have been very different if any of my father's brothers had married a black person." Angela concedes, "I did have issues with black people."

Angela's experiences reveal how deeply her involvement in several hate groups bumped into and against her own life choices. She explained the slow and lengthy process to extricate herself from the movement. The transition was neither easy nor direct. For Angela, trapped in a series of relationships with abusive boyfriends and insincere colleagues, her journey to freedom was a rollercoaster of public and private conflicts, all masked behind the face of a vicious bully her friends called "Angie."

In her youth, Angela was attracted to kids with devilish vices and a rebellious streak. From her pre-teens to late 20s, her life was a non-stop track of disregarding rules and making bad choices. Those years included a convoluted series of interconnected confrontations and paying little attention to laws. Her choice to enter the ranks of neo-Nazis was elevated in intensity when she started to mingle with Hammerskins, the most violent of all skinheads.

Her entry into a web of progressively escalating hate was expressed through her tattoos, Nazi images, and the propaganda she used to win over other young people feeling just as detached from their surroundings as she was. She spoke their language.

Angela's criminal path covers an assortment of misdemeanors and felony arrests, along with time in courts, jails, and prisons. Her crimes often overlap and merge with previous incidents in a chain of sometimes connected and sometimes disconnected events, not all of which were charged as hate crimes.

In 2006, I met Angela at the Starbucks in a Florida strip mall near Orlando. She responded thoughtfully and candidly to questions about her life in the movement. Mellow and subdued, she looked no different than any other young, self-directed American woman, unfazed by fashion or circumstance. Jeans and a somewhat conservatively solid-colored blouse offered a contrast to the black, studded clothes she wore during her days in the movement. She often speaks with a steely intensity, halting and sometimes anxious, with an occasional glint of humor. She threads a conversation in which words are a sobering reminder of a harsh past, each sentence weighed carefully to punctuate a singular, unmistakable meaning: "That life is behind me."

Born in 1975, the oldest of three children, Angela grew up in a universe filled with difficult decisions and few mentors to guide her. At her family home in Cooper City, Florida, household religious conflicts abounded, along with family disagreements. From an early age she learned to navigate around her father's Baptist background and her mother's Catholic roots.

Angela considers religion at least in part responsible for her earliest rejection of conventional wisdom. She attended a private Baptist school in addition to studying Catholicism. She describes that time as rough, mostly because too much religion was being forced on her. She wanted to remove herself from religion completely. Caught between opposing Christian theologies, she became rebellious. Racial and ethnic differences were another source of confusion at home.

School afforded little opportunity to understand or appreciate ethnic diversity. Angela remembers "maybe one black student and no known Jews" through elementary, middle, and high school. She believes her father's entrepreneurial acumen as the owner of various small businesses allowed her access to a private elementary school.

While she was still in her early teens, Angela fell into deep turmoil and confusion at a time when her parents' marriage was disintegrating. After they divorced, she lived with her mother. The family's economic status nosedived from the relative comfort of a two-parent income to "the other side of the tracks." As a consequence of events leading to her parents' divorce, Angela was forced to leave private school before entering sixth grade. In the public K-12 system, her conflicts with black students became difficult to endure.

Angela said that at her first public school, "I was threatened and abused by black kids simply for being white. I had no good experiences with blacks before that. I had no base from which to relate or judge blacks. Until then, I hadn't even considered other races. Blacks were in a separate category than other people of color."

Parental role modeling was inadequate for Angela to form objective judgments about people of color and other "minorities," often magnifying gut-level conflicts about how to respond to human differences. "I had no one to help me confront issues. I got many of my ideals from my parents. It would have helped for my parents to be more attentive to my issues, in addition to their own."

As she struggled to make sense of the people around her, ambivalence and uncertainty led to bigger disputes with family members, schoolmates, and friends. Wherever she went, she felt out of place. As her behaviors at school became more unsettling and unmanageable, with loud disruptions, disobedience, and breaking rules. Her parents sought outside help from counselors and psychologists, to no avail.

Angela first came to the attention of law enforcement in 1989 while she was 14 years old when she and a friend tried to sneak into a movie theater without paying. Caught and kicked out, the two walked around the corner to a store where they bought wine-laced coolers. A police officer noticed the two out-of-place young females with alcoholic beverages in their hands. Youth and the lack of a criminal history kept the two out of jail. Instead, both were sent to counseling.

During Angela's early years she grew more disconnected from her family. Friction with schoolmates and feeling rejected at every turn contributed to an overwhelming loneliness. To compensate, she found comfort in cigarettes, alcohol, sex, and drugs, all in greater proportions as the years went on. As the struggles got more difficult to endure, she became fearful. She still didn't fit with the people around her and they didn't fit with her. Fear turned to anger. A dark attitude grew along with dark clothes and a tough exterior. She told a college audience years later, "At the time, I didn't like myself, inside or outside. It was far beyond a bad hair day."

Between the ages of 14 and 15, she was an easy catch for an undisciplined crowd seeking excitement and recognition. She told me, "This was a time when everything was very confusing. My family had been torn apart. I felt alone and unwanted. I was very unhappy with my life and the world in general. The counselors and psychiatrists didn't help. None of them seemed to take the time or say the words I needed. I was hanging out with a bad group of kids, and I kept getting attention. I was like, 'Wow, I'm really cool,' because I keep getting in trouble and they all like me."

Over the following year, Angela's anger and frustration led to further anxiety and disconnection. In the 9th and 10th grade at Cooper City High School, Angela felt her life crumbling around her. She moved from one crowd to another, finally meeting a group willing to accept her as one of them.

At long last, barely into high school, she found a peer group with whom she could fit, a cluster of racist skinheads who convened under the name Strike Force. With Strike Force, she was able to express her anger and was appreciated for it. Unlike other friends and family, skinheads listened to her rants with great interest.

By making her feel her rage was not her fault, her skinhead friends redirected her frustration to focus on specific groups demanding greater civil rights and more social power at the time: Jews, blacks, gays, and immigrants. She recalled her Strike Force friends "started pounding stuff into me, giving me pamphlets and books to read. They were younger than me by a year or two. Through them I met adults who lived by themselves and were in [larger and more] organized hate groups."

Through her peers, Angela was convinced that as power shifted to "minorities," white power was being undermined. Once she was accepted into the fold, her conflicts could be crafted to influence similarly misguided souls to join Strike Force.

Among her first tasks was to write and circulate promotional materials for the group. To do that, she blended in at venues where young people met. "We would take other [hate groups'] propaganda and make our own fliers. We would post them all over, drink beer, and hang out."

The hate movement influences angry people to see that their problems are really not their own. Instead, the movement espouses that individual problems are the fault of "minority" groups usurping white power. This is an especially effective technique to win over loners and young people who don't fit in with their peers. If the fights failed to win over believers, violence was a useful outlet for the group's anger and an effective way to air its ideology.

Drawn to a shadowy element to begin with, by age 15 Angela started to blossom in the movement. She met with skinhead disciples whenever possible. Their personalities and temperament were an ideal match with her own. "They were angry all the time. For me, that was the perfect thing. I was angry and didn't like myself. They got into fights and called people names. They didn't have a *reason* to be pissed off all the time; they just were. To me, they were the coolest thing." Angela bonded to her skinhead friends with the awestruck fervor of a rock star groupie. "*Belonging,*" she said, "far outweighed the consequences of being hateful." For the first time in her life, she was part of a group.

Angela and her skinhead cronies occasionally clashed with non-violent *anti-racist,* skinheads, better known as SHARPs, Skinheads Against Racial Prejudice[17]. ""Many anti-racist skinhead groups are extremely violent," Angela explained, "[SHARP] tactics were the same as ours, but their beliefs are different." By now more deeply entrenched in an extremist enclave, she had an even stronger commitment to her colleagues, with purpose and a newfound outlet for pent up negative energy – finding comrades; "I recruited people, the same as I was recruited."

At the age of 17, Angela was involved in a variety of racist skinhead groups, taking a leadership role in many, including starting chapters and operating them on her own. "I finally found people that understood me and wanted me around. I could be angry all the time and start fights. The more I did it, the more I was liked. I even started to get a good reputation going as someone not to mess with."

By the time she hit her middle teens Angela already looked and acted the part: dark clothes, a threatening demeanor, and her first tattoos – a flaming Celtic cross on her right calf, five-inch high male and female Vikings on her chest. She believed her grasp on life was finally connected to a viable cause: Build the movement. She remembers walking along beaches near Hollywood and Palm Beach convincing teens and 20-somethings to consider the two questions that best demonstrated her leadership skill: "Don't you want to be something? Don't you want to be proud of what you are?" Her persona and rapport made her a natural recruiter for other misguided teens.

Her youth, body art, and deceptively unruffled self-confidence telegraphed "cool." Angela used her physical assets to get young prospective recruits to listen. Her image made it easy to strike up a casual conversation, use the jargon of the day, and convince people to make the same kind of life changes that meant so much to her. Her goal was to just get them involved.

Through most of 1993 and part of 1994, when she was 18 and 19, Angela was living with a new group of self-professed skinheads, this time in Palm Beach. The skinheads with whom she was living were affiliated with Aryan Nations, the neo-Nazi and white supremacist organization. Lest her humble abode be confused with any part of an otherwise peace-loving neighborhood, Nazi and Confederate flags waved proudly from their roof.

Angela had been dating one of her roommates, Rob, who brought Angela into the Palm Beach Aryans. He was a Gulf War veteran, 10 years older than Angela, with a penchant to be physically and emotionally abusive. She acknowledged, "I was naïve. I hadn't dated an older man before. I thought I was special for an older man to be dating me." Not long after she and Rob started dating, Angela learned she was carrying his child. Not exactly the model couple, their early romance was also marked by Rob's sporadic surges of abusive language, put-downs, and physical violence.

Rob introduced Angela to his friends, most of whom were other racist skinheads. One evening, they were at a raucous party where a heated conversation became progressively violent. When fists started to fly, a "friend" of Rob's pulled out a knife and stabbed Rob in the face. "When I tried to help [Rob] off the ground, the guy was still trying to get at him. In the heat of the fight, the man kicked me in the stomach." Shortly after the kick, a miscarriage brought on a slump into depression. "In the movement," she said, "we were taught the best thing a white woman could do is breed." Although she was disheartened by the failed pregnancy and a mishmash of internalized emotional conflicts, Angela found solace in being surrounded by neo-Nazi skinhead friends. "I felt like I belonged there."

One night in 1993, Angela and Rob were driving around Palm Beach County. Two skinhead friends, a married couple, following them in a separate vehicle. Two adolescent boys were with them; one rode in the car with Angela and Rob, the other rode in the car with the married couple.

Without an apparent reason, Rob drove into a parking lot. The other car followed. Angela could tell Rob was irritated and looking for a fight as he climbed out of the car. She said, "He demanded that I accompany him." Feeling uneasy, Angela chose to stay in the car. Rob gruffly demanded, "Do not leave this car!" He climbed out, grabbed something from the back of the car, and walked toward a nearby building.

"I knew something was up, I didn't feel good about it," she explained. Conflicted over Rob's command for her to sit tight, Angela walked over to the couple in the second car and asked if she could join them, describing Rob's exceptionally angry mood and her own pessimistic intuition. His friends refused to let her join them, believing Rob would have a reasonable explanation. Dejected and angry, she returned to Rob's vehicle.

As Angela strolled to the car, Rob dashed back. Appearing tense and agitated because she had contradicted his order to stay in the car, he rushed Angela to get inside and tossed something into the backseat. He leaped behind the wheel and sped off, continuing to rant and fume about how Angela had so recklessly left the car when he had distinctly told her to stay put. The other car followed them out of the lot. Unknown to anyone at the time, Angela's brief excursion to the other car proved to be at her peril.

Shortly after they returned to their home, Angela walked up behind Rob and his friend as they leaned over an outside water spigot. She saw Rob put something under the running water. "He was rinsing blood off a crowbar." She tried to piece together what Rob had done after he left their car. Even years after her time in the movement, the details were unsettling to talk about.

Angela learned that while they were driving, Rob had seen three women walking toward the entrance of a gay club. After they parked, while she and the other couple waited, Rob walked up behind the women and, in a quick swing of the crowbar, struck one of them in the back of the head. Angela later learned the injuries were significant, although not life-threatening.

Shortly after the assault, police arrived at their home with its defiant flags flying at full mast. Following skinhead protocol, Angela answered the door, using her gender as a shield to protect Rob. "He's not at home," she lied. When the officers described the incident in the parking lot, they explained an eyewitness had observed a vehicle, a car matching the description of Rob's car with plates registered in Rob's name.

Ever the obedient comrade and partner, Angela denied any knowledge of the episode while Rob hid inside the house. As the questioning continued she became acutely aware that, although the police were onto Rob's car being at the scene of the crime, the questions were directed more toward her than to Rob. When the police left their house with no one in handcuffs, she and Rob both breathed a sigh of relief.

Soon after the interrogation, Angela decided to leave Rob and hit the road. Hoping to "get away from the bad experiences that kept happening in Florida," she set out on a cross-country excursion with no particular destination. She lived with a friend in Iowa for a few months where she also visited neo-Nazi groups. From there she moved to North Carolina. By then the crowbar incident was a fading memory.

On April 9, 1994, Angela was traveling with a couple of skinhead friends when they made a stop in Mountain City (Johnson County), Tennessee, to visit some neo-Nazi friends. Still living in North Carolina at the time, her travels had led her to a group recognized at the time as among the most aggressive, vicious, and inhumane elements in the movement. "I visited the Confederate Hammerskins, part of Hammerskin Nation," a kind of skinhead franchise. "As time went on," Angela recounts, "the events I was involved in got more and more serious. I was breaking the law . . . and the more I did, the cooler it seemed."

It helps to know what makes Hammerskin Nation different from other skinheads. Every skinhead group tends to create its own unique identity and specialty. The Anti-Defamation League (ADL) identifies Hammerskin Nation as "the most violent and best-organized neo-Nazi skinhead group in the United States." According to the Hammerskin Nation website, the organization is "a leaderless group of men and women who have adopted the white power skinhead lifestyle. We are blue collar workers, white collar professionals, college students, entrepreneurs, fathers and mothers." ADL notes Hammerskin Nation members "have been convicted of harassing, beating or murdering minorities." Confederate Hamnmerskins represent the southern United States from Texas to Florida. One of the group's key functions is the production and promotion of hate rock music.

Angela described her Tennessee stopover site as "a backwoods town where the main entertainment for the week is drinking beer in the parking lot of the local grocery store." It was on one of those Saturday nights that she and her skinhead buddies decided to head out to the store and, in her words, "mess with the teens." As is not uncommon when a group of young raging white supremacists confronts a group of half-lit rowdies having a good time, a fight broke out. No particular damages evolved from the skirmish.

But things started to go south when local police showed up, asking questions and taking names. Angela, powered by her 18-year-old beer-infused defiance, refused to give her name to police. After flunking an on-site sobriety test, she was charged with public intoxication. Being below the legal drinking age didn't help. The night was a long way from over.

On the way to the police station, Angela became agitated when one of the arresting officers called her a "skinhead slut." Boozed up, enraged, and pushed beyond her limit, she unlaced a boot from her foot and used it to pound against the glass partition separating her from the officers. The police were not amused. This lack of decorum earned her additional charges of disorderly conduct and destruction of city property.

She said that at the police station, "They threw me in the drunk tank until an off-duty female police officer was called in to search me." When the officer arrived in street clothes and started poking and prodding, Angela lost it. By then "an army of other officers" had gathered around her. Now totally out of control, she was subdued only after a large male officer, whom she describes as weighing "at least 300 pounds," sat on her chest so others could remove her boots, socks, jacket, and jewelry.

She recalls coming to her senses the next day, in a cell inside the jailhouse of "some hick town in Tennessee." The place was no high-security fortress. The cells were separated by cinderblocks pasted together with caulking rather than cement. She said, "You could just peel out the caulking, communicate with other inmates, and pass cigarettes through the gaps." She also learned that inside this particular jail, other accused offenders worked regular jobs and served time only on the weekends.

Angela spent weeks in the Johnson County Jail before her case appeared on the docket in the same one-room courthouse where all cases are heard. "The judge had to be 100 years old," she huffed, noting that at several points through her trial, "he was nodding out on the bench." Taking a plea, she was found guilty of the charges. Because she intended to return to Florida as soon as humanly possible, she agreed to an option to report her probation by mail. The mail-in probation involved "filling out papers every month and sending payments to the Johnson County Probation Office from wherever I was." Once again free to roam the countryside, albeit on probation, Angela headed back to the Sunshine State.

On May 26, 1994, just shy of two months after her meltdown in the Tennessee cop car and two weeks after returning to Florida, Angela took advantage of a balmy evening to celebrate her 19th birthday. She set out drinking and carousing with a small group of skinhead friends.

That evening, while heading toward a convenience store in Hollywood, the skinheads got into a heated tussle with a white gang (not a skinhead group) on a sidewalk next to a busy street, a few blocks away from their destination. Tempers flared. Fists flew. During the melee, one of the non-skinhead gang members hit a male skinhead in the face with a brick. The man was knocked unconscious, bleeding from a gash in his chin.

Full of fury and disbelief over their friend's injuries and being on the losing side of a fight, the skinheads collected themselves and decided to leave the scene and regroup at home. Before any clear strategy evolved, Angela took control. She and a skinhead friend returned to the convenience store in a seething rage. By then, police had been called and were on the scene. When Angela saw members of the opposing gang still in the store, "I just freaked." She started hurling derogatory names. She and her friend were promptly charged with disorderly conduct.

At the police station, Angela felt a twinge of relief when she heard bail for her buddy was a mere $50. "I can handle that," she thought. Expecting the same bail for the same offense, she was stunned to hear *her* bail was much higher.

It turned out that while Angela was in custody, the crowbar confrontation that had been in legal limbo for over a year returned with a vengeance. Hollywood police discovered an outstanding warrant accusing Angela of aggravated battery related to the still-unsolved incident with a crowbar in Palm Beach County. Police claimed Angela swung the crowbar, not Rob. The warrant for her arrest was a dramatic surprise to Angela because, she has maintained consistently, she did not leave the parking lot and did not wield the weapon. The crime, she says, was actually committed by Rob. Despite her assessment of reality, she was behind bars in the Hollywood jail, now facing a charge of aggravated battery, in addition to disorderly conduct. She managed to bond out of jail for a later court trial, but the case was far from closed.

For the fight in the convenience store, Angela appeared before a black female judge. Ultimately, the judge assigned two years of probation and sentenced Angela to 50 hours of community service for the disorderly conduct charge, 25 hours in a black church and 25 hours at a Jewish community center.

Ignoring the judge's leniency, Angela scoffed at the sentence and, after only a few hours, ignored the remainder of her community service. "I didn't complete the time and I didn't finish the probation," she told me. Years later, Angela explained that her arrogance and lapses in judgment were a product of youth and inexperience. "I was 19 years old and thinking I was a criminal mastermind. I would do the minimum to get by without more trouble." Her attempt to avoid the sentence would eventually catch up with her.

Angela opted to go to a jury trial for the Palm Beach County charge of aggravated battery from the crowbar incident. The crime was pinned on Angela because during the trial an eyewitness, and at least one of the three women involved in the assault, identified Angela as the person who actually struck the victim. Her skinhead colleagues offered little support. The male friend at the scene of the crime who refused to let

Angela into his car that night, refused to testify on Angela's behalf. She later learned that man had charges pending against him from an unrelated crime and knew if he showed up to testify he'd be legal toast. Ultimately, despite her repeated claims of innocence, Angela was found guilty and spent time in a county jail.

Ahhh, skinhead friends.

She assumed that, "Since I didn't do it, I couldn't be convicted of it." She was assigned a public defender, whom she refers to as incompetent. She explained, "The lawyer failed to actually provide any defense. For instance, the victims admitted to being intoxicated, which he didn't question. Also, if the woman was hit from behind, how could she see me run up from behind her? He didn't dispute any of the information. That simply made no sense at all." Plus, "The public defender had me appear in court in a granny dress," Angela says, rolling her eyes. "The dress was hideous; floral print, oversized, with a broken zipper in the back. I still shudder when I think about it."

The image is indeed comical. By then Angela's tattoos included a ring-sized image on the middle finger of her right hand, a swastika, a triskelion, SS bolts, a flaming Celtic cross on her right calf, a four-inch wide Reich Eagle with a Celtic cross in its claws on her right outer thigh, and the word "skins" tattooed on her right hand between her thumb and first finger. To the jury, the image of a heavily inked, tough-as-nails, neo-Nazi woman posing as an Earth mother must have looked like a dramatic contradiction.

Fashion statement aside, the public defender's scanty research and courtroom theatrics had little effect to sway the court in Angela's favor. The defense stacked up against a prosecutor who focused on Angela's background as an active racist skinhead with a criminal history. Rob, Angela's former boyfriend whom, she affirms, actually wielded the crowbar, was never even subpoenaed to testify.

Days after her conviction, Angela was astonished to learn the judge who heard the case "didn't feel right" about Angela's verdict. After requesting a review of the issues, the judge declared a mistrial. In Angela's words, "The judge believed the prosecutor chose to use my [ideological] beliefs as a motivating factor and cause for punishment. [The judge] said my beliefs were hateful, but not against the law, that my civil rights were violated."

Angela was given a choice between a retrial or a plea bargain. "Rather than risking another trial, I took the plea bargain," she said. The plea included two years of house arrest; one year with an ankle monitor, another year without the device, and a third year of probation. "I took the plea because I had the shit scared out of me for being found guilty of something I didn't do." She was convinced that if the case was retried, she'd be facing time in prison. Instead, the probation would end early – as long as she stayed out of trouble. Taking strides to reconstruct her life, Angela moved in with her mother and stepfather.

During her time on house arrest, Angela obediently wore her ankle monitor for a full year without incident and reported to a probation officer (PO) as ordered. The second year without the ankle monitor was another story. "I went on the lam for a few weeks without reporting to my PO." She was considered Missing in Action from her probation obligations, prompting a probation violation. During that year (1995), Angela says she got into a scuffle with a group of anti-racists, yet another violation. The prospect of a free future was looking more and more bleak. But this time she had an unexpected advocate on her side, her probation officer.

In the months after her last fistfight, Angela felt a growing level of mutual trust and began to confide in her PO. Among other disclosures, she told the officer that she was trying to distance herself from the movement. "We had a good relationship," Angela told me. "He was concerned. He knew I had been trying to serve my time. I had been doing well and not getting into trouble."

Confidences aside, Angela was obligated to tell her probation officer about her probation violation, which she did, prompting a report up the line. She believes that, partially because of her genuine interest in getting away from a life of hate, "My probation officer withdrew the violation of probation charge. From that point on, I did really well. I was on probation for another year, until February 1997. My third year of probation was terminated early because I had done so well."

At 22, she was once again a free woman. With the probation behind her, she moved to the warm shores of South Carolina. She also continued sending monthly payments to the Tennessee Court to pay restitution for damages to the police car. Much to her delight, an administrative adjustment in the Johnson County Probation Office proved to be in her favor as well. According to Angela's reasoning, "The office closed. No one contacted me." In her words, restitution payments were "successfully terminated" when the office ceased to exist.

After years of crimes, legal charges, and court cases, Angela began to weigh the consequences of nonstop drinking, fighting, and abusive boyfriends – as well as the arrests, and the feeling she was constantly running away from cops. The emotional burden was becoming more than she expected when she became a neo-Nazi skinhead.

In 1995, Angela had a change of heart. On April 19 of that year, roughly two months after the crowbar trial, news broke about the bombing of the Murrah Federal Building in Oklahoma City. Like other white supremacists, Angela soon learned that the alleged bomber, Timothy McVeigh, had carried out the crime according to the sinister plotline of *The Turner Diaries*[18], the neo-Nazi novel involving a futuristic war.

Non-stop media coverage of the aftermath and the victims lasted for days. One photo stirred Angela's emotions to the core, the striking image of a first responder carrying the body of a lifeless child in his arms. "When I saw that picture, I suddenly realized I was getting older." She told me that the photo made her think more meaningfully about life, children, and eventually being a parent.

The Oklahoma City bombing clinched a decision for Angela. "That's when I ran away from the movement. I quit seeing my [skinhead] friends. I quit going to the bars and places where we would hang out."

The transition created a crushing stress for a young, single woman trying to navigate life away from the comfort of a group that had embraced her when no one else would. Returning to her family didn't seem viable at the time. Angela began to realize much of her physical and mental freedom was still under the control of her former skinhead groupies. For most of the past seven years, the bulk of her decisions were made by the group – what to do during the day, where to go at night, who to spend time with and who to shun. Individual choices were limited to the most mundane.

As soon as she dropped out, her adopted skinhead brothers and sisters turned ugly. With indisputable clarity, they exposed the spiteful underbelly of the movement by showing what happens when a hate group is ignored by one of its own. "They shot at my house and shot at my car. They made [physical] threats against me and members of my family." An inescapable string of threatening phone calls made every moment miserable. The pressure was more than Angela could bear. "I felt I would be found wherever I went unless it was a place where I knew no one at all. I also had zero resources so it was impossible for me to make a big move at that time."

Resigned to defeat, her brief fascination with a life free of the movement came to an abrupt end. "I decided to return to the movement." Opting to reenter the group she tried to abandon, Angela felt obligated to prove to her oh-so-loyal teammates that her experimental escape was a foolish blunder and that she was truly committed to skinhead ideals. A half-hearted attempt was not enough. She had to reestablish her trustworthiness at an even *higher* level of dedication.

She defined her comeback with great forethought. "This time," she reasoned, "I'd be the best damned skinhead there ever was. I would *prove* there won't be a better racist than me." Her intention was now focused on earning the recognition of white supremacists *nationwide*. Now that the desire to ditch the movement was over, tending to her cascading legal problems became her highest priority.

When I met Angela for our first in-person interview in 2006, she had been out of prison for five years, roughly eight years had passed since her final and complete separation from the movement. Lingering anxiety from Angela's failed defection in 1995 appeared evident in a sudden emotional catharsis. While describing a difficult epoch, Angela took a deep breath and exhaled wearily. Her body sagged, arms falling to her sides. "I didn't have the strength to fight them," she sighed, a stony expression spanning her face. She reaffirmed that, even after Oklahoma City, the energy she needed to release her from the movement was simply impossible to muster.

When she returned to the movement after the threats and gunshots, she was driven by a born-again allegiance to hate. She read every book she could get her hands on, every pamphlet, and handout about hate groups, skinheads, Hammerskins, and other extremists. She replicated her colleagues' brutal behaviors with a new fervor, frequently in a drunken state, calling people names, initiating fights, and creating public disturbances with little or no provocation. Her skinhead colleagues, she says, "just egged me on."

After falling headlong back into the fold, Angela was hell-bent on a mission to expand the movement. She scrounged the resources to travel around the U.S., meeting skinhead groups in racist enclaves, cementing personal connections wherever she went. With a possessed fanaticism, she spread the word and, ultimately, recruited new skinheads wherever she went.

Her comeback was marked by a revolutionary zeal. Yet, on the inside, she still harbored a growing discontent over a loss of independent thinking. Around her 23rd birthday, after becoming part of yet another group of neo-Nazi skinheads in Broward County, Florida, discomfort turned to distress. By then, her hate mask included a patchwork of over a dozen unmistakable neo-Nazi tattoos, enough recognizably racist ink to cause any progressive passerby to wince. Dark clothes and high red-laced Doc Marten boots rounded out the steely don't-mess-with-me veneer of a proud neo-Nazi. Anyone in the movement would recognize the red laces and SS bolts as symbols to note some sorry victim shed blood in her quest to be the best skinhead ever. But, her biggest challenges were yet ahead.

Traveling back to central Florida from South Carolina, Angela moved in with another group of skinheads. Prior to her arrival and without her knowledge, her Florida roommates had stolen some stereo equipment. Not long after her arrival, Angela was dragged into a police investigation when officers arrived at the door of her latest residence.

While she was being questioned, police found a warrant claiming Angela violated her probation for not completing her community service hours from the fight outside the Hollywood convenience store. She was extradited to Broward County, not far from where the fight took place, and sent back to court. This time she found herself before the same black female judge who had assigned her probation and the original community service hours. Angela explained the circumstances of violating the probation. The judge reinstated the original community service sentence, which, Angela said with a nod, "I completed the second time."

In February 1997, after completing her community service and probation for the aggravated battery charge from the crowbar incident, Angela was once again a free woman. With those crimes behind her, she moved to South Carolina – with a clean slate.

In 1998, at age 22, after years of involvement in a handful of violent far-right extremist groups, Angela entered the major league of hate when she met Ray Leone, an active member of the World Church of the Creator (WCOTC), one of the most infamous hate groups in the U.S. throughout the 1990s and an international reputation as a racist, white supremacist, anti-Semitic organization.

Angela knew WCOTC. Years earlier, when she first entered the movement, she had written articles for WCOTC's predecessor organization, Church of the Creator (COTC). COTC changed its name in the 1990s when leader Matt Hale took over the group. WCOTC is now called the Creativity Movement[12].

By the time Angela joined Leone, some of the group's leading members had already been convicted of serious hate crimes and malicious harassment felonies, including first degree murder, weapons possession, plotting to blow up Jewish and black landmarks, among other crimes, and WCOTC was already advocating Racial Holy War (RaHoWa), with a global mission "to attain a white world without Jews and non-whites."

Leone was five years younger than Angela and her second abusive partner. At the age of 17, Leone was already well connected with larger, national hate groups. Angela had already known Matt Hale, WCOTC's national leader, and Jules Fettu, leader of Florida's WCOTC. Through a circuitous chain of events, Fettu would later reappear in Angela's life. Hale would soon to be serving a 40-year sentence in federal prison for soliciting the murder of a federal judge in Chicago.

As the relationship with Leone progressed, Angela recalled, "I shared Ray's violent tendencies. We had a way of playing off of one another, inciting one another and butting heads." As part of WCOTC, she and Leone started recruiting new members along the beaches of South Florida. "We actually recruited whole families, not just teenagers," she told a reporter in 2005[19].

Reflecting on the experience, Angela told me members of the COTC "call themselves religious, but don't believe in God. To them, everything is a Jewish conspiracy." But, the anti-Semitic nature of COTC and its members failed to resonate with her. She later said that when she was 15, "I dated a Jewish boy. I had no problem over his being a Jew. It didn't even cross my mind," she said. "In most of the [neo-Nazi and white supremacy] organizations I was involved in, they considered blacks as 'mindless' or of inferior intelligence to whites. One popular perception among people in those groups," she observed, "is that blacks are being used by Jews."

Barely a year went by crime-free before Angela was again involved in another collision with Florida's finest. On March 29, 1998, Angela and Ray Leone were driving through Hollywood with three others in a car driven by a skinhead friend. Angela recalls a day of heavy drinking and, later, an argument at a local club that turned into "a huge bar brawl." The argument rose to heated banter over *The Turner Diaries*. Plied by a constant stream of alcohol, and provoked by the book's subversive plot, the four skinheads began cruising the streets on the lookout for small businesses that could be a suitable robbery target like those suggested in the novel. According to *The Turner Diaries*, larceny is an easy mechanism to fund racist causes, all the more expedient when the sites are liquor stores, porn shops, and places believed to promote or harbor any form of vice or debauchery.

Their car passed an adult video store, the perfect venue for a hit. Their friend stopped the car. They sat for a few minutes, observing the store and plotting their moves. As a group, the five reasoned that funds from a robbery would allow one of them to register with WCOTC and, after taking a cut of the cash for themselves, any remaining funds would be sent to "the church."

As they chatted, Ray openly considered shooting a black man who happened to walk by the car, a potential witness. Talked down by the others, no shots were fired and the unsuspecting man passed by, unscathed and unaware. Then Ray left the car with a loaded handgun.

Angela and the others were thrust into the role of lookout. Scanning the surroundings, Angela watched as Ray entered the video store wearing a mask hastily crafted out of a torn shirtsleeve. A few minutes passed before Ray returned to the car.

On the floor of the store, a pistol-whipped clerk struggled to regain his composure, his cash register emptied. "We didn't even know the extent of his injuries," Angela told me. The prize was less than $500. The four friends went back to the apartment where Ray and Angela were living. They divided the cash. Without the knowledge of the others, Angela stashed "a couple hundred dollars" for herself and Ray before the two headed out on another road trip.

"Shortly after the robbery," Angela told me, "we went on the run because law enforcement started making arrests in an unrelated hate crime case Ray was involved in." The previous incident involved an unprovoked attack on a black man and his son outside a concert in Sunrise, Florida. "We knew Ray was wanted for that offense." While they were hiding out in Illinois, the two learned through the skinhead grapevine that one of their other accomplices in the video store robbery had been arrested on a warrant for the concert beating. Although Angela was not with the others when the previous crime was committed, Ray had been intricately involved.

What they did not know at the time was that a skinhead sister, the second woman who served as a lookout during the armed robbery at the video store, had given police the names of all those involved in the incident. Once the suspects were identified, the other accomplices were also arrested for their part in the beating at the concert in Florida. They, too, identified all the players in the video store robbery. Angela and Ray Leone, oblivious to being turned in by traitorous colleagues, were traveling with warrants out for their arrest.

In September 1998, Ray was arrested in Chicago, taken into custody for his role in the concert beating, and later indicted for his role in the armed robbery as well. Angela left Chicago, driving directly to Florida, anticipating news of Ray's fate, but unaware she, too, would soon be indicted for the robbery. She roamed freely for three weeks before being arrested.

On October 2, 1998, after five months on the run, Angela was taken into custody for her role in the video store heist. Like the others, she was charged with use of a firearm in the commission of a crime. Because videos sold in the store had been shipped between states, the robbery charges also included conspiracy to interfere with interstate commerce, thereby making the case chargeable as a federal offense. Angela reasons, "The feds were adamant about getting skinheads. They wanted a maximum sentence for us."

Ray and three other skinhead accomplices in the video store offenses pleaded guilty to federal conspiracy and other charges and were sent to prison. Facing similar charges, Angela went through a series of hearings and legal motions before taking a plea bargain. She was convicted and sentenced to federal prison for seventy months. After a sentence reduction for cooperating with the authorities, she served three years [1998 to 2001].

The period between early 1998 and late 1999 was a turbulent time for Angela. She spent time in courts, testifying against former colleagues, and serving time in prison for her own offenses. After her arrest for the armed robbery at the video store, Angela spent one night in the Fort Lauderdale jail before being transferred to the Federal Detention Center in Miami, where she was placed in solitary confinement with no explanation for her isolation. She believes she was singled out because of her tattoos and apparent racist "attitude." With little more than her brain to entertain her, the experience chipped away at her resistance. Her life would never be the same. [Federal prisons may assign prisoners to solitary to protect inmates against harm from others in the prison population. The appearance of racist and neo-Nazi tattoos is believed to put prisoners in danger.]

"When I was initially arrested, I felt that my role was minimal in the robbery. I didn't feel and/or take responsibility when I was first incarcerated. However," she said, "relatively early during my time in prison, one of the most valuable lessons I learned was about taking responsibility for all of my words and actions, including – and especially – the robbery. I am one-hundred percent responsible for all of my own actions, words, decisions."

Angela learned how a successful plea bargain works in the federal system. "It means acknowledging and taking complete responsibility [for what you did]." By being as truthful as possible to herself, she now reasons that the circumstances at the time "precipitated the way I view my role and level of responsibility, not only in the robbery, but in other aspects of my life."

In interviews and presentations to college audiences Angela talks candidly about her role in the video store robbery and the personal insights she gained from her time in prison. She acknowledges she could have stopped the crime – "I didn't say, 'Hey guys, you could hurt somebody or kill somebody.' I did nothing. And for that, I went to federal prison for three years."

Prior to their convictions for the armed robbery, Angela had considered marrying Ray Leone. The abusive lover and crime leader was now serving time in the same institution as she. By sheer coincidence, shortly after getting situated there, Angela was seated in front of Leone on a prison bus headed to a legal hearing. They were both in shackles. In the midst of a subdued but increasingly heated dialogue, Leone grabbed Angela's arm in a grasp tight enough to leave bruises.

Ray Leone's grip represented another turning point in both their relationship and her involvement in the movement. With his pointlessly malicious gesture to grab her arm, Angela instinctively understood that, for her, the romance was over. Without quite realizing it at the time, she had reached the end of being controlled by bullying skinheads and the starting point of thinking independently. The insight gave her one more issue to mull over during her time in prison.

After weeks in a solitary cell at the Miami Federal Detention Center, Angela was moved to a section that housed a diverse mix of women that her limited inner circle of friends had never stretched to accept. After solitary, she remembers meeting people from all over the world, representing all races, cultures, and ethnicities. Human interaction was a welcome relief, even with people from groups that had been the object of her white supremacist wrath. She began to talk with several black Jamaican women with whom she was cautious, yet friendly.

As they talked, Angela slowly became aware that the life experiences of some of the Jamaican women aligned with her own history. They, too, came from broken homes and long-term poverty. They had experienced the same frustrations over class and social status, always wanting more than they were able to get. They, too, had struggled with alcohol and substance abuse, and coped with abusive partners.

Angela knew the anger of many black women could be real because she had seen it in the eyes of those she had confronted over years as a skinhead heavy. She had not realized before they talked that her new friends tackled a near-lifelong battle with internalized fear. As they chatted, Angela bonded with the women over conversations about clashes with police, the legal system, and abusive men.

The friendships with her new Jamaican inmate friends deepened quickly. One of the woman stood out as particularly sympathetic. She was interested in Angela's stories and Angela in hers. After a rocky start, their conversations went into uncharted territory. "When we first met, she hated me because I was a racist and was convicted for a hate crime." Yet the two continued to relate their pasts. In Angela's words, "We compared our lives before prison. We both had violent pasts. She had been involved in a gang. We knew we didn't want to go back to our previous lives [after prison]. We wanted to be different."

Angela and her new friend talked about their youth and adulthood, their likes and dislikes, high points and low points in their lives, all with little restraint. As their conversations progressed, a long-suppressed impulse from Angela's early years began to come alive, one that until then was effectively shielded behind a fortress of clouded emotions. Angela found herself looking forward to their exchanges with unusual anticipation. Each one-on-one talk grew more intense than the last. As her desire for more depth and intimacy increased, Angela was not certain where their conversations – or her emotions – were leading.

By using prison-style caution and discretion, the two managed to get assigned to the same cell, at least for a brief time. She said, "It was my first same-sex relationship. I fell head over heels in love." Angela declined to identify the woman by name.

Not long after the affair began and before Angela knew which prison she, Angela, would be assigned to, her Jamaican girlfriend was moved. When her girlfriend left the Detention Center for prison, Angela wasn't sure the two would ever see one another again. Shortly after the move, Angela was assigned to the same federal prison in Tallahassee, Florida, where her girlfriend had been assigned. They occasionally talked to one another, yet by the end of her prison term, Angela's effort to reignite the relationship proved futile. "When I was released, she still had more time to serve," Angela explained.

After a period of not talking, the two women reconnected through social media. Over time, their communication tapered to a memory. As she described the relationship, the pace and tone of her words, made it clear that, to her, "The separation was difficult." After a series of relationships with abusive men, an understanding soul, much less an unexpected lover, was a welcome relief.

Over the years, her parents' rule still seemed to lurk in her mind: *Just don't come home with a black man or a woman.* "In my youth, I felt I *could* be gay. But that [rule] caused me to bury and deny any issues I had about sexual orientation." Yet, even rigid parents can change. After the two women were separated and Angela was still in prison, Angela notes with a smile in her voice, "My mom helped get letters from her to me."

In a follow-up interview, Angela told me, "We re-established contact several years ago, although we have not seen one another face-to-face again." But, the relationship with her Jamaican girlfriend had a significant effect on Angela's separation from the movement. She explained, "I'll never forget our time together. She gave me hope that I could be a different person. We used to daydream about how to make it work on the outside. With her, I could start to see a completely different future for myself. My time with her was an enormous experience – to have been with another woman. This was the opposite of what I had been doing. It was freedom for me, even though I was in prison. That time was the freest I had ever been in my life. I was able to let go of what other people would say or do to me."

Without question, Angela's tattoos had a profound impact on her interactions with prison staff and inmates. Because incarcerated members of hate groups tend to have a subculture of their own on the inside, no matter how her markings were interpreted, Angela was either a point of attraction or aversion. She could easily be lured into joining other neo-Nazi inmates, a common occurrence during incarceration. If she failed to associate with like-minded prisoners, she could be labeled a traitor for showing swastikas and other outward signs of the movement on her body, but not uniting with other white supremacists. That dynamic would make her a target for anyone associated with a hate group.

Inmates with no interest in hate groups were likely to form their own opinions, pro or con, and act accordingly. Liberal-leaning prisoners would reject her out of hand, without so much as a chilly hello.

To her benefit, Angela's crime was a federal offense for which she served her time in a federal prison where inmates are protected against threats or attacks over race or other personal issues, including their involvement in a recognized hate group. In state penitentiaries, prisoners have less protection against such harassment, simply because cultural disputes are rarely if ever allowed as a reason for making cell reassignments. Were Angela in a state prison, her options to avoid offenses from other criminals would have been just another fantasy. In a federal institution, were such an offense to occur, she could request a cell change.

On more than one occasion Angela was sexually provoked in aggressive ways by both men and women in prison. However, she was not bothered enough to request a reassignment. It was a comfort to know federal protection was possible when and if she needed it.

While she was incarcerated, Angela remembers running into a white supremacist friend, an accomplice in the same video store robbery for which Angela was convicted. According to Angela, "She was the one who turned us in to the police." In prison, she said, a separation order kept the two apart "because officials didn't know what I would do to her." Angela explains that the woman owned the gun used during the robbery. "It was her gun. It was her car that was used." When the other woman went to police, Angela said, "She changed a few details so that she appeared less involved and I looked more responsible." Ratting on the other guy is part of the domino effect in the hate movement; implicate others so you look clean.

Angela contends a similar get-the-co-conspirator-before-he-gets-you pattern was how she ended up in prison. She was drawn into a legal web regarding the hate crime at the Sunrise concert in which Ray Leone beat up a black man and his son, a crime in which Angela was not present and was not involved. Although she was not a part of that offense, some of her buddies from the video store were. When an accomplice involved in the Sunrise beating, a man who was *also* a part of the armed robbery at the video store, took his case to trial, his testimony implicated Angela in the subsequent crime.

Multiple arrests and overlapping bias crimes are often part of a hate criminal's rap sheet. Angela tried to unscramble two interconnected malicious harassment events, the beating of a black man and his son and the armed robbery at the video store. Angela's words reveal how friendships within the hate movement mark the limits and fallacy of "belonging" within a hate group. Friends to the end – then, watch you're back.

In Angela's words, "The domino effect went like this: The other woman involved in the robbery case got dumped by a boyfriend who was also involved in that robbery *and* the concert hate crime. She implicated all of us involved in the robbery but wasn't taken into custody immediately because law enforcement needed her help. Other arrests were made in the concert hate crime based on the initial information from the other woman. Ray Leone and I found out that arrests were being made in the crime at the concert. Others involved in both the concert hate crime and the video store robbery were arrested and gave more information.

"Ray was arrested in Chicago for concert hate crime and extradited back to Florida. Sometime during the few weeks following Ray's arrest, indictments came down for both Ray and I for the robbery, but we weren't actually both indicted for the armed robbery until I was arrested and officially in custody. We gave information to police and others were arrested for other [unrelated] crimes. Those individuals also gave information to police. Only one person in all the cases took his case to trial. That was Jules Fettu, who I eventually testified against." In 1999, Fettu, leader of the World Church of the Creator in Florida, 26 at the time, was sentenced to five years in prison in 1999 for his involvement in beating the man outside the Sunrise, Florida, concert while the victim's 17-year-old son was forced to watch.

During the 1998 to 1999 turmoil and prior to her testimony against Fettu, Angela was temporarily housed in the Broward County Jail. Local authorities wanted to keep her close to where the Fettu case would be heard. After testifying, she was returned to the Federal Detention Center in Miami before ending up at the Federal Correctional Institute in Tallahassee.

Angela remembers a setback that occurred in the Broward County jail before she was moved to Tallahassee. On an emotional level, she was still separating herself from the neo-Nazi mold and white supremacist ideology. She measured her progress to detach from any remaining ties to the movement by the amount of time she spent not having negative reactions to non-white people.

At the county jail, Angela became friendly with a female singer from a heavy metal band. The woman had no known connections to a hate group. Angela knew the woman only by name. "I had gone to her concerts."

In Angela's words: "She was Jewish, gay, and a heroin addict. She hated black people. Now she was in jail. At the time, I had already made changes, met new [non-racist] friends, and was progressing in a transition out of the movement. When I was thrown in with this woman, we spent our days making fun of and criticizing black people." The rock idol status of Angela's new friend may have had a subconscious influence; however, she said that while her perspectives were evolving, "It was easy to fall back into the same bad habits."

Angela's combative nature continued in prison. She believes two jail fights she was involved in were not race related, although "one was with a black girl." The other was an insignificant tussle "with a white girl over changing a TV channel." The fights, she explained, "contradicted all the progress I had made. It was like I slipped back into my old self. I have no explanation for it." Once she moved out of the county jail and away from the singer, she was back on track toward a clean break from the movement.

After being released in 2001, Angela recalls feeling a sense of loss and confusion, complicated by a sexual disorientation. "The process of coming out as a [former] skinhead is very similar to coming out as gay," she explains. The conflicts of a new and different lifestyle left her unsure of where to turn for friendships or intimacy. "It was easy to find lesbians in prison. After I got out, I had no idea there was a whole gay community living their lives on the outside." To her, the realization of a "community" for LGBTQ people correlated to her earlier discovery that the hate movement could offer a safe harbor for misanthropic teens. Making adjustments was a whole new dare, one she felt woefully ill-equipped to maneuver.

For 18 months after being released from prison for the last time, Angela went back to pursuing sexual relationships with men. "After that time, it took me a while to realize why I wasn't happy [sexually]." Without women, she went back to feeling like she didn't fit. "In order to have sex with men, I had to watch porn with women." Finding a new [gay] community allowed Angela to rediscover herself and warm up to a whole new approach to humanity. Online chat rooms posed a new technique to connect with other people. "At the time, I saw myself as lesbian – not bi-sexual. I spent years with women."

Not one to be comfortable with her own status quo, in 2009, long after her release from prison for the last time, Angela fell in love with a man, leading to a pregnancy that ended in a miscarriage. "We broke up months after that." While exploring her sexual self, she told me, "I came to a point where [trying to qualify or quantify] gender and sexual orientation didn't work for me. There comes a certain freedom when one stops trying to fit into a box that doesn't fit. It's important to me to be with someone who finds his or her own happiness. It has taken me years to get here." Her thoughts represent a monumental advancement for a person whose life choices were constantly plagued by an inability to find a place where she could fit.

Angela looks back at her lesbian prison romance philosophically. "I don't know if I did it to prove something to myself or to break from the movement. Maybe it doesn't matter. What I got out of the relationship was so enriching as to change me spiritually. I could do all the soul searching possible, but couldn't change until I had the courage to do it." Today she considers herself pansexual[20].

Angela reflects on a tormented past. "During most of my time in the movement, I felt dead inside. I used to self-mutilate. I burned myself, used razor blades, and would bite my lip until it bled. When I woke up in the morning, I knew I wasn't where I should be. I was emotionally unavailable." Looking back, she saw that living the image of a skinhead thug bestowed a self-contradictory reward. [Being a neo-Nazi skinhead] "was a chance to feel something. Emotions arose. It was exciting."

Asked how prison changed her, Angela focused more on her struggle to reestablish herself within the context of her own core values. "Prison changed everything. I don't believe *the system* rehabilitated me. It wasn't prison as an institution that changed my life; it was the experiences with the people I met. The system gave me a place to rehabilitate *myself.*"

The experience was enough to convince her that prisons are "overburdened, understaffed, and employees are underpaid. I don't believe the resources are there to counsel and rehabilitate everyone who enters. For those who *want* to learn from their mistakes, they can do it."

Being behind bars also gave Angela time to reflect on other events that she had overlooked during her time in the movement, situations that today give her pause. "One example was when I lost a male friend who was my age. We were both 21. Since then, I think about this sweet kid and what he would have been like if he didn't get involved in the movement. Later I learned that all but one member of a group I was a part of had been killed. I was angry, but didn't equate [their deaths] to the movement."

Another life-altering event transpired when Angela lost both of her grandmothers within a two-week period. At the time, she was separated from her family, living with skinheads in another state. "I felt bad for not being near them and not with them when they died. Shaking her head from side to side, she went on, "At the time, even that [loss] was a small sacrifice for being accepted into a group."

In prison, Angela recognized education as an avenue to self-worth and fulfillment. She took advantage of the opportunity to attend free classes. The coursework led to a Certificate in Business Education. Her newfound thirst for knowledge inspired her to pay it forward by teaching fellow inmates to read. She also had an occasion to scrutinize how her values had shifted from her childhood, into the movement, and after prison, in a development largely outside of her own control.

In an online "Open Letter" published in 2002, Angela describes the emotions she experienced through her transition out of the hate movement. Her words reflect nearly identical statements voiced by other defectors. In the letter, she writes:

"Being wanted was a great feeling and one that I had not felt in many years . . . The turnaround was a true epiphany. I could wake up in the morning, look in the mirror, and even when I was in prison, I actually liked who I was looking at . . . To completely understand the depths that can drive someone into a life of hatred is not an easy thing to do, but maybe a necessity if we are to prevent others from becoming involved. If I would have had someone that understood what I was going through with real-life understanding, I believe I would have turned out different. It would have made such a difference to me to speak with someone who had actually been through or felt the emotions that I was going through."

Within a few years of her final release from prison, Angela started talking openly about her escape from the movement. The first time she spoke publicly about her experience was when her probation officer taught a criminal justice class at Barry University and asked Angela to give a presentation about her life. After that, she became a speaker with the Anti-Defamation League (ADL). Among other messages she delivers, Angela tells groups, "I am still working on forgiving myself. I'm closer every day."

A low-key, yet stirring public speaker, Angela frequently regales audiences at colleges and universities with the story of inner turmoil. She said, during her talks, "I used to try to cover up my tattoos, but I don't anymore. I've come to realize that my tattoos add to who I am today and there is no good reason to run from my past." As part of her toned-down and self-effacing persona, she rarely wears a dress and heels at such events.

After exposing the inky signs of her past during a presentation to one college group, a woman in the audience offered to persuade her husband, a plastic surgeon, to remove Angela's tattoos. The gesture was gratefully accepted. Over time, her remaining tattoos were tattooed over to conceal the original images. All but one.

At our interview in Florida, Angela raised her hands to her mouth and turned down her lower lip to reveal the single remaining tattoo. A blue imprint hidden across the inside of her lip reads: "*Sieg Heil,*" a common tattoo for hardcore skinheads. Aside from the sensitivity of laser surgery there, she declared confidently, "No one sees it, so I probably won't get that one removed."

In 2016, Angela told me about "another epiphany," explaining . . . "I found the forgiveness of self that I had been missing. I realized that I cannot expect others to forgive me or to fully realize the impact and power of kindness and compassion if I did not have the ability to see that in myself."

What makes Angela's story so extraordinary is that her experience mirrors that of other women defectors who have faced the very same emotional turmoil as well as the physical threats, terror, and violence from other white supremacists.

In 2016, during one of our last interviews, Angela told me that Ray Leone, her Hammerskin ex-boyfriend and ringleader of the video store robbery, had contacted her within the past year. He told her, "I was fucked up at the time . . ." Angela declined to give more detail about the conversation.

Ray's comment suggests that, like countless other defectors, he may have fallen silently out of the movement, merging back into the mainstream with so much dexterity as to be just another unfamiliar face in the neighborhood.

Since she left prison, Angela has received an Associates Degree from Broward College and Bachelors and Masters Degrees in Interdisciplinary Studies from the University of Central Florida. Her academic focus was on Women's Studies and Social Concern.

In addition to serving as a resource to many community groups, Angela is a founding member and Deputy Director of Life After Hate[21] (lifeafterhate.org) a non-profit "dedicated to inspiring individuals and communities to a place of compassion and forgiveness for themselves and for all people." The organization relies on the "powerful stories of transformation and our unique insights about extremism gleaned from decades of experience" in order to create change. One of Life After Hate's programs, Exit USA, specifically helps former members of the white power movement leave hate and violence behind.

For her part, Angela explains, "Because I know the deep impact that kindness and compassion had on my own life and process, I have a moral and spiritual responsibility to give back in a positive way after all of the negative energy I put out into the world. I also feel that I have a responsibility to serve as a voice for those who, for whatever reason, cannot raise their own."

By 2018, Angela realized the importance of self-care. Some 17 years after exiting the movement she said, "I have been doing the work, personally and at Life After Hate, since day one." That has included coping with the psychological burden from her role in the hate crimes she was a part of and personal therapy.

Asked how her speaking engagements at colleges, universities, and community groups were going, she took a breath, continuing slowly and deliberately, "I can't do that anymore. I've pushed myself since 2001, without paying enough attention to my physical health. I can let go of the speaking. I don't need it for my ego and I no longer do it out of a need to make amends. I know talking about my experience is important and useful to tell young people leaving the movement about my experience. But, I have to pay attention to myself."

Angela says she still greets every day with intellectual curiosity and continues to examine her values. "Honesty is at the top of the list, with equality a close second." With a measure of thoughtful counterbalance, she comments, "Every human being deserves kindness and compassion and every human being has the ability to offer kindness and compassion to others. I try to transform my worst experiences into something positive that might save lives – and help me heal."

As she helps former extremists regain inner strength, Angela occasionally looks back at her own life in open wonder, rising above a violent past, yet careful to conceal the glow of a master craftsperson eyeing a piece of fine furniture in which every tiny detail fits.

Frank Meeink

FRANK MEEINK OFFERS A WILD PERSPECTIVE ON the hate movement. Were his talks to college audiences cleared by a censor, every other line would have at least one bleep. His quirky stories flourish with the kind of crusty language and earthy humor that causes some to smile and others to cringe. How he was pulled into the movement, his bizarre escapades as a skinhead and Christian Identity leader, and what he's done since he left the movement merge together raunchy laugh lines with memories of horrific skinhead terror sprees and a spirit of redemption. His funniest lines are often at his own expense.

Rocky Balboa is, to some extent, responsible for Frank's punch. The character, a native Philadelphian boxer portrayed by Sylvester Stallone in the movie *Rocky* and several sequels, was Frank's childhood idol and adult role model. Balboa beat the odds to become Heavyweight Champion of the World. The character influenced the way Frank dealt with his frustrations – through left hooks and drop kicks to defenseless victims on the same streets Rocky roamed.

As a skinhead heavy, Frank's footwork danced around the law, dodged his own goofy screwups, forged unexpected friendships with members of gangs on his Philadelphia turf and fought a string of

The author has received permission from Hawthorn Press to use excerpts from Frank's book, *Autobiography of a Recovering Skinhead.*

addictions. Eventually however, he became an unlikely superstar to at-risk kids.

Like other high profile former skinheads, Frank's life is occasionally rumored to be the basis of the 1998 drama *American History X*, in which Edward Norton plays a neo-Nazi who serves three years in prison for voluntary manslaughter, changes his beliefs, and abandons the hate movement. The film more accurately merges the life trajectories of *many* former white supremacists and extremists, including those profiled in this book. Celluloid avatars aside, Frank is a one-of-a-kind character in his own right.

Born Francis Steven Bertollini in Philadelphia, Pennsylvania, on May 7, 1975, Frank's Irish mother chose her maiden name, Meeink, as Frank's surname so he would not be perceived as Italian. Frank describes his parents as "lower working class," unsympathetically referring to his Italian-American father as an alcoholic and his Irish mother as a drug-dealer. He recalls the humiliation he felt whenever food stamps instead of cash were used to buy groceries. He refers to both parents as "crack heads." He uses few kind words to describe his step-father, flashing back to memories of beatings and mean tirades at Frank's expense.

Frank's family was raised Catholic, but he says, "We were not very religious." They went to church only on Christmas and Easter. His parents divorced before his third birthday, after which Frank moved in with his father, whose home was "a drug environment." He lived there until he entered the ninth grade. By then his mother had remarried. Frank moved back to live with his mother and step-father in a Philadelphia row house on the outskirts of a mostly Irish neighborhood. Halfway down his block, the neighbors were mostly Asian and black. He recalls cultivating relationships with non-white friends.

Frank recalls that his father was not systematically racist, but had friends of color, some of whom his father met working as a bartender or dealing drugs. His mother, he remembers, commonly used racial epithets at home. In school, Frank was aware of race, ethnicity, and other differences, many in a negative context. He remembers, "When black kids jumped me, like fights in parks or at school, I would always join the white kids. It was payback time. I was getting tortured by black kids, in some way or another, every day." Through his early years Frank was no stranger to mean people. He grew up surrounded by Philadelphia's notorious street gangs. Through much of his youth, he was on both sides of beatings – giving and taking.

Frank went to [George Wharton] Pepper Middle School, located in a Southwest Philadelphia industrial zone where a majority of students were bused from other neighborhoods. "People knew Pepper was a bad school, a tough school where 90 percent of the students were black. White kids would get beat up and robbed [by blacks]. White boys ran to school. We'd get rolled, get our shit robbed. I never thought about a good day at school – we just tried to avoid fights." When he grew a bit older, he played sports against ethnic teams, mostly black.

From an early age, Frank excelled in sports, a way to counter his less than stellar academic performance. He says, "I was unnaturally fast. My legs were ahead of me when I ran, faster than me." He was pegged as an athlete for his strength, played several sports, and especially excelled at hockey.

He calls his middle school and early high school years "the lowest time of my life," with particular emphasis on the ninth grade, the most tumultuous. That year discontent showed up at school and at home. Forcing him to repeat the eighth grade did little to increase his chances of scholastic success the next year. Instead, he harbored grudges and resentments. Shortly after he entered ninth grade, Frank's life took a new direction when he got chummy with his cousin "James," not his real name.

In 1989, a month after his 14th birthday, Frank's mother and step-father kicked him out of their house. That year an aunt and uncle took Frank to live with their family on a farm in Lancaster, Pennsylvania, known for peaceful eccentricities and the Christian traditions of the region's Amish people.

His relatives were not part of the Pennsylvania Dutch community. Not by a long shot. When he entered their home, he came face-to-face with two prominent flags; one a Confederate battle flag, the other sporting a black swastika. The walls were covered with news clips about skinheads. Frank bunked with his cousin James, whose bedroom was draped with Hitler regalia. James introduced Frank to his friends who were clearly neo-Nazi skinheads. In Frank's words, "The guys James hung out with looked cool. I looked up to them." The die was cast.

After being ejected from an unstable household and drawn to the tightknit clan of James's friends, the skinheads offered a feeling of structure and purpose; a new family, one that let Frank blow off steam about black kids at school and gripe about people who were different. He was rewarded for contradicting political correctness.

Frank adapted to white supremacy with all the fury of a long-term radical. In his book, *Autobiography of a Recovering Skinhead*[22], he tells about recruiting new members with his favorite line: "You don't have to be picked on ever again . . . " His strategy, he writes, was to bypass "smart guys, rough guys, nerds, and especially good looking guys," whom he saw as "too competitive." His favorites to enlist: "Guys with cars. They got friends."

Years later, sitting in the cocktail lounge of a Seattle hotel, he told me about how the relationship with his cousin unfolded. "I liked hanging out with James. His friends talked about how a multi-racial society doesn't work. I knew what [they] were talking about. I went to school in West Philly. I would tell them about myself. They asked questions about me and my life. My parents never asked how I was or what's new. James's friends were older. They drank beer and gave me beer." Not long after connecting with James, Frank was binge drinking a 12-pack every day.

Frank remembers the night "the guys" shaved his head, his informal initiation into the skinhead world. Soon he was with his new skinhead buddies when they confronted a victim at a bar. Without describing the victim in any detail, Frank got a gut impression of what was happening and was immediately infused with a memorable emotion. "I saw the fear in his eyes. That was the best. I LOOOVED it." For the first time in his life, the mutual admiration allowed Frank to feel like he belonged to a nuclear family. He was hooked.

Before moving in with his cousin's family, Frank recalls looking at race and religion differently, saying, "My animosity toward blacks was already there because of the fights at school, [but] I had no reason to hate Jews. I knew no Jews in South Philly; I'm not even sure any lived there." Being exposed to the deep anti-Semitism he experienced around James's family made it easy to adopt negative stereotypes.

Over the next several years, Frank separated from James's skinhead crew and shifted allegiance to a variety of anti-Semitic and other white supremacist groups. With their encouragement, he committed a chain of hate crimes from Philadelphia to Springfield, Illinois. Often, the crimes he committed slipped between the cracks of local, county, state, or federal law enforcement. "We would often do horrible things to people, homeless people, gays, other people . . . Horrible things." Much of the harassment was never reported to police.

When Frank was 14, an incident occurred while he was hitchhiking home at night from a friend's house. The scene would provoke his anger more than any "minority" confrontation could. Among other events detailed in his autobiography, the following excerpt describes a scenario in which he was picked up by a middle-aged man:

> We were speeding east on Highway 3, shooting the shit about sports, when he reached across me, opened the glove box, pulled out a revolver, and shoved the barrel into my temple. He held the steering wheel with his knee and used his free hand to unzip his pants.
> "Suck me," he said.
> "No fucking way."
> "Your choice, kid." He pulled back the hammer.
> He kept that fucking gun cocked, jammed into my skull, the whole goddamn time. When it was over, he dumped me on the side of the road.
> I memorized his license plate and he sped away.

Frank found a way to assuage the inhumanity and lingering outrage from having been raped. He writes, "Later that night, I jumped a random queen in Center City. I bragged to the other skinheads about how I'd brutalized him, but I never breathed a word to them about what the man in the car had done to me." It was neither the first nor the last of his merciless gay bashings.

Over a two-day period in early 1990, at age 15, Frank was embroiled in a vicious string of hate crimes. With five guys from a South Philadelphia skinhead group called the South Street Crew, Frank sprayed a swastika and "Seig Heil" on the side of a Polish American Club.

The crew returned the next day, wielding a ragtag display of weapons: a bat, a hockey stick, a metal pipe, and a tack hammer. When they saw two white male students walk toward them in an isolated area devoid of onlookers, they pounced. In the midst of the mayhem, a skinhead hit one of the two men in the head with the tack hammer. Frank remembers leveraging the man's neck against the pavement with his boot while another skinhead jerked the pointy end of the hammer from a bloody wound. When one of the skinheads shouted "Cops," they packed into a vehicle and fled, chugging beer, laughing, and convincing each other the man's injuries were not that big of a deal. All but the victim walked away. Frank says an investigation was conducted, but no arrests were made. Years later Frank confirmed he was never questioned by police and the case has never been linked to him or anyone in the South Street Crew. In commenting on the tack hammer scenario, the following passage from Frank's book follows the same thinking voiced by other defectors, a concrete example of white supremacist and Christian Identity reasoning:

> "I truly believed I had a permission slip from God to kick anybody's ass if they disagreed with me, looked at me funny, didn't look at me at all. I thought I was doing God's will by raining down 'Justice' on those who violated his commandments. The thing is, I only enforced the 'commandments' [Christian] Identity preaches; I never thought twice about the other ten God handed down to Moses . . . "

By the end of 1990, not yet 16 years old, Frank had dabbled in a Ku Klux Klan group, been ejected from the Klan, and been enthusiastically accepted into a male-only white supremacist group called Strike Force. The group was not directly related to the Strike Force skinheads Angela King was a part of around the same time.

Strike Force was part of the anti-Semitic Christian Identity (CI) movement. Frank recalls his entry into CI theology: "For the first couple years I was in the hate movement, I attended Christian Identity Bible study." In 1991, at age 16, Frank was named Pennsylvania Chapter Leader of the group.

As another example of Frank's one-of-a-kind style, this first-person account of an otherwise grim development gives all the color that is Frank Meeink: Somewhere around age 17 while he was on the lam, Frank spent a night in a Terre Haute, Indiana, home where his employer allowed him to crash. After a depressing night of listening to country music and drinking as much beer as he could consume, Frank stripped to his boxers, wrote a suicide note, and slit his wrists. He then walked to the balcony in a daze. He describes neighbors seeing a bloody half-dressed stranger on the rail of a friend's home. They called 9-1-1, believing Frank had murdered the tenant. Frank panicked at the sound of sirens. With warrants out for his arrest in at least three states, he had reason to be antsy. Using clever ingenuity, he barricaded the door with all the furniture he could move and headed to the outside balustrade with visions of a short jump to find help and stop the bleeding.

In relating the story to audiences, Frank pauses to chuckle, rolling his eyes while explaining one slight miscalculation. Between the time he blocked the door, and his anticipated leap to the street, it became confoundingly clear that the apartment door opened outward – not in. A SWAT team turned the knob, swept aside the obstacles, and promptly took Frank to a mental health care facility, better known to Frank's crowd as "Krazy Kate's."

Two years later, at a holiday party on the afternoon of Christmas Eve, 1992, Frank and his skinhead buddies had a testy run-in with Jake, a member of the anti-racist organization Skinheads Against Racial Prejudice (SHARP). Earlier in the day, he and Jake had negotiated an electronics deal that had not gone Frank's way. With a force behind him, he confronted Jake to level what he saw as a lopsided bargain.

Frank already had a reputation as a SHARP hater, confirmed by a two-word tattoo on the inside of his lower lip: "SHARP KILLER." In an obsessed rant, Frank viciously criticized anti-racists, opening a free-for-all fight focused on Jake. "We beat the shit out of him." Frank and company left the scene of the assault. But that wasn't the end of it.

A more serious drama unfolded after the initial assault, when Frank returned to the party with a shotgun. Among other threatening gestures, he describes putting the gun barrel on Jake's forehead. Rather than pulling the trigger, his steel-toed Doc Martin boots pounded Jake's face.

Without Frank's certainty of why a skinhead buddy would take a video recorder to the party, much less use it to record a fight, the beating ended up on videotape. As he writes in his book, the camera recorded every punt, including Frank sputtering the words, "We should just kill this fucker."

Recording the ambush was one mistake; keeping it was another.

At the time, Frank was employed as a talk show host for a television show called *The Reich*. By some quirk, the tape mysteriously passed through the TV station where he worked. The beating video provided indisputable evidence of Frank's involvement in a crime. The recording eventually fell into the hands of a television executive who forwarded it to police. Frank was arrested for being at the center of the incident.

Frank was convicted on charges of aggravated unlawful restraint (kidnapping) and assault with a deadly weapon. He was sentenced to three to five years in prison, not the first time he was behind bars. He told me, "I was in jail much of my teenage life," including time for a home invasion offense, another stint for ethnic intimidation, and again for a gay bashing. But, this sentence would be the most memorable.

After the trial, Frank bounced from one prison to another before ending up at Shawnee State Penitentiary in Vienna, Illinois, about 340 miles south of Chicago. While he was at Shawnee, he became the father of his first child (a daughter). He was more immersed in coping with cellmates, prison gangs, and organized hate groups than thinking about being a parent.

At Shawnee, Frank ran into members of the Aryan Brotherhood and Aryan Nations. By then, Frank was marked with the usual array of neo-Nazi ink, 30 images in total, over his arms, hands, head, and a five-inch Celtic Cross in a flaming circle on the side of his neck. The name of his former Christian Identity group, "Strike Force," appeared across the back of his neck. The words "Mad in Philly" were tattooed across his shaved head. His tattoos tripped a signal to the other neo-Nazis that he was an ally. He learned that anyone connected to the movement was automatically considered part of Aryan Nations.

A jock at heart, Frank deflected from the Aryan cellmates by focusing his attention on sports. His powerful legs and quick moves became a line of defense for teammates on the prison football field. It didn't take long for Frank to see he was the only white boy in the lineup.

While Frank was at Shawnee, he met Abel, a one-time drug kingpin from East St. Louis, Missouri. Abel, a towering 6'6" black man who became "born again" in prison, had seen Frank with a Bible and invited him to come to Abel's nightly Bible study. That evening, Frank joined five black inmates with whom he held hands and recited the Lord's Prayer.

Abel's friendship freed Frank to look more deeply into his misunderstandings of race and faith. Earning Abel's trust had a monumental impact. Frank began to warm up to his own religion and a growing affinity to black people. His position as the sole white guy on the prison's black football team was another testament to his transition. He was beginning to see that by slowly breaking down deep-seated African American stereotypes and biases, he was gradually separating from the ideology that had been guiding his life. Moreover, he had become friendly with black men in a profoundly meaningful way.

It was during his time in prison that Frank began to detach from the movement.

After his release, a tortured, but brief relapse occurred when Frank learned that a close skinhead friend had been murdered by a black man. He immediately returned to the skinhead mentality. In the spirit of friendship among colleagues with whom he shared a criminal history, he set out to show his respects. At a beer party in honor of the fallen comrade, Frank ran into a group called Axis Skinheads, former friends who caught wind he had left the movement.

Not happy to see a traitor, the neo-Nazis ambushed Frank before he had a chance to slip away from the makeshift memorial service. As he was being kicked with unforgiving force, among the faces watching from the sidelines, he saw his cousin James. Under the grueling scrutiny of members from other skinhead groups, including his own former crew, he arose from the battering and, for the last time, walked away from his skinhead and now enemies.

After years of being wrapped up in white supremacist ideology, Frank would have occasional setbacks as he transitioned away from hate. At one point, it became apparent that his progress to accept African Americans did little to defuse a lifelong anti-Semitic conflict with anyone he perceived to be Jewish. That's when an unexpected learning opportunity arose in the form of an employer.

Like other heavily tattooed former white supremacists, Frank made an unappealing employment candidate. At the end of an agonizing effort to find work, he was offered a part-time job moving furniture at an antiques dealership whose owner was unfazed by the swastikas and neo-Nazi image blazing on Frank's neck. One snag for Frank: he surmised that the shop owner, Keith Goldstein, was Jewish. But, flat broke and with no other prospects in sight, he took the job with serious reservations.

After many "oy vey" comments and what he saw as his boss's stereotypical behaviors, Frank slipped back into anti-Semitic thinking; he suspected he was being shortchanged in one of his first paychecks. While he was weighing whether it was wise or dumb to question his boss so early into the job, Keith called Frank in for a one-on-one meeting. Before Frank had a chance to voice his complaint about being cheated, Keith handed him a $100 bonus and asked him to stay on full time.

Another culture barrier shattered.

Years after his exit from the movement, Frank was drinking a non-alcoholic beverage at a bar in St. Louis. Across the room he eyed Jake, the anti-racist SHARP victim at the center of his conviction and prison sentence. Jake resurfaced after one of Frank's post-rehab sobriety stretches. Heeding the advice of a former Alcoholics Anonymous sponsor who encouraged him to "clean up the wreckage from your past," Frank nervously approached Jake in a gesture of atonement.

The two exchanged social niceties, an anxious strain after their last encounter in a courtroom. Then came an odd turn of guilt and personal accountability; as Frank was thinking about his role in beating Jake and pillaging through his belongings, it was Jake who apologized to Frank, sorry that he went to the police. Frank theorizes Jake's apology was part of his own clean-up-your-past work.

Frank told me the conversation with Jake went on for over an hour. "We talked about life and friends. He knew I was changed. He could see it in my eyes. I haven't seen him since then." For

Frank, the encounter was one more indicator the movement was a shadow from his past.

Just a year after his release from prison, the April 19, 1995, bombing in Oklahoma City, topped all news headlines. After the initial reports, Frank knew instinctively the incident would be connected to the hate movement. Like other defectors rattled by the photo of a first responder carrying a fatally wounded child from the wreckage, he too, was haunted by the image. With the movement behind him, the photo caused Frank to think more deeply about what he could do as a *former* white supremacist.

He decided to tell the FBI everything he knew.

After answering a barrage of FBI questions, an investigator urged Frank to share his story with the Anti-Defamation League. Guidance from his ADL contacts inspired Frank, the former Christian Identity poster child, to use an innate talent that could dissuade young people from getting involved in gangs or organized hate. He went back to the ice rink.

With help from the ADL, Frank created a nonprofit organization that fosters spirituality and provides children and young adults with a positive team experience. His brainchild, Harmony Through Hockey, was designed to nurture self-esteem. The organization strives to bring culturally diverse communities together by promoting racial harmony through team building and athletic competition.

Still coping with remnants of his own transition, Frank became an ADL speaker, lending his voice to oppose anti-Semitism and any form of hatred. He pitched the idea for Harmony Through Hockey to his closest ally at ADL, with the vision of attracting youth from an array of cultural backgrounds. He preferred kids with no skating experience. Frank explains his logic for selecting diverse hockey players for the teams: "They wear too much equipment to see their skin." Plus, he said, "No matter what color they are, they're all going to land on their asses."

Confident in Frank's turnaround, leadership potential and vision, an ADL lawyer connected him to the owner of the Philadelphia Flyers, who facilitated sponsorship and support from the team. Frank's ADL mentor also secured an agreement with the local Department of Recreation to provide rink time to Frank's youth team, with a request that Frank be head coach for the new program. The ADL put Frank on the road to promote the Harmony Through Hockey concept to other cities. He endured an ambitious schedule, with unwavering ADL support. Then came, well, a hiccup. A hotel bill from Frank's tour revealed a charge of roughly $500, itemizing just how deeply Frank had reached into the mini-bar in his room.

Frank was called to task, although gently and with support. He responded to the kindness by owning up to an alcohol binge. Building on the theme, he also confessed to a more than $200-a-week cocaine habit.

With unrestrained encouragement from the ADL, Frank dried out after a series of rehab programs spanning five years, each punctuated by periodic returns to booze and prescription narcotics.

It was evidently easier for Frank to give up his addiction to hate than to break his dependency on controlled substances. He says his first four years after leaving the movement were filled with alcohol and drugs, leading to at least one more suicide attempt.

Another one of Frank's obsessions is his reputation as a Romeo, strengthened over years inside the male-dominated neo-Nazi culture. In a single month around his 21st birthday, he became father to two children from two mothers – each unaware of the other. By age 26, he had fathered a daughter and two sons, one of whom later lost his life in a car accident.

Related only obliquely to his romances, a woman in a college audience asked Frank to explain the role women play in the hate movement. Frank speculated how women defectors may answer the question. "Some women serve as nurses in the race war, but the basic plan is to make babies and hang out with the bad boys."

In the fall of 2001, Frank married Valerie Doyle, a woman strong enough to rein in his former exploits in favor of a family and a future. When we last spoke in 2016, Frank told me he is happily married. He and Valerie have one daughter, born in 2010.

As is the case with many defectors, Frank told me that a "Jewish doctor" offered to remove Frank's racist and neo-Nazi tattoos. Since then, any that were not removed have been altered or covered with obscuring images. Frank hastens to add, "But I still love tattoos."

Over his lifetime, Frank's religious beliefs were unable to fit into any traditional container. Before getting entangled in the movement he had already drifted away from Catholicism. When asked about his faith years after the movement, Frank said, "To the extent that I am committed to a different way of living, yes, I have a relationship with God." He added that meeting Abel in prison inspired him to become "born again."

Since he left the movement, Frank speaks out more as a reaction to political issues than about his own religious interests. In one radio interview he gave his assessment on where the white supremacy movement is headed – and why. "If political rhetoric doesn't change, we're on track for a civil war in the U.S. We are growing so far left and so far right, there is no compromise."

In an interview in 2009, Frank looked back at the rise of the Tea Party. He told the reporter: "All the Tea Party's issues – Pro-Christian, anti-abortion, anti-immigration, anti-left wing, pro militia – those issues fit into the same list as the hate movement. Hate is the same in both." In a separate interview in 2011, Frank included MoveOn. Org, in his criticism, "Not that I think the Tea Party is a racist group, but it attracts racists. MoveOn.Org is so far left that anything to the left is right. Same with the Tea Party. It's so far right that anything to the left is leftist."

Since he left the hate movement, Frank joined others profiled in this book as a co-founder of Life After Hate, the organization created by former violent extremists and is committed to compassion, education and countering hate and discrimination. Frank also continues to stay involved in Harmony Through Hockey long after its move from Philadelphia to Des Moines, Iowa.

Arno Michaelis

ON AUGUST 5, 2012, WADE MICHAEL PAGE entered a Sikh gurdwara (place of worship) in Oak Creek, Wisconsin, fatally shooting six people and wounding four others. Arno Michaelis, a proud Wisconsinite, feels responsible for the tragedy, even though he had no connection to the gunman. "If someone gave Wade Page a hug on the day he walked into the temple, maybe he wouldn't have done what he did," Arno told Fox News. Feeling all the residual guilt of a hate group defector, he added, "I paved the way to create the environment that created Wade Michael Page."

Arno is the quintessential "former," the term he prefers to identify defectors from the hate movement. Arno was the sparkplug most responsible for creating Life After Hate, the international organization that helps defectors cope with separating from the movement. In the uncanny way he describes his own life experiences, many crude and unpleasant, he reflects knowingly on the victims he hurt along the way. On the flip side, he talks respectfully about those who helped him recognize his own internalized inferiority. The contradictions in his life bring a smile to his face and a soft chuckle, more as a way of assessing the learning experience than aiming for humor.

The author has received permission from Arno Michaelis to use excerpts from his book *My Life After Hate*.

Arno is a tall man with a muscular build and a booming, gravelly voice. In March of 2014, we met in the cocktail lounge of a downtown Milwaukee hotel. Thick muscular arms, sheathed by multi-colored tattoos, poked out of the pushed-up sleeves of a dark hoodie. After 10 years of sobriety, he swigged a non-alcoholic beer.

Arno was born in 1970 and grew up in Mequon, Wisconsin, a small town north of Milwaukee that he remembered as "virtually all-white." Considered a gifted child, he was raised in a loving, intact family. He described his mother as a woman who appreciated multiculturalism.

As he spoke, Arno sketched a childhood similar to that of other defectors. "I grew up in a middle class neighborhood. My dad was an alcoholic, but he was functional.'" Arno drew a gloomy picture of his parents' marriage, but said they stayed together for the sake of the family. Despite the conflicts at home, he said, "I always had people who looked up to me and wanted to be my friend. I was never unpopular and without friends." That would change.

"As I got older and my parents became constantly miserable, I wanted to move away. If I wasn't physically moving away from them I was growing emotionally separate. My father was mostly drunk. I grew into a bully on the school bus; it was stimulating and led to fights at school. When I was in high school I started drinking alone. I was a rebellious, boisterous kid."

Over the seven years between 1987 and 1994, Arno shaved his head and adopted the threatening look of a skinhead. In that time, he unleashed a reign of terror on Jews, ethnic "minorities," gays, and others as an active player in the white power movement. In 1997, at the age of 27, he became lead singer and front man for Centurions, a white power punk rock band. He guided the band to sell over 20,000 CDs, earning him the title "Reverend of Racial Holy War." Not to be confused with the surf rock band from California popular around the same time, the songs of Arno's Centurions doubled as a call to violence. Racist lyrics were part of their show, with lines like, "The blood is gonna flow . . . This planet is ours/We'll ever fight/Until the world's white!"

Shortly after graduating from high school, Arno adopted the racist beliefs embraced by Church of the Creator (COTC), the Christian-based neo-Nazi group later named World Church of the Creator (WCOTC). In his autobiography, *My Life After Hate*[23], Arno writes about spending two weeks at a COTC training camp in Otto, North Carolina, learning paramilitary maneuvers. He remembers the group's social order well, writing, "In 1989, COTC was as anti-Christian as they were anti-Semitic. Even as a punk rocker, I saw Christianity as a problem. So, COTC was attractive to me. I liked the group's notion of survival of the fittest. The more I got involved, the more I saw COTC as a way of saving the white race." He later said the camp also gave him an appreciation for wild macho behaviors and drinking to excess.

In his late teens, Arno started the group Skinhead Army of Milwaukee (SHAM) with other collaborators. The group, renamed after a series of violent internal clashes with other skinhead groups, continues to have an international following today. After leaving the movement, Arno avoids identifying the group by name explaining, "Any mention of the group, even in a negative reference, gives more power to the group, power that a neo-Nazi organization does not deserve and is not entitled to." He adds, "It's okay to say I was a co-founder of the largest organized skinhead organization on earth."

Arno sees the hate movement in general, and specifically WCOTC, as a survivalist lifestyle in which the white race rules all others. Sliding back into the WCOTC vernacular, he mocked, "We have to fight for our rights and the right to procreate. We were living to nature's laws."

During his time in the movement Arno assumed an identity in which " . . . all that mattered was the color of my skin." Contrary to what he calls "skinhead protocol," he acknowledged, "Black guys would make me scared. [With them], I had to be out front and as hostile as possible. If you showed any softness, they'd get you. That may or may not have been true. But they never came after me." Flexing toned biceps had its advantages.

In 2011, Arno was interviewed by the Forgiveness Project, a London-based nonprofit that promotes forgiveness. He told his story of a 1989 Thanksgiving dinner with his mom. At the meal, he said, "I was vehemently and drunkenly spouting off my [racist] views." Midway through the rant his mother announced, 'Well, Mr. Nazi, did you know that you're one-sixteenth Indian?" The newsflash did not go over well.

"That completely shut me up," he recalled. Later that night he went back to his own house and continued to guzzle one beer after another.

When I asked how his own racial background helps or hinders his interactions with people of color *today*, he waxed philosophical. "I really don't identify as Native American. Maybe I should. My family doesn't. I have all the respect and admiration for Native Americans, but to now claim I'm part of that heritage would not be honorable."

Like most others interviewed for this book, Arno was arrested many times. Unlike them, however, he never experienced a long-term prison sentence because of a hate crime. After one arrest in Ohio for Assault and Destruction of Property, Arno spent weeks in a Cincinnati jail awaiting his fate. He described the incident as if the details were plucked out of a cheap novel.

On the night of the assault, he was staying at the home of a skinhead friend. A raucous party was in full swing when he met a woman. "I wanted to get into her pants, so we went outside." A tall hedge separated the house from a hotel. The two were in the bushes when a hotel security guard flashed a light on them.

As Arno tells the story, "The guard left us alone. We ran back to the party to tell what happened." Ticked that one of their brothers was confronted by a hotel employee, three revelers thumped their way next door. They kicked through a locked glass door and used a hotel phone to beat the guard that found Arno and his woman friend.

Shortly afterwards, Police escorted the guard to the party house to identify the assailants. The guard singled out Arno as the one who beat him. But, Arno asserts adamantly, "I didn't do it . . . " Arno insists that although he was in the bushes with the woman, he was at the party when other skinheads pummeled the guard.

Arno likes to point out one occasion in which his own white privilege reigned supreme. He remembers going to a white power rally in Chicago with a group of Milwaukee skinheads circa 1989-1990. "We were driving through Midlothian, Illinois, in a 1972 Buick LeSabre with a gin mill in the back seat." While they were driving, one of the guys chucked a gin bottle out of the car. Two white cops saw the bottle fly, stopped them, and asked the men to get out of the car. All the guys had shaved heads and were sporting swastikas and other tattoos. Arno says that, in addition to driving with alcohol in the car and all passengers sloshed, the driver had no driver's license.

So, what's the penalty for a circle of drunk, bottle-throwing, white skinheads tooling through Illinois with alcohol in a vehicle driven by a man with no license? "They let us go." Years later, as an understatement to racial profiling, Arno commented, "If we had been black kids, we'd probably still be sitting in jail."

Today, Arno spends time studying the behaviors of players in the white power movement. He describes the incidents that led to his separation from skinheads as falling into one of three categories: Unexpected Kindness; Disturbing Events; and Cultural Issues.

"Unexpected kindness [happens] when people I was hostile to treated me with kindness." One particularly meaningful incident involved a server at a local McDonald's Arno frequented at the time. The server was an older black woman. "She always tried to have a conversation with me. That made me uncomfortable." Arno distinctly remembers her reaction when she delivered his meal shortly after getting a swastika tattooed on the back of his finger. "I didn't want to hurt or offend the woman." When the server glanced down at the tattoo, he instinctively covered the tattoo with his other hand. The woman saw the gesture and asked, 'What's that on your finger?' I said, 'It's nothing.' She said, 'I know you're a better person.' I picked up my food and never went back."

The woman's bold display of compassion and empathy was so compelling that Arno wasn't sure what to do. Later that same night he got into a fight. It took some time for him to understand what was happening. He said, "I was trying to create distance between that incident and the movement."

Arno described one "Disturbing Event" that helped him separate from the movement. He said the incident, unfolded "when a young skinhead friend told me he beat up 'a [Latino] kid' and left him crying in an alley. This guy looked up to me as a leader in the movement. What I said was, 'Well little ones grow up to be big ones.' I didn't have the courage to tell him what he did was fucked up. I couldn't because I was out there preaching race war rhetoric." Arno knew that to have told the young man it was wrong to hurt a Latino child would have weakened his own reputation. "In truth," he said, "I don't know whether or not he actually beat up a kid. In any case, I thought the man's behavior was wrong. Once again I tried to distance myself from the human parts of me."

Arno cited a "Cultural Issue" that evolved after watching Seinfeld episodes. He knew the star of the show and most of the cast were Jewish, and many of the themes featured situations unique to Jews. Years later Arno recalled discovering the ambiguity. After a day in which he and his skinhead buddies harassed Jewish victims, Seinfeld's humor would have them rolling on the floor.

On a similar cultural theme, Arno said that one of his favorite movies of all time is *This is Spinal Tap*, the 1984 Rob Reiner cult satire about a group of heavy metal rockers in their waning years. He said his band watched the fake documentary often. "After practicing songs about Jews as the scum of the earth, we'd pop in *Spinal Tap* – [a film] conceived, produced, and directed by Jews. That movie influenced our music."

Still reflecting over his skinhead years, Arno was amused to learn he was not the only racial extremist football fan to secretly root for his home team, the Green Bay Packers. "In the movement," he explained, "You can't be a Packers fan because most of the athletes are black; whites are a minority [on the team]. We didn't want to watch football because white men are not physically dominant in the sport. In the white power narrative, teamwork and discipline are lost. So, I would go home alone to watch the Packers." He said that, in a moment of weakness, he once told a skinhead buddy about his attraction to the Packers. "I was surprised when he told me he did the same thing all the time."

"The irony of these stories is ludicrous," Arno smirked, adding, "You know you're a hypocrite."

Since he left the movement, Arno has become a Buddhist who likes to "meet aggression with compassion." His vow is to "not continue the cycle of violence." Following Lakota tradition, he says, "To love your enemy is the same as what Jesus aspired people to do." He calls himself a "peace warrior," a sensibility that, he said, "is particularly important to convey to white men."

In his book, *My Life After Hate*, which was published two years after the election of President Barack Obama, Arno comments on political trends taking place across the U.S. at the time. He writes, "Events that have taken place since President Obama has been inaugurated concern me deeply. In the eyes of birthers, Deathers[24], Townhallers[25], and Tea-Partiers, I see the fiery refection of who I used to be."

Arno takes every opportunity to share his story and motivate others to leave the ranks of white supremacy. In an MSNBC interview in 2016, Arno summarized the major catalysts that inspired him to leave the hate movement. In his words:

> "What drew me out of the movement was the kindness and forgiveness of people that I had claimed to hate. There were times when a Jewish boss, a lesbian supervisor, black and Latino coworkers treated me as a human being. They treated me with kindness when I least deserved it. That indicated to me how wrong I was and also how much better life would be if I left this kind of self-imposed hell I was in behind. It's important to understand that living with this racist mindset, you're in fear of the world around you constantly, all day, every day. Once you can get a peek outside it and see what life can be like when you don't look at all other human beings as your enemy it becomes a no-brainer to make that decision to leave."

He writes in his autobiography, "By 1994 I began to feel I had an identity of my own. For the first time I allowed myself to listen to whatever music I wanted to listen to, and watch whatever TV shows I wanted to watch – not just what had been approved by the white power movement." He often closes interviews and talks to student groups and others with one constant that always seems to be present in his persona: "I'm always gonna be kinda rough around the edges."

Life After Hate (LAH), the organization Arno founded with other former extremists, is unlikely to have grown beyond a handful of activists, much less the thousands of members around the world who attend

LAH meetings or use its website, were it not for his innovative first step. Arno launched the organization as a quarterly online publication in January 2010. The newsletter aimed to connect and communicate with others who had left the movement.

In June 2011, the six founding members [Sammy Rangel, Angela King, Arno Michaelis, Christian Picciolini, Tony McAleer, and Frank Meeink) met at a conference in Dublin, Ireland, called "Summit Against Violent Extremism" and began working collaboratively to form what is known today as Life After Hate. The organization was certified as a non-profit later that year. Since then, LAH has helped more than 100 men and women leave extremist hate.

By the end of 2018, disagreements among the LAH founders have affected the unity and focus of the organization. The latest dynamics are covered in the chapter What Makes Defectors' Stories So Important under the subheading "Conflicts at Life After Hate." Despite the differing personalities and unique perspectives on the founders' contributions to the organization, LAH continues to inspire former extremists to a place of compassion.

AUTHOR'S NOTE: Like the other five defectors profiled here, Arno's life has a history of discriminatory behaviors, poor decisions, and hateful actions that harmed innocent people. He chooses to look ahead. Coming after more detailed narratives, this chapter focuses more on Arno's philosophical growth, a process that guides him to compassion, and his effort to help other defectors do the same.

What Makes Defectors' Stories So Important

WHAT ARE THE TRAITS AND CHARACTERISTICS that defectors have in common? Did they grow up in a racist or hateful environment? Were they loved as children and young adults? In what ways did their core values change – before, during, and after their involvement in the movement? Do their stories reveal how everyday *non-extremists* can tolerate, if not embrace, categories of people they may neither understand nor appreciate?

At first, the answers were somewhat unpredictable. Then patterns emerged.

The profiles in this book are not intended to constitute a definitive study. For more answers, I turned to researchers who examine the hate movement, including experts at the Southern Poverty Law Center (SPLC) and Anti-Defamation League (ADL). I talked to criminologists, police officers, attorneys who work with hate crime defendants, and prosecutors who work with victims. I also interviewed two social scientists, Caitlin Carlson (Seattle University) and Randy Blazak (Portland State University), who spent six months and a year, respectively, undercover inside a hate group as part of their research.

Defectors rarely discuss their past. They'd rather will it away like a bad dream. The courageous defectors profiled in this book share histories and behaviors consistent with academic studies and other scholarly research. Yet, courage does not make them heroes. Their stories include vile language and unpardonable crimes against innocent people. In most cases, no one knows that better than them.

Together with more scientific examination, the narratives from this relatively small sample, and details from other defectors, offer a window into a rarely seen universe and an opportunity to explore real life experiences from those who have lived in that mysterious world. The patterns tell a great deal about how the hate movement operates, why it is so difficult to abandon, and most important, raise public awareness about ways to thwart the most routine practices white supremacists and other extremists employ to attract newcomers and sustain their hurtful work.

Extremists abandon hate groups all the time, although the vast majority of defectors rarely, if ever, discuss their past, much less to a large public audience. Studies find multiple reasons why a defector abandons hate; however, no single reason fits all.

According to a 2015 study by Bryan F. Bubolz and Pete Simi published in *American Behavioral Scientist*[26], "the three primary means of defection are (1) expulsion, where individuals are forced to leave the group at the demand of other members or leaders; (2) extraction, where an outsider forces an individual to leave, sometimes through the use of kidnapping and deprogramming; and (3) voluntary exit, where individuals leave as a result of their own decision."

One study found that others defect because of a lack of loyalty among members and the ways younger members are manipulated by veterans. The research added that some become upset when members of their group spend too much time on activities that involve alcohol consumption instead of focusing on their political and ideological agendas. Still others burn out because of the demanding lifestyle and guilt produced from engaging in violence. The vast majority of defectors came to realize they were violating their own core values in deference to a white supremacist ideology.

No data exist to quantify or even estimate the number of defectors in the U.S. Nor do we know how many active members populate hate groups today. What we do know is that defectors change their beliefs and simply disappear. They'd rather forget the experience. Exposing their stories opens them to retribution, most of which is inflicted by former comrades. What we learn from the valiant ones who do tell their stories provides insights into the movement overall.

This book explores the backgrounds and behaviors of former members of organized hate groups. "Lone wolf" extremists are more difficult to identify. Their actions, however, conform to the same patterns we see from those who are members of a group.

Fundamentally, all hate extremists come from the same cloth. The threat from a growing number of hate groups is only one element to consider. In recent years, the number of lone wolf extremists has reached epidemic proportions. Loners commit violent crimes based on the same issues that motivate members of hate groups. Three of the nation's recent and most brutal hate crimes – at Mother Emanuel African Methodist Episcopal Church in Charleston South Carolina, at the Pulse nightclub in Orlando, and at the Tree of Life Synagogue in Pittsburgh – were all committed by lone gunmen.

After their crimes, loners are often found to have a history of direct or indirect contact with a specific group, generally through social media and online connections. Bias crimes by loners massively outnumber those by members of hate groups. Single perpetrators are rarely possible to identify *before* they commit a crime. Aside from the major incidents of malicious harassment, many loners commit their crimes spontaneously, after some provocation; for instance, seeing a person, a couple, or a situation that crosses their philosophical or ideological boundaries.

Among the more surprising discoveries among defectors is that most grew up in a loving household environment, free of heavy-handed racism. A few with violent histories in the movement told me their parents would not tolerate racist language at home. Bryon Widner, whose sister and brother had both been part of skinhead groups before him, said, "I was raised to be non-racist." Frank Meeink said that although his mother used ethnic slurs, "My father was not *systematically* racist."

George Burdi, whose profile was deleted after evidence surfaced that he had not truly separated from the movement, told me his parents were accepting of everybody, adding, "Until the end of high school, I had no racist leanings at all." He later served as front man for a white power rock band known for stinging diatribes and its name, RaHoWa, short for Racial Holy War.

I would be remiss to not add that, although most I talked to said their parents were not racist or did not tolerate racist language in their homes, some made subsequent comments suggesting they may be unintentionally covering a degree of ingrained shame or a memory lapse. For example, one later refers to a parent's use of an ethnic slur. [This is, after all, America, a nation in which race has always been a divisive issue and we live in an era in which few news days go by without racism raising its ugly head.] Either way, the possibility of one not being completely candid about their family's views on race decades ago was insignificant in relation to their own transformation – and not worth challenging.

In the past few years, a new round of defectors has outed themselves in new, heavily promoted biographies, autobiographies, television documentaries, and other media formats, all telling similar stories. Some of the most recent defectors include individuals whose family background represent a departure from many who preceded them. Two in particular, Megan Phelps-Roper and Derek Black, skew the overall data because, unlike others, they grew up in households firmly entrenched in the hate movement. Megan's grandfather is the founder of Westboro Baptist Church, the anti-Semitic and rabidly homophobic group commonly seen protesting at military funerals, alleging an implausible link between military service and homosexuality. Derek gained attention after he exited the movement in an op-ed piece published in the Sunday *New York Times* (November 2016). Derek's story is expertly told in *Out of Hatred: The Awakening of a Former White Nationalist*[27]. Derek is the son of Don Black, a former leader of the Alabama KKK and founder of the white nationalist site Stormfront. His mother's ex-husband and Derek's godfather is David Duke, former Ku Klux Klan Grand Wizard and Louisiana State Representative. On this dimension alone, Megan and Derek deviate from the norm – if there is a norm.

Connecting Points

What does it take for someone to become a revolutionary right wing extremist intent on harassing people for just being themselves?

Overwhelmingly, the single most common reason individuals join a hate group is the need to connect with like-minded others. More than half of the 35 defectors I interviewed said that before they joined the movement, they "didn't fit in" or were detached from any identifiable circle of friends. In one way or another, all biographies and autobiographies by or about defectors touch on an overpowering "sense of belonging" as the main magnet that kept them in the group after being initiated.

Defectors told me about experiencing internalized discontent to the point of self-abuse manifested through alcohol or drug abuse, cutting themselves, and thoughts of suicide prior to, and often during, their involvement in the movement. Before they joined a group, many described themselves as lost, or out of sync with their peers. Many fell prey to the tactics of recruiters who seized on their social awkwardness. Also, prior to getting involved, many had no stable, ongoing, or long-term motivational commitments such as hobbies, career goals, raising children, or maintaining a home. Others talked about finding an ironic solace in their love of hate rock and white power music, writing lyrics, rehearsing, and performing.

Testy relationships at home led some to accept hate-filled colleagues as a substitute family. With their new friends, they could share unrestricted stories about whatever rubbed them the wrong way, issues peers soon molded to conform with a whites-only mentality. For others, family and friends preceded them in the movement and were directly responsible for their getting involved. Kerry and Kay Noble, who joined CSA before its leader guided the group to an extremist ideology, relocated to the farm to reunite with friends they first met at another Christian organization. For others, no known previous connection to a hate group precipitated their own involvement. Julie Miller, who had known white nationalists, was lured into the National Alliance by the chance acquaintance with the roommate of a traveling salesman. One person I interviewed said he was persuaded to join a hate group in his 20s while he was in the U.S. military. Arno Michaelis and others were seduced by the lyrics of hate rock/white power music. Studies conducted by various researchers between 1997 and 2014 (Tore Bjørgo, 1997; Kathleen Blee, 2002; Joseph A. Schafer, Christopher

W. Mullins, and Stephanie Box, 2014; Pete Simi and Robert Futrell, 2010) identified the most common reasons individuals are attracted to hate groups, including: "sympathy for the group's ideology or political position; anger because of immigrants, leftist antiracists, or the authorities; [for] protection against enemies or perceived threats; a search for excitement and thrill seeking, the violent and militant aspects of the group; the perception that it provides a substitute family, and the search for status and identity."

Many if not most individuals do not make the transition from personalized discontent to extremism on their own or by encouragement from family members or friends. They are pushed and prodded by hard-selling recruiters, charismatic leaders, followers who already drank the proverbial Kool-Aid, and an ideology that supports their personal dissatisfactions. Defectors said that although it may take weeks or more to fully adopt a group's belief system, neophytes are easily drawn into recruitment strategies that capitalize on the need to be with others who can "talk openly about things that piss them off," a phrase voiced by many.

Leaving the Movement

Perhaps the most apt description of what influences defectors to leave the movement and return to their own core values is summarized in what Arno Michaelis told an MSNBC reporter in 2015: "What drew me out of the movement was the kindness and forgiveness of people that I had claimed to hate." Arno goes on to describe a Jewish boss, a lesbian supervisor, and black and Latino coworkers treating him like a human being "when I least deserved it."

Among all connections between defectors, the most essential to capture is that, like Arno, *every other defector I talked to* left the movement after developing a similarly meaningful personal relationship with at least one person they previously "claimed to hate." As the profiles describe in detail, when each defector realized their perceptions of an entire category of people were inaccurate, they were no longer able to see that group through the same lens. They were on common ground.

Falling in love is also a major motivator that nudged defectors closer to compassion. Each spoke eloquently to describe the meaning of loving someone in a category they previously devalued or despised. Perhaps the most dramatic change evolved when Angela King fell in love with a black woman. The impact from such a deeply moving experience altered their values forever.

Many talked about the birth of a child as their springboard out of the movement. Bryon Widner spoke passionately about being at his wife's side for the birth of their son. Frank Meeink and Arno Michaelis had similar experiences.

Time in prison also helped. Those who were incarcerated talked about their time in a prison cell as an opportunity to seriously reassess their lives. This trend does not suggest that prisons rehabilitate inmates as the system was intended to do. As Angela King explained so well, it is not necessarily the *institution* that changes lives. In her words, " . . . it was the experiences with the people I met. The system gave me a place to rehabilitate *myself.*"

Many also realized that the ideology of the hate group they became a part of had so profoundly altered their own core values that they were blinded by a charismatic leader's words and misguided directions. For detached souls, belonging to a pseudo-family helped sweep them into a group consciousness, one in which independent thinking was a fault. Only by seeing through lies, hypocrisy, distorted reasoning, or unmitigated hatred were they able to return to their own sensibilities.

As each told me about the pivotal moments when a new emotional event helped them see they were no longer on their own path, how love could conquer hate, their demeanor changed. The voice of even those with the most violent histories became noticeably softer. They spoke as if a dumpster full of garbage had been taken off their backs.

Recruitment

Hate group recruiters have narrowed their techniques to a science. Among the most popular are placing flyers on windshields of cars parked at sporting events and night clubs and distributing handouts at high schools in person. Music venues are scouted to attract unsuspecting novices. White power music, a multi-million-dollar industry, is another access to a built-in audience of people willing to at least listen to hate-filled messages. According to the SPLC, "The digital media marketplace owned by Apple Inc., boasts the sale of more than 21 million songs every week, from a catalog of more that 26 million songs that, as of September 2014, included at least 54 racist bands."

Angela King found success chatting up young sun worshippers at beaches along the Florida coast, asking, "Don't you want to be something? Don't you want to be proud of what you are?" Bryon Widner's "look-for-the-loner" routine was masterful for its simplicity. He sought out unhappy people sitting alone at parties or in bars and convinced them their problems were not because of *their* failures. In a highly cleaned-up paraphrase, Bryon's message was more like, "Hey man, it's not you, the problem is Jewish financiers who own Hollywood and the banks, it's the blacks and immigrants taking jobs from qualified white people, it's the gays who walk all over common decency . . . " Bryon would close his pep talk with an invitation to "have a beer with us." Before his listeners knew what was happening, they were joining the group in acts of malicious harassment.

Frank Meeink's favorite recruitment line was, "You don't have to be picked on ever again . . . " He also learned how to avoid certain people, particularly "smart guys, rough guys, nerds, and especially good looking guys," because they were unlikely to stay loyal to the group even if they did join.

The characteristics hate group recruiters most commonly look for in prospects form a blueprint to detect behaviors that presage hateful prototypes, including:

- Social awkwardness, standoffishness
- Disconnection or isolation from family, friends, classmates, neighbors, and others
- Frequent anxiety or frustration
- Anger at the slightest provocation
- Use of language that reflects negatively on other people: put-downs, name-calling, ethnic slurs
- Blaming others for one's own inadequacies
- Difficulty with social engagement, e.g. not talking or shutting down during routine conversations in bars, at parties and other events
- Few commitments to focus their energy

Prison

As discussed elsewhere in this book, prisons are a fertile breeding ground to cultivate hatred. While many defectors I talked to started to change their beliefs while they were in prison, at least one (who chose not to be identified by name) was drawn *into* the movement through connections made while he was serving time. The Aryan Brotherhood, a white supremacist and neo-Nazi prison gang, is estimated to have 15,000 to 20,000 members currently in or out of federal and state prisons. According to the FBI, the Aryan Brotherhood makes up an extremely low percentage of the entire US. prison population, but is responsible for a disproportionately large number of prison murders.

Age

The ages of hate crime offenders vary. According to a report released by the FBI in 2013, of 2,527 known hate crime offenders in 2012, 68 percent were 18 and over; 32 percent were under 18. Three years later, the FBI reported 83.8 percent of individuals who committed hate crimes were 18 and over, with 16.2 percent under 18. While informative, these data do not provide a solid indicator of when individuals are most likely to join a hate group or commit a hate crime.

Based on the backgrounds of the six defectors profiled here and consistent with other research, high school can be a pivotal time for misdirected youth to be lured into extremism. Frank Meeink, Angela King, and Bryon Widner entered the hate world while they were between the ages of 14 and 15. Arno Michaelis got involved around age 17. Julie Miller joined the National Alliance while she was 25. Kerry Noble entered The Covenant, the Sword, and the Arm of the Lord (CSA) when he was barely 30 years old.

Significant Emotional Events

Morris Massey, Ph.D., emeritus professor of Social Psychology and former Associate Dean and Professor of Marketing at the University of Colorado in Boulder, theorized a concept he presents in a series of training videos and talks, titled "*What You Are Is What You Were When.*" From the late 1960s and through the 1970s, Massey's research centered on his finding that humans develop their personal core values by the time they are 10 years old. Those values, he maintained, remain unchanged over a lifetime, unless or until we experience a "Significant Emotional Event." Such a catalyst, no matter how brief or superficial it may seem to anyone else, can be life-changing and come from anywhere; a book, a romance, the birth of a child, or the death of a loved one.

Three defectors referred to being emotionally shaken by the same iconic photograph in which a first responder is carrying a lifeless child after the Oklahoma City bombing. Seeing the photo was a reflection of their own childhood and, in an instant, pushed them to examine their future and how the values driving their behaviors in the movement had veered so far from their core.

Every defector's story tracks back to memories of significant emotional events. Arno Michaelis talks about the gut-punch he felt after a black server at McDonald's glanced at a swastika recently tattooed on his hand. Her words brought Arno's guilt to the surface in a way he could not escape. For Kerry Noble, the same result was ignited by the thought that, had he actually set the timer on the bomb he carried into a gay church, he would have been responsible for "killing people in the act of singing *my* hymns, praising *my* God."

One of Julie Miller's emotional crises came from listening to speaker after speaker at the KKK family event where she met Bryon Widner, her future husband. As each venerated presenter rambled on about family values, she knew firsthand how they treated women and children. When Julie saw the sexual abuse of a young woman at that family-oriented festival, the blatant hypocrisy was her last straw. That emotional event helped her see how far she had veered from her own values. For Bryon, falling in love with Julie and the birth of their son were instrumental to his transformation. Childbirth allowed him to realize his commitment to be a dad trumped being the leader of his skinhead crew.

Curious similarities appear in some defectors' stories. The common attributes between Angela King and Frank Meeink are the most uncanny. Born three weeks apart, both had self-absorbed parents who divorced during their childhood. Both were accused of being mentally unstable to the point of being committed to in-patient treatment. Both were harassed by black children at school. Despite having Jewish friends and neighbors during their childhood, both were vehemently anti-Semitic as neo-Nazi skinheads, each with a visible swastika tattooed on their bodies. Both entered the movement in their teens. Both were moved to the core by the Oklahoma City bombing photo.

Most defectors have a newfound appreciation of personal values that most non-extremists take for granted. They have been through an emotional grinder, withdrawing from families, navigating rocky relationships with new adolescent friends, and joining or leading violent attacks on innocent people. By consciously altering the values that accompany hate, they demonstrate to the rest of us how the progression of negative emotions from activist to advocate and advocate to revolutionary can indeed be reversed.

Extremists' values evolve. In a country with a long history of racism, sexism, homophobia, nativism, and religious hostility, opportunities to criticize marginalized people as "undeserving" or "inferior" imply that white privilege or any "entitlement" is a one-way ticket to everything they want. White supremacists see superiority as their advantage, their exclusive right, and are willing to do anything to keep it.

To a detached, disengaged, and angry personality type, demonizing others is a tantalizing seduction. It is easier to blame others for one's own deficiencies than to self-examine how to correct them. Once a person is sucked into the hate vortex, the progression moves from talk to action, from having a brewski to organizing a "bum roll" – and beating up anyone who doesn't conform with white norms.

In assessing one's core values, it is exceedingly important to measure the difference between the extent of love – and hatred – expressed toward others. Implied in the stories of defectors, although not stated directly, is that when one is alone or feeling abused, irrational thinking escalates. While hate is rigid, love is open and can be seen as a pathway to vulnerability, or worse yet, to rejection. Revealing vulnerability can be interpreted as weak or inferior. It's a tautological trap for someone trying to escape a hateful environment.

Mental Stability

Accusations of mental instability by family members is another thread connecting many defectors. Angela King, Bryon Widner, and Frank Meeink were all subjected to therapists, or institutionalized at some point, despite their strong objections.

With no reflection on any individual, mental illness is often said to be endemic among those who commit violent hate crimes, despite inadequate scientific evidence to back up the claim. In an article for the online Milwaukee Journal Sentinel, Jody M. Roy, Ph.D., Professor of Leadership Values at Ripon College, wrote, "Hate is not a mental illness. It is an inversion of fear of the unknown other into an illusion of power . . . Mental illness entangled with hate is a particularly toxic brew. But hate, served straight, also can be deadly."

The research project cited at the beginning of this chapter from the journal *American Behavioral Scientist* found that 32 percent of the study sample reported they had experienced mental health problems "either preceding or during their hate group involvement;" 44 percent reported "suicidal ideation" at some point during their lives; and 58 percent reported problems with alcohol and/or substance abuse. The authors note that substance abuse is listed as a form of mental health problem in the *Diagnostic Statistical Manual of Mental Disorders*.

Sexual, physical, and mental abuse is inescapably evident in the mainstream culture. By living in a universe overshadowed by hate, it follows that the rate of abuse against women in the hate movement would be higher. Angela, Julie, and other female defectors talked about being attracted to "bad boys" and, in turn, being physically abused by those same boyfriends and spouses. Yet, although recent news stories report white nationalists and neo-Nazis being convicted of domestic violence offenses, I could find no definitive study to confirm the rate of domestic abuse inside the hate movement.

Family Background

A common element connecting white nationalists and other extreme right wing reactionaries is the inaccurate assumption that "minorities" reduce white peoples' access to education, housing, jobs, upward mobility, and other advantages. Such accusations come at times when the U.S. unemployment rates are at historic lows, universities are raising tuition as a matter of supply and demand, and the overall economy is on an upswing. Does the belief of diminished access originate with a person's family, from institutional history, the media, or from some other source? Hints are found in the background of each defector.

The defectors I talked to were mostly raised in lower income families with a few from more middle class roots. In some cases, as with Angela King, the family's economic status worsened after her parents' divorce. While class and economic status varies widely among them, a very high percentage of defectors come from broken homes. An estimated 50 percent of U.S. marriages end in divorce, yet the rate of split families among the defectors I interviewed is over 90 percent. One exception is a former black separatist I interviewed whose parents never married, although they stayed together for at least 60 years, until his father's death.

Of those whose parents divorced, some suggested that growing up in two households was partially responsible for their feeling detached and isolated, factors that attracted them to the sense of belonging for which hate groups are notorious. Arno Michaelis said he grew up in a middle class neighborhood and was raised in a loving intact family.

Although only one said so directly, others made references to a divided family, one in which they felt disconnected from one or both parents and siblings, causing them to question how deeply they were loved. Some however, acknowledged having little regard for one or both parents as they matured, or even more commonly, an outright animosity for *step*-parents. This was especially true among defectors from families in which one or both parents abused alcohol or drugs, a condition they, too, coped with before, during, and after their involvement in the movement. At least three, Bryon Widner, Arno Michaelis, and Frank Meeink, became clean and sober after abandoning the world of organized hate.

Racial/Cultural Friction

Many defectors profiled in this book relate stories of cultural conflicts with race, ethnicity, religion, and sexuality starting at an early age. Some grew up in racially charged cities where race and ethnicity were virtual time bombs.

Angela King, who had little direct exposure to black people before joining a skinhead group, found herself befriending a cluster of black Jamaican women in a Florida prison only because she had no one else to talk to after weeks in solitary confinement. Soon she discovered that her fellow inmates came from backgrounds very similar to her own, that is, from low-income families, and a history of substance abuse, troubled relationships, and barbaric boyfriends.

It is not surprising that white supremacists and other radical right wing extremists in the U.S. are almost universally heterosexual white Christians born on American soil. Eventually, newcomers to the movement believe anyone else does not deserve to share the planet with them and "all those other people" are a threat to the eternal purity of the white race.

Religious Values

Religious differences are clearly a primary driver behind many extremists' motivations. All of the defectors I talked to who described their religious background said they were raised Christian and, while they were in the movement, had an extreme hatred toward non-Christians. More than half said one or both parents were Baptist; the remainder Roman Catholic.

Many defectors changed their religious denomination or their faith for various reasons before, during, or after they left the movement. The conversion often followed a new relationship. All remained Christian in their post-movement lives, including at least two who today consider themselves "born again." After leaving the movement, others veered away from religion altogether, some in a quest for greater independence.

One former black separatist I spoke with told me religious shifts played a major role in his life while he was in the movement. Both parents, he said, were less-than-devout Baptists, although they were both committed to strong Christian values. He became a separatist while he was in prison, where he converted from Christianity to Islam. Years later, his return to Christianity was responsible for his transition away from black separatism.

Some defectors change their religion during or after their time in the movement, often due to a new spiritual direction resulting from their eventual enlightenment. For many, notably former neo-Nazis and followers of the anti-Semitic Christian Identity (CI) theology, their perceptions – or misperceptions – of Judaism were a significant part of their hatred. Kerry Noble and Frank Meeink, both raised Christian, were heavily involved in CI groups.

Three defectors I talked to said they were first drawn to the hate movement through World Church of the Creator (WCOTC), an organization identified by the SPLC as a hate group. The "religion," formed in 1973 "for the survival, expansion and advancement of the white race," was later repackaged to include a global focus. WCOTC is now called the Creativity Movement.

Connecting the names of hate groups to Christianity is no more than a ruse to mask beliefs that would make Christ cringe.

Anyone who reasons that "common sense" will keep extremists within the margins of reasonable Biblical interpretation does not understand how *uncommon* common sense is inside the movement. [After a 30-year career as a cultural competency professional, my experience suggests common sense is not that abundant in the mainstream either.]

Among the more bizarre discoveries from my interviews is the extent to which, as a theological tenet, some religious-oriented extremists base their superiority on the notion of being among "God's chosen people." For example, the CI interpretation of the Bible views white Christians as the chosen people. Black separatists believe only people of African descent are among the chosen.

In the words of one defector, the term "chosen-ness" connects being chosen to "a covenant with God by virtue of Jewish descent from the ancient Israelites," that is, Jews have been the chosen people going back to the Exodus from Egypt around the 12th Century BC, give or take a couple hundred years, depending on whom you ask. Within hate groups, the notion of being whimsically consecrated as "God's chosen people" is as competitive as it is incomprehensible.

Anti-Semitism and race have propagated American hatred for well over 150 years. During the Civil War, General Ulysses S. Grant issued an order expelling Jews from the sections of Tennessee, Kentucky and Mississippi under his control. The decree was later rescinded by President Lincoln.

The hate movement got its start before the Civil War with groups such as an American nativist political party that operated nationally in the mid-1850s. Known as the Know Nothing Movement, followers were primarily anti-Catholic, xenophobic, and hostile to immigration. During

Reconstruction, the Ku Klux Klan mobilized as a vigilante group to intimidate Southern blacks. Over the years, the KKK has extended its reach to attack Jews, immigrants, gays and lesbians, Catholics, and others.

Since then, leaders of hate groups have taken great liberties in their interpretation of Christian doctrine. Many, like James Ellison, the leader of Kerry Noble's group, CSA, get their spiritual guidance "directly from God." Such was the case when God told Ellison to take a second wife and enjoined CSA members to follow. Many CSA couples saw through the absurdity and bolted in a mass exodus, while others, including Kerry, were so under Ellison's spell as to consider polygamy a realistic option. Besides Ellison, however, no others rushed into a quest for additional spouses.

Perhaps because most of the defectors I interviewed left the movement before 2001, one talked about hate crimes they committed against Muslims. Within months after 9/11, anti-Muslim hate crimes skyrocketed. Since then, Muslims have been among the top targets of hate groups and individual extremists.

Hate and Substance Abuse

Alcoholism plays a huge role in the hate movement. It incites both members of groups and lone offenders alike to commit hate crimes, often spontaneously. To an alarming degree, hate crimes are committed by individuals, in groups or alone, who were intoxicated at the time. Most defectors I talked to describe a struggle with alcohol while they were in the movement.

This trend raises questions about why extremists drink to excess. Is it because they need alcohol to fog any chance of moral persuasion that could return them to responsible thinking? Is it because many hate groups do not tolerate drug use? Is it because they simply can't manage their desire for a drink, or something else?

A 2016 research project reported in the *Journal of Research in Crime and Delinquency*[28] examined common precursors to violent extremism. The study found that 73 percent of subjects reported having problems with alcohol and/or illegal drugs. More specifically, 64 percent "reported experimenting with illegal drugs and/or alcohol prior to age 16."

Many defectors say they learned to manage their alcohol consumption after leaving the movement. At least three of the defectors profiled here, Bryon Widner, Arno Michaelis, and Frank Meeink, became clean and sober after leaving the movement. All three came from families in which one or both parents abused alcohol or drugs.

A tendency toward other addictive behaviors may give credibility to the belief that hate itself is an addiction.

Relapse

Angela King and Frank Meeink talk about relapses in which they returned to the hate movement after an initial separation. Both later left the movement permanently.

Sociologists have discovered it is fairly common for one to return to the hate movement after an initial exit. A study cited earlier found that some extremists "stay in the movement for decades or even entire lifetimes, but these cases are the exception rather than the rule." The same study noted "a number of difficulties associated with exiting such as ongoing emotions of guilt, ideological relapse, and maintaining social ties with current members of the white supremacist movement."

Another reason for relapses is threats and intimidation from members of the group a defector would like to leave. Angela King told me about a relapse after first leaving a skinhead group in 1995. Soon after, her house and car were shot at and she received multiple threatening phone calls. She decided to return with a vengeance. Three years after her reentry, Angela was arrested for her role in the robbery of a video store in which a clerk was pistol-whipped. The conviction ended with a two-year prison sentence, time that allowed her to reexamine her values.

Frank Meeink also had a brief return to his former skinhead group that may not truly qualify as a relapse. After leaving the movement, he ventured into a memorial service honoring a former colleague, at which he was confronted by a group of skinheads and severely beaten as members of his own former crew stood idly by. The skirmish marked the end of Frank's skinhead days.

Rivalries and Competition

Rivalries are common in the hate movement. Defectors confirm that extremists are not particularly swayed by reality or rational thinking.

That thinking often turns into competition between opposing hate groups. To achieve their objectives, hate groups often use low-cost and generally stealthy maneuvers designed to . . .

- Attack unsuspecting victims
- Outwit the enemy before [the enemy] outwits you
- Hide in plain sight
- Live alongside targets as if you belong there
- Infiltrate the military and police forces
- Use the same techniques to control victims as law enforcement agencies use to control criminals
- Gather (better yet, steal) all the weapons one can amass

Those trends do not suddenly end when an extremist decides to abandon hate.

Seldom reported in the news, battles between groups for more power or larger turf happen somewhat routinely, as do fights between members of the same group. When Bryon Widner co-founded Vinlanders Social Club, one of the group's goals was to take over the North American white power scene. Bryon also intimated that financial friction among the Vinlanders occasionally led to serious disagreements, including violent fistfights between members.

For some of the more high-profile defectors, specifically those most quoted in news stories, television programs, and films, the tug-of-war continues long after their departure from the movement. Disagreements took a nasty turn around 2016. Since then, post-hate friction and competition has erupted between the original six founders of Life After Hate (LAH), the nonprofit they created to inspire individuals toward a place of compassion and forgiveness. For an organization created to help former extremists cope, the feud has taken a nasty turn.

Conflicts at Life After Hate

Arno Michaelis, Angela King, and Frank Meeink, all profiled in this book, were among the original founders of LAH, as were Sammy Rangel, Tony McAleer, and Christian Picciolini. Rangle, is a former gang member and author of the autobiography *FOURBEARS: The Myths of Forgiveness*[29].

McAleer is a former member of the White Aryan Resistance (WAR), a white supremacist neo-Nazi organization founded and led by former KKK Grand Dragon Tom Metzger. Picciolini, the former leader of two separate white supremacist punk bands, wrote an autobiography in 2015, *Romantic Violence: Memoirs of an American Skinhead*[30] which was updated and republished in 2017 under the title *White American Youth: My Descent into America's Most Violent Hate Movement – and How I Got Out*[31]. In 2018, Picciolini produced an MSNBC series titled Breaking Hate, about himself and his work to help active extremists leave the movement.

Arno Michaelis is largely responsible for creating LAH in 2010, first as an online publication. In recent years, as LAH has matured and increased its work and membership, Arno believes some of the original founders "hijacked" the organization from him, while continuing to claim they created it.

After his departure from the nonprofit in 2017, to the chagrin of other LAH founders, Picciolini formed a new organization called the Free Radicals Project. From its website, the group helps defectors, as well as those considering an exit from hate, with a process focusing on "non-aggressive, community-led methods of individual resiliency-building, reconnection, cross-cultural immersion, and making amends."

Having two organizations competing to serve similar purposes may help defectors soothe the fears and anxieties both groups set out to assuage. On the other hand, if followed as written, the guiding principles behind both LAH and the Free Radicals Project provide a workable path to resolve the competition between the two organizations and between the original LAH's founders.

Ongoing hostility between colleagues bonded together in a fight to heal the psychological remnants of the hate movement is part of the collateral damage from being involved in groups that breed and strengthen hatred and fear. There is no magical switch to flip off at the end of such a destructive experience.

As defectors from hate use their past experiences to disclose compelling stories, their talent monetizes a despicable history through the success of publications, speaking engagements, and other ventures. As such, their ethical standards are often called into question for capitalizing on the harm they caused during a violent time in their lives. Few are free of the accusations.

"I Didn't Do It."

An odd correlation connects stories from three subjects profiled here who proclaim adamantly that, although they played a role in the offense for which they were arrested, they really "didn't do it."

Primarily because Angela King was identified by an eyewitness, she was convicted for committing a hate crime outside a gay bar in Florida. Although she served the time and accepts responsibility for her part in the incident, she has consistently said she was in a parking lot at the time of the assault and that it was her boyfriend who swung the crowbar that hurt the victim.

Similarly, Arno Michaelis stands firm on his claim that, although he had a run-in with a hotel security guard when he momentarily left a skinhead event for a romp with a woman, he was not present when *other* skinheads assaulted the victim. He, too, said, "I didn't do it."

One person I interviewed several times, George Burdi, was arrested in Canada for kicking an anti-racist activist whom he was later convicted of brutalizing after he led a white power music performance by his hate rock group (RaHoWa). He has told reporters, and reiterated to me in a phone interview, that despite the allegations, he did not commit the crime, although the victim identified him as the offender.

Angela, Arno, and George Burdi nonetheless acknowledge being present and having a role in the crimes they were accused of committing. Are they telling the truth? I raise this question not as an accusation or oblique indictment, but to question how or why crimes by 43 percent of those profiled here suggest an element of innocence. Is this a product of lingering internalized guilt from the cumulative effect of their time in the movement, a way to appear *less* guilty, or is it purely the clean truth? Although they all acknowledge taking part in the offense, to what extent does indirect participation in a hate crime absolve those on the sidelines of responsibility?

Body language, vocal intonation, and speaking patterns tell a lot about what's going on in the mind of a someone asked to reveal their past. Some described emotional events that enabled them to see what they had become inside the movement, their explanations broken by long pauses, deep breaths, tears, and outright sobbing. Many seemed a bit quick with polished responses, likely the result of repeatedly answering the same questions from reporters and researchers looking for a pithy soundbite.

Their stories help us examine our ability to resolve our own ignorance and keep our actions in check – and be more aware of the words used, and actions taken, by the people around us. In the end, we see that even uncompromising and overly dogmatic thinkers can be dissuaded away from extremism to become less judgmental, more inclusive, and deeply compassionate.

Amid the mishmash of all they've gone through to achieve a sense of empathy, further examination is unlikely to serve much purpose. The bigger point to capture is that, if extremists can change their beliefs, anyone can.

Atonement/Restitution

While courage does not equal heroism, most of the defectors profiled here have done remarkable work to compensate for the misery they caused to victims during their time inside the hate movement and to atone for and remedy the harm. All are proud of their accomplishments since they left the movement. Most are engaged in some form of community work.

For example, without the founding leadership of Arno Michaelis, and five other defectors, the national organization Life After Hate, despite its internal conflicts, would not be there to help others find the off ramp and pull their lives back together. Today Angela King serves as LAH's Programs Director.

Kerry Noble has served as a consultant to the FBI and works with several LGBTQ organizations to help them understand Christian Identity and similar Christian-based hate groups. Like other defectors, Kerry meets with students in K-12 schools and colleges, spreading the gospel of post-hate reform. Frank Meeink created Harmony Through Hockey, "a nonprofit to give young kids a chance to stay out of the way of violence and have fun in the process."

Defectors take every opportunity to promote the importance of self-forgiveness to maintain their focus, and they encourage others to do the same. Their self-reflection helps the rest of us come to grips with the volatility of the human equation. Through their experiences we can appraise our own disposition to unwittingly practice hurtful behaviors. Their stories help us examine our ability to resolve our own ignorance and keep our actions in check, if not those of the people around us.

With so many angry people wandering through communities today, enraged by whatever issue incites them, from politics to racial inequality, how many are one argument or one impulse away from letting hate kidnap their better judgment?

Hate affects every person on the planet. When people are hurt, they are unable to function to the best of their talent. Relationships are damaged, families are broken, children become confused, communities are threatened, and safety is uncertain. The moral imperative to slow or stop hate is a burden for which we are all responsible.

After connecting a swath of circumstances that defectors have in common, one broad conclusion is that the latest research available from federal agencies, universities, and independent researchers is woefully inadequate to guide extremists away from the allure of organized (or disorganized) hate. The need to examine the consciousness of individual (loner) extremists, organized hate groups, and the soaring occurrence of hate crimes nationwide is grossly underfunded. Instead, government resources appear to be more committed to counting the number of hate crimes and data analysis than to stopping the rising tide of white supremacist violence.

As Life After Hate wrangles to stay focused on its lofty goals amid internal conflicts, the outcome of one federal funding request from the nonprofit reveals how a similar rift between presidential . . . administrations is no less contradictory. When it took control of the White House, the Trump administration promptly discontinued a federal grant of $400,000 that had been awarded to LAH under the Obama Administration.

In 2017, an article published in the *American Sociological Review*[32] asserts, "The U.S. white supremacist movement represents one of the most enduring political subcultures in American history yet is surprisingly one of the least understood."

PART TWO

The Anatomy of Hate

First They Came

First they came for the Socialists,
and I did not speak out
because I was not a Socialist.

Then they came for the Trade Unionists,
and I did not speak out
because I was not a Trade Unionist.

Then they came for the Jews,
and I did not speak out
because I was not a Jew.

Then they came for me,
And there was no one left to speak for me.

Martin Niemöller

Martin Niemöller (1892–1984) was a German Protestant pastor and a leader of the church's opposition to Hitler. He was interned in Nazi concentration camps for seven years, from 1938 to 1945.

Introduction/Overview

INSIDE THE HATE MOVEMENT LIES A Pandora's Box of mysteries and haunting ogres. Part Two offers a deeper view into the mechanics of the movement, why the information at our disposal is unreliable, how hate groups started and why, after nearly 250 years into American democracy, this beast is not yet under control.

Centuries of blatant racism, religious bigotry, and blissful ignorance have fueled a crusade that continues to isolate people into two camps: "Superiors" and "Inferiors." Despite efforts to stop organized hatred from morphing into domestic terrorism, the best we have to show for it today is a series of convoluted laws, complex definitions, and mindboggling data that fails to measure up to common sense.

This chapter builds on the premise that **The Father of All Hate Groups Is The United States Government.** As a four-year veteran of the U.S. Navy during the Vietnam war and a strong believer in democracy and my country, I do not make that statement lightly. [True Confession: I originally wrote this line to say "The Mother of all hate groups . . ." before friends reminded me that mothers had no power to make the decisions alluded to below.]

This premise of governmental influence is based on a long tradition of historical policies and practices adopted and enforced by Presidents, legislatures, and courts that, together, have served as a strategic blueprint

171

to restrict or limit Constitutional rights of selectively chosen immigrants and American citizens based on such variables as skin color, race, nation of origin, gender, religion, sexual orientation, gender identity, and others. These are the very same categories of people targeted by hate groups today.

From the oldest surviving nationwide racist hate group, the KKK, to the skinhead groups and lone extremists of today, the message to people they consider "inferior" mirrors those of government agencies in the past and, to some extent, today. In short, the message is: we don't want you here.

The difference between government actions and the hate movement is that a government functions with authority and a moral tone that is implemented through a systematic process. The hate movement is a consortium of rogue groups operating to similar ends, but professing their own dominion within an incoherent structure that defies morality.

In the beginning, government policy escalated from the desire of early settlers to use native land for their own purposes to taking part in the mass genocide of indigenous people. Pioneers didn't appreciate that the continent they coveted was already occupied long before a white person ever set foot on it. Since then, colonialists have turned their takeover into entitlement and an endless occupation. Today, white supremacists operate with the same power and similar techniques to dominate the lives of people they believe are less worthy of the privileges they are entitled to and enjoy.

That tradition has been maintained under the administrations of successive Presidents, confirmed by Congress, and endorsed by the U.S. Supreme Court. The latest efforts, currently coursing their way through the process, are designed to cut off entry to the U.S. by citizens of primarily Muslim nations, retract rights previously extended to transgender people, and stop Mexican and Central American immigrants at the border. The latter practice includes the use of military force, separating families, and locking up children in cages.

As years passed, antiquated restrictive and exclusionary policies were abandoned as the nation's social conscience grew. Those outdated codes of institutional conduct were replaced by new policies and standards to match the latest concerns over which category of people posed a more contemporary threat – or *perceived* threat. In most cases, the trauma continues to affect families, neighborhoods, and communities.

Part Two explains why **what most Americans know or believe about hate groups and hate crimes is misleading, grossly incomplete, or dead wrong.**

No one wants to be in the dark and we certainly don't want to be seen as ignorant or bigoted. On the contrary, thanks to decades of vocal advocates lobbying for and demanding social justice, most Americans today are more culturally aware than previous generations. This is particularly true among millennials and the Generation Z demographic born between the mid-1990s and mid-2000s. More communities and work environments now aim to establish meaningful relationships with neighbors and employees from different cultures and backgrounds. Yet, others are constrained into a framework of languages and cultures that can be difficult to understand from the dominant paradigm.

Then there are those who are fully content living in the sameness of their own isolated superior bubble.

Five main reasons underscore why Americans are uninformed about the hate and extremism that permeates every state in the nation and most cities as well.

The first is **faulty information.** The information available to news consumers, especially statistics from federal government agencies, starting with the FBI, is often intricately detailed and specific, but the FBI accepts and distributes questionable data as fact, excluding critical information we need to know.

Second, **the bewildering breadth of the hate movement.** The number of organized hate groups is one indicator of the immensity of the movement. That number ebbs and flows with each passing year. But it does not include lone extremists, nor does it account for the members of groups that disappear every year. Few Americans are truly aware of the power and extent of American hatred.

Third, **not all hate crime victims are protected equally.** Understanding the definition of a hate crime is a confusing proposition.

Because each state defines a hate crime differently, what qualifies in one state may not be the same in other states. Discerning the legal implications of hate crimes laws is confusing for anyone, including many experienced lawyers and judges.

Fourth, **each state's hate crimes statute defines which categories of people are protected and which are not.** In some states, the populations most targeted by white supremacists and radical right wing extremists are not protected by their state's law. Contrasting a comprehensive and inclusive federal hate crimes law against state laws that exclude specific groups of people is a confusing overlap of legal differences. Do you know what groups are protected in your state?

Fifth, **legal exclusions.** Through a succession of policy decisions made at the highest national levels, the U.S. government has excluded or restricted entire groups from the Constitutional rights and freedoms enjoyed by the dominant population of white, Christian, straight, able-bodied men. Even though those policies have since been repealed, reversed, or thrown out, the history of exclusion has served as a model for Americans to emulate.

Understanding other cultural dynamics can also create a deeper awareness of hate groups and hate crimes. Some of these include: the power and privileges of the dominant culture, how a lack of meaningful relationships affects our acceptance of others, and the nefarious ways some organized hate groups obtain their resources.

Subsequent chapters also explain the role of mainstream and social media in conveying information to news consumers, a critical factor in changing public opinion about the hate movement. The influence of Christianity-based hate groups and black nationalist hate groups is also explored, as well as how fear affects extremists as strongly as it does their victims.

Finally, what we know about hate adds up to a 9/11-size cataclysm happening in slow motion right in our own backyards.

Part Two unpacks how these issues boggle our ability to learn the truth about hate groups and hate crimes and why old traditions are unlikely to change without the support of vocal citizens who favor fairness and equality over denial and exclusion.

Faulty Information

TWO SEPARATE AGENCIES WITHIN THE U.S. Department of Justice, the FBI and the Bureau of Justice Statistics (BJS), are charged with reporting the number of hate crimes committed in the U.S. every year. Each agency uses a different methodology to gather data. Each process has pros and cons. Together, both efforts were created so Americans can learn the extent of extremism in their communities. To be most effective, it is essential that this two-pronged process to measure the impact of the hate movement is undertaken with candor and transparency.

[Note: the terms hate crimes, bias crimes, bias-oriented crimes, and malicious harassment have the same meaning and are used interchangeably.]

Fuzzy Numbers

In theory, the FBI gets its numbers from more than 16,000 law enforcement jurisdictions across the country. According to its formula, each municipal, county, and state police department, as well as every university and port that employs a police force, sends annual numbers to their state police headquarters regarding how many crimes of all types were committed in each jurisdiction, including a breakdown of hate crimes.

In turn, state police forward aggregate numbers to the FBI in the form of a statewide report broken down with specific results from each agency. The FBI data come from reports made by individual victims and identifies them (and their offenders) by gender, race, ethnicity, and other variables. Police departments range in size from single-officer units to those with more than 30,000 officers. Each police force submits its own hate crime totals for FBI analysts to examine and report to citizens through various channels of communication. That's the way it's supposed to work.

In contrast, the BJS gets its numbers from a comprehensive inquiry called the National Crime Victimization Survey (NCVS), which measures the number of all types of crimes. In 1972, the U.S. Census Bureau started conducting the NCVS for the BJS. The study tracks crimes committed against victims in the same nine categories protected by federal law, albeit with consistently higher totals than FBI reports. Through its in-depth survey, the BJS also examines perceived motivations, as well as the demographic characteristics of victims and offenders.

The BJS website describes its process this way: "Each year, data are obtained from a nationally representative sample of about 135,000 households, composed of nearly 225,000 persons, on the frequency, characteristics, and consequences of criminal victimization in the United States." One person with expertise in the BJS process clarified that the BJS hate crimes statistics are not produced every year and that BJS has done a total of three studies, the first two examining two different multi-year periods and the third reexamining the data from the first two. Another expert said that although the data may not be compiled every year, victimization surveys are nonetheless sent to respondents every six months.

Each BJS respondent answers a list of 80 or more questions regarding whether they have been the victim of a crime during the previous survey cycle and other information. From the responses, the BJS is able to calculate (an estimated) number of hate crimes committed in the U.S.

In order to be counted by the FBI, a hate crime must first be reported to police. Crimes calculated by the BJS do not require that every incident be reported to police. The difference in the numbers obtained by the two data sources is dramatic. On closer inspection, the outcome raises as much doubt as it does alarm. But, one reason sirens aren't blaring is that the BJS data rarely reaches the population.

Through no fault of the agency, BJS hate crimes reports seldom get the media attention they deserve.

Among the most positive elements from the BJS studies is it's consistent finding that more than half of hate crimes are not reported to police. Were these data not substantiated by the BJS, FBI reports would be accepted at face value and go unchallenged for their lack of candor and transparency about unreported crimes.

The Difference Between Hate Crime "Incidents" and "Related Offenses"

The FBI Hate Crime Statistics Report released in November 2018 stated that law enforcement agencies throughout the U.S. reported a total of "7,175 hate crime incidents and 8,437 related offenses in 2017." The totals represent an increase of 1,054 (17.2 percent) nationwide above the 6,121 hate crime incidents and 7,321 related offenses reported in 2016. It is important to understand the terminology used in FBI reports. This can get a bit complicated and tedious, which is part of the reason it is seldom reported by media.

The FBI's Uniform Crime Reporting (UCR) Program defines a hate crime (also known as a bias crime) as "a committed criminal offense that is motivated, in whole or in part, by the offender's bias(es) against a race, religion, disability, sexual orientation, ethnicity, gender, or gender identity." The FBI goes on to state, "The 'crime' in a hate crime is often a violent crime, such as assault, murder, arson, vandalism, or threats to commit such crimes. It may also cover conspiring or asking another person to commit such crimes, even if the crime was never carried out. 'Bias or Hate Incidents' are acts of prejudice that do not involve violence, threats, or property damage."

The FBI's Criminal Justice Information Services (CJIS), defines a hate crime incident as "one or more offenses committed by the same offender, or group of offenders acting in concert, at the same time and place." The incident explains what happened, while related offenses are what occurs within each incident. The number of offenses will always be higher than the number of incidents because each incident contains one or more offenses. FBI reports refer to hate crimes as "single-bias incidents" and "multiple-bias incidents."

Because the FBI specifies that one incident may involve multiple offenses, the Bureau reported 7,175 hate crime incidents in 2017. Within those incidents, 8,437 offenses occurred.

Rarely do media reports distinguish a hate crime *incident* from a *related offense*. Instead, incidents are almost always reported as the total number of hate crimes. That is because incidents are far more important. Related offenses, although useful to be aware of, are more numerous, yet different. The distinction is that a single hate crime incident may involve multiple related offenses. For example, say a radical extremist is arrested for using offensive racial and anti-Muslim language against an imam at a mosque (assuming the incident legally qualifies as a hate crime). If the same offender is also arrested at the same time for setting the mosque on fire, the verbal harassment charge and the arson charge are two separate crimes. Those two crimes together would be counted as one incident, but as two related offenses.

In the scheme of things and on a national scale, the gap between the number of incidents and related offenses is seldom significant. Any hate crime is worthy of community-wide attention. Residents also deserve to know all of the types of crimes happening where they live and how often they occur, whether they happen during a single event or separately. Do we need to protect ourselves more against verbal threats – or against arsons? Are the offenses in a neighborhood primarily beatings – or do they involve firearms and other weapons. Are our local police prepared for all possible types of crimes? Do they require special training because one type of crime is more prevalent?

The burden to clarify misinformation or a lack of information about hate crimes in any community is on government agencies and the media, two institutions not known for their ability to work collaboratively. Community organizations often inform their members when it believes either institution has failed to report hate crimes accurately.

On its website, the FBI states, "To ensure uniformity in reporting nationwide, all contributors [police departments] must conform to the FBI reporting guidelines and definitions." Uniformity cannot happen when critical terminology includes fine-line distinctions and is difficult to interpret.

The lack of clarity around specific terms contributes to public confusion about what truly constitutes a hate crime. In short, this is a murky issue for *anyone* to understand, including police officers and journalists. As a result, news reports rarely explain the difference between "incidents" and "related offenses" when FBI data are released.

While hate crime numbers are steep and abominable, the combined number of all hate crimes does not reflect reality. Just because a crime did not legally qualify as a hate crime doesn't mean a hate crime did not happen, nor does it mean the intent was not to harass the victim because of his race, skin color, religion, sexual orientation or other variables. What it may mean is that the crime didn't qualify as malicious harassment in the state where it took place. But, that same offense may qualify as a hate crime in other states. This is covered in more detail in a subsequent chapter.

In the end, hate crime victims don't care much about dissecting laws or terminology. Their concern is to bring peace of mind to their community and justice to their offenders.

Bureau of Justice Statistics Data

While definitions may be difficult to interpret, numbers are more definitive.

According to the BJS report released in June 2017, "**U.S. residents experienced an average of 250,000 hate crime victimizations each year from 2004 to 2015.**" Victimization does not necessarily imply the crime was reported to police or that a perpetrator was arrested or prosecuted. The FBI numbers rise and fall with each annual report. BJS numbers stay fairly consistent, although the data are not analyzed every year. Historically, the FBI's hate crime numbers tend to increase more than they decrease.

The void between the estimated 250,000 hate crime victimizations reported by BJS studies over the past 15 years and the 7,175 by the FBI (or 8,437 if one includes "related offenses") in 2017 is a staggering disparity of at least 242,800 crimes. One would expect that wide gaps in such a critical slice of public information would raise the hackles of elected officials and community activists. They do not.

The gaping hole between the two counts is no secret. Both agencies report their numbers every year. However, the statistical difference is rarely reported by the press or through social media. In an era when both hate groups and hate crimes have been increasing and the people they harass need to be more informed, what we get is an ambiguous lack of transparency.

Which agency is more believable, the FBI or the BJS?

Even though the latest FBI total of hate crime incidents is just over three percent of the BJS total, few explanations are forthcoming. The two methodologies used to obtain the data unquestionably make a difference. The FBI relies on numbers from police departments, whereas the BJS uses survey responses directly from citizens.

For two federal agencies analyzing hate crimes data to obtain such widely divergent outcomes seems a dubious return on the nation's investment in processes designed to discover truth.

To some extent, BJS estimates are calculated by a technique somewhat akin to that used by the Neilson Ratings to measure television audiences, although with very detailed feedback from anonymous respondents. The BJS survey form includes questions about all crimes, not just hate crimes.

For a crime to be classified as a hate crime in the BJS National Crime Victimization Survey, a victim must provide at least one of three types of evidence: (1) the offender used hate language, (2) the offender left behind hate symbols, or (3) police investigators confirmed the incident was a hate crime. Because the NCVS reaches some 225,000 Americans, BJS obtains more data than the FBI is able to gain solely from roughly 16,000 police departments. But, the quantity of information is far less important than the quality.

Although the BJS data is analyzed less frequently than annual reports from the FBI, perhaps the biggest limitation of BJS data is that surveys are based on self-reporting. With no in-person follow-up process to certify accuracy, reliability can be questioned. Nevertheless, community organizations consider the BJS estimates more realistic. Hate crime numbers offered on the Southern Poverty Law Center website, for example, are more closely aligned with the BJS estimates than the FBI count.

Another disconnect lies in the number of police departments that actually report hate crimes to the FBI every year. Police departments voluntarily submit hate crimes to the FBI. In 2017, the FBI noted that 16,149 law enforcement agencies "participated" in the Hate Crime Statistics Program. But, and this a big but, only 2,040 jurisdictions (12.6 percent) actually reported hate crimes to the Bureau.

What the FBI fails to distinguish is that 14,109 police departments in 2017 *implied* zero hate crimes in their jurisdictions by submitting no report at all. Only when a police department distinctly reports "Zero Hate Crimes" to the FBI, does its report mean no crimes were reported to, or processed by, police in that jurisdiction.

When no report is filed, the FBI is unable to discern whether (1) no hate crimes actually occurred, (2) that a police department made no hate crimes arrests, or (3) the department is negligent in reporting crimes that may have indeed occurred.

The FBI does, however, caution in its annual report that its mandate does not allow the Bureau to "estimate offenses for the jurisdictions of agencies that do not submit reports." That is, if a police department does not report how many hate crimes occurred within its purview in any given year, the Bureau assumes none took place. Between 2015 and 2018, the number of agencies reporting hate crimes increased by over 11 percent each year, a step in the right direction. The FBI calls those jurisdictions "participating agencies." The term is a misnomer. Not all participate.

In its most recent report covering crimes from 2017, data were submitted by 895 more jurisdictions than those that reported hate crime numbers the year before – 16,149 in 2017 versus 15,254 agencies in 2016. More police departments reporting hate crimes contributes to an analysis that is more reliable and more credible.

But, not having a full picture from all police departments diminishes the validity of the entire FBI reporting process. Plus, the high number of agencies that do not submit data to the FBI defeats the purpose of the Hate Crimes Statistics Act passed by Congress in 1990 and modified in 2009. The law requires the U.S. Attorney General to collect data on crimes committed because of a victim's race, religion, disability, sexual orientation, or ethnicity, i.e. hate crimes. The law, however, does not require states to provide data to the FBI. The logic of this process is like a mother telling her bad boy child, "Tell your father what you did." That kid is on his own.

What's more challenging is that some of the states or individual jurisdictions that report Zero Hate Crimes or fail to submit complete reports to the FBI have a long history of racial violence and brutal conflicts over religious differences, immigration, and other social issues. Communities need more certainty in the data they receive from police departments and the FBI in order to provide adequate security where it is most needed.

Certainly, it is *conceivable* that many jurisdictions experience no hate crimes in a given year. The need for caution arises when a community doubts its local police department over the number of hate crimes arrests made and the number it reports to the FBI every year.

For example, some may find it a bit surprising that Georgia, home to one of the largest number of hate groups in the U.S. (41 in 2018), would report data from only six police departments out of 493 statewide – a mere 1.5 percent of the state's law enforcement agencies. In 2016, even fewer jurisdictions in Georgia reported hate crimes.

Similarly, wouldn't it raise a red flag at the Texas State Legislature or at local media in the Lone Star State, to learn that out of 1,009 police departments there, only 75 submitted data to the FBI?

Does the low number of reports submitted to the FBI suggest that the term "participating agencies" is permissibly more elastic in some cities, counties, and states than others? Since the FBI data is a voluntary process, what happens when people who live in a certain jurisdiction believe more hate crimes occur there than are reported to the FBI?

One more city and state stand out as having potentially improbable statistics from the 2018 FBI report. Missouri is a state historically rife with racial conflict. In 2018, 24 hate groups were based there. The city of Ferguson, where Michael Brown was shot and killed by a white police officer in 2014, is one of 630 law enforcement jurisdictions in Missouri that either reported no hate crimes that year or failed to submit any report. More recently, only a trifling 25 agencies reported hate crimes statewide in Missouri during 2017 – while 600 did not.

Ferguson reported no hate crimes to the FBI between 2014 and 2018. Although the police shooting of Michael Brown was not deemed a hate crime, can one deduce that a young black man's death was an anomaly and violence against African Americans never happens in the city of 21,201? Another oddity: In 1970 the population of Ferguson was 99 percent white and one percent black; in 2018, it is 67 percent black and 29 percent white. At that rate of demographic change, racial tension is more likely to increase rather than decrease. With greater tension comes a greater likelihood of hatred based on skin color and race. The facts just don't line up as believable.

When the FBI releases annual hate crime counts to the media, the announcement suggests that most local and regional law enforcement agencies nationwide submit hate crime statistics to the FBI. Ostensibly, the FBI analysis identifies the number of crimes committed against each protected category in every jurisdiction. Most print media report the numbers with great fanfare.

But, because the gross imbalance between the FBI count and the BJS numbers are almost never reported by mainstream or online media, local government agencies, state legislators, and citizens believe the FBI data tell the whole truth. The inability to accurately count hate crimes is even more problematic in areas where a false sense of security leads marginalized populations to believe their lives are not at risk.

Why Some Police Departments Do Not Report Hate Crimes

It takes time for police to compile and submit hate crimes data to federal authorities. A lack of adequate staff to follow through with reporting requirements is one reason some police departments say they are unable to submit paperwork to the FBI. This may be true in departments with few staff.

Sometimes an offense is not reported because the evidence is too weak to substantiate a hate crime charge, in which case the offense is reported as a different kind of crime, one not motivated by bias. Another possibility is that police haven't investigated a crime adequately to confirm the offense was motivated by prejudice toward the victim.

Among the most critical problems with police reporting is that victims don't always report hate crimes incidents to police. The Police Chief in a municipality where a known hate group has resided for several years said his city generally reports zero hate crimes to the FBI. He explained that although he suspects hate crimes happen there, "If a victim doesn't report a crime to us, we can't report a crime to the FBI."

Other than jurisdictions that truly experience zero hate crimes, why other police departments do not file hate crimes reports with the FBI is a mystery. Since no consequences are likely to befall delinquent departments, a bigger mystery is why agencies are allowed to contradict the requirements of a federal law.

Another reality exists to explain why police may choose to submit no hate crimes report to the FBI. It is in the best interest of any police department to appear as though they have hate crimes under control. To have experienced no hate crimes under their watch, police chiefs look good for protecting their citizens from domestic terrorism and have a reason to applaud the local force for its positive work to keep extremists at bay. And local elected officials, who are generally responsible for hiring the chief, have a positive statistic to use in their next campaign.

Whether attributed to staffing challenges, tight budgets, politics, insensitivity, laziness, or blatant racism, spotty police department reporting results in FBI statistics that do not reflect the full spectrum of American extremism.

Federal agencies are not meeting their responsibility to communities that rely on accurate data to make reasonable policing decisions. Allowing police departments the discretion to file a hate crime report to the FBI leaves accuracy and accountability hanging in the balance. In the meantime, the rumor mill among community groups is abuzz with stories about hate crimes that occur in public settings, at places of worship, at sacred sites, inside community centers, and homes. But are they rumors?

Is it plausible that law enforcement agencies in racially volatile jurisdictions and more than 11,000 other U.S. cities, can experience not even a single bias-motivated crime – not one swastika painted on the wall of a synagogue or mosque, not one noose hanging from a tree in a black neighborhood or over a colleague's locker, not one gay bashing, and not one violent anti-immigrant attack against a fourth generation Asian-American whose ancestors escaped a war-torn region where U.S. bombs leveled their city?

People who live in regions where race relations have reached lethal proportions have to raise questions about the extent to which the numbers their government says are accurate truly mean anything. But they can't dispute facts they don't know about.

Further, is it realistic to expect federal change while Donald Trump is President? The Trump administration has relied on guidance from recognized white nationalists serving as presidential advisors. The chief executive's social media announcements also consistently vilify citizens protected within the Hate Crimes Prevention Act, specifically immigrants, Muslims, and transgender people.

Garbage In, Garbage Out

While the FBI data have the strength of a sound statistical analysis, a major limitation is that law enforcement agencies that do not submit data to the FBI bear no consequences for sidestepping the Hate Crimes Statistics Act, thereby creating a porous requirement. By reporting "zero hate crimes," or by not submitting any report at all, police communicate to the public that the communities they protect have experienced no hate crimes and perhaps that's true.

Given the disproportionate number of police departments that opt out of the process, the FBI data are misleading, woefully incomplete, and only questionably reliable. Those who believe their local police are more likely to rejoice when zeros or few hate crimes are reported to the FBI because police are doing their job. Nonbelievers, more likely to be members of marginalized communities, may suspect police are not doing their job and, as a result, the entire community is not being protected.

Data omissions raise serious questions. In the FBI's 2018 hate crimes report, Georgia reported data from eight of 409 agencies; Alabama, from four of 334. The entire state of Hawaii does not appear in the Bureau's state-by-state breakdown because officials there generally decline to participate in the FBI data gathering process.

Whether by default or deliberate omission, when a large percentage of the nation's police departments suggest, "no hate crimes happened in our jurisdiction last year," police *appear to be* effectively managing crimes against all citizens – and the favorite targets of hate groups *appear to be* safe from the extremists who live around them. Other research suggests that neither is a reasonable or a safe assumption.

Because FBI statisticians sort through the data they receive and calculate accurate analyses accordingly, the agency is effectively doing things right. It is not doing the right things. The right thing is to ensure that every law enforcement agency submits accurate data and the public is informed of the results.

The "False Zero Phenomenon"

After decades researching hate groups and hate crimes for the Southern Poverty Law Center. Mark Potok refers to unreported numbers in FBI reports as the "False Zero Phenomenon." He explained: "For example, [if] the Montgomery, Alabama, Police Department misses the FBI deadline for reporting hate crimes, the Alabama State police pencil in a zero. There may have been hate crimes there, but they just don't make the deadline and don't report anything. In that case, the 'false zero' creates an assumption that no hate crimes were committed in Montgomery."

An unexpected outcome of periodic victimization surveys is that BJS data often sheds a light on issues beyond an accounting of hate crimes. Potok lauded the NCVS for remarkable discoveries, including this: "At a time when no one really believed there was much sexual assault in the country, either because it was considered shameful to report a rape or other reasons, the NCVS uncovered rape to be very prevalent in the U.S." When photos of missing children appeared on milk cartons all over the country, Potok continued, "Most Americans had the impression this was a huge problem with tens of thousands of stranger-abducted children. The NCVS was able to show that well under 100 kids were abducted every year."

Asked about the reliability of either the FBI or BJS data, Potok commented that based on in-depth, statistically representative data, "The FBI's Uniform Crime Reporting system relies on input from police departments, many of which choose to opt out of the system by not submitting data, by their inability to differentiate a hate crime from another type of victimization, or by their reporting zero crimes." BJS data, he concluded, "is considered much more reliable than the FBI data."

Accountability for the number of hate crimes in the U.S. must start with numbers that pass a smell test common sense people trust as credible. Today, scholars and legal authorities who study the hate movement and examine bias crime statistics every year deem the results of current government practices to be of limited value to anyone who accepts and passes on the information as fact, including elected officials, teachers, and journalists.

More vexing is the occasional FBI gladhanding over reportedly low hate crime numbers in any given year. In its 2013 report, the FBI praised itself for the lowest number of hate crimes committed since 1991, the year it first started to tally hate crimes. Despite the glaring omissions and questionable zeros, the FBI's annual process extends a license for police departments to operate autonomously. This is not how trust is built between federal agencies, local police departments, and any marginalized population that finds itself in the crosshairs of white supremacist extremists, not to mention their family, friends, coworkers, neighbors, and community groups.

With all the data Americans now have at their fingertips about hate crimes, and reasons to doubt the reliability of those statistics, two questions come to mind: One, do either the FBI, BJS, or their parent agency (DOJ) have the resources, experience, and cultural authority to effectively and efficiently account for all hate crimes committed in the U.S.? And two, if not, why not?

The Bewildering Breadth of the Hate Movement

WHAT WE ARE LED TO BELIEVE about hate groups and hate crimes is not the fault of any person's or institution's deliberate intent to deceive as much as it is a product of overwhelming information that is poorly organized into categories by talented people juggling unreliable numbers. Toss in weak or nonexistent hate crimes recordkeeping by police departments, plus questionable statistical variables between the FBI and BJS, and even the best analyses are debatable. Add a hint of media spin and the end result is a misinformed public that assumes everything that shows up in the news is true.

Number of Groups Versus Number of Extremists

The number of hate groups in the U.S. fluctuates year to year. In 2019, the Southern Poverty Law Center cited 1,020 hate groups in the U.S. While groups like SPLC and the Anti-Defamation League commit a Herculean effort to track extremists, knowing the number of identifiable hate *groups* doesn't really tell us much without knowing the number of *people* in any given group. Additionally, one group with 1,000 members is not necessarily a bigger threat than ten groups with five members each. A handful of violent inner city Hammerskins can be much more dangerous than 100 weekend Klansmen in the Ozarks.

"It is impossible to determine the number of people in hate groups," says Mark Potok, an expert on the radical right and former Editor of the SPLC quarterly magazine *The Intelligence Report.* "The numbers are often overestimated by groups and kept secret. The leader of a group may say they have hundreds or thousands of members when they actually have 14. The number of groups is the best index we have, although that count is admittedly imperfect."

Another factor to weigh in counting extremists is that when any hate group disappears from a yearly total, the *people* who were part of a former group do not disappear with it. In California, the state with the most hate groups, the number of identified hate groups leaped from 68 in 2014 to 83 in 2019, according to the SPLC Hate Map. During the intervening years, California extremists whose groups disbanded or no longer exist, didn't just vanish into the desert. One can reasonably speculate that some will continue to victimize, albeit independently or with like-minded friends they seduce into joining them.

The hate movement has morphed away from crimes that were once perpetrated by members of groups to a majority of offenses now committed by individuals, many with no known connection to a hate group. Prosecutors say that malicious harassment crimes often occur spontaneously out of impulsive circumstances motivated by the perpetrator's state of mind.

Similarly, one person's extremist thinking can influence fair-minded friends out on the town to participate. In their capacity to act on internalized hate, some are prone to violence by any situation they encounter in public. The trigger may be a driving vengeance for anything that violates their sense of what is "right." That may be a building they believe deserves to be vandalized because of what it represents or a person who doesn't "fit in our neighborhood" because of their skin color, race, religion or some other perceived difference.

Consider this common formula for hate: Combine a hateful person with alcohol, a weapon, and testosterone-fueled bravado. Enter a visible "minority" or a couple on a street, no witnesses in site. In such a scenario, to an extremist, anti-*anything* thinking takes over and logic is replaced by a compulsion to destroy property, harass people, and cause harm.

Experts who study hate groups say politics is a prime factor affecting the hate movement. Platform positions of political candidates can affect the number of hate crimes committed in any year. Some candidates are transparent in broadcasting negative perceptions of certain "minority" groups, while others advocate for peace and offer more inclusive messages about ways to unite communities.

The election of the nation's first African American president caused higher numbers of extremists to organize and become active, believed to be motivated by race-related concerns about a black Commander in Chief. In the three years after the first election of President Barack Obama in 2008, hate groups rose 10 percent, from 925 in 2008 to 1,018 in 2011. Despite consistent efforts to unify diverse populations through his two terms in office, Obama maintained a centrist administration in the face of opposition from radical right wing groups.

During Donald Trump's first year in office, the number of hate groups in the U.S. rose 11.2 percent from 917 in 2016 to 1,020 at the end of 2018. In this case, the bump is believed to be in support of the president's overtly right wing agenda. As president, Trump's tacit support of white nationalists and opposition to other specific categories of Americans has emboldened the hate movement to become more visible and more active.

Through the 2016 presidential campaign, candidate Trump questioned the acceptability of immigrants, particularly those from Mexico, Syria, and other Middle Eastern nations. As a contender, Trump promised to impose restrictions on Muslims entering the U.S. Within his first few months as President, Trump achieved the promise. President Trump signed Executive Order 13780 in 2017, which limited travel to the U.S. from five majority Muslim countries (Iran, Libya, Syria, Yemen, Somalia) as well as North Korea and Venezuela. The order also bars entry for all refugees who do not possess either a visa or valid travel documents. The order was upheld by the U.S. Supreme Court in 2018.

Trump has continued to mobilize the hate movement through negative messages about Muslims, immigrants, Mexicans, Africans, transgender people and has proposed policies designed to limit their freedoms. He also openly disparages women, overweight people, and others. Coming from the nation's top leader, members of the hate groups that target people in categories the President disapproves of interpret his words as a legitimate reason to actively victimize them.

According to numbers updated annually by the SPLC, over a seven-year span, the total number of U.S. hate groups has leaped from a 599 groups in 2000 to 1,020 in 2017. [See Table 1]. More alarming, the number of hate groups does not include individual extremists, so-called "lone wolves," whose crimes vastly outnumber those committed by members of organized groups.

Table 1:

Numbers of hate groups identified by the SPLC 2008 to 2017

Total # of Hate Groups 2008 to 2018										
2008	2009	2010	2011	2012	2013	2014	2015	2016	2017	2018
926	932	1,002	1,018	1,007	939	784	892	917	954	1,020

When it comes to counting hate crimes, annual data gathered by the FBI show that in the nine years from 2008 to 2017 hate crimes *declined* from 7,783 in 2008 to a low of 5,479 in 2014. The numbers rose again in 2017 to 7,175. [See Table 2] Hate crime numbers are always in flux due to such variables as political dynamics, the status of civil rights and human rights, and the power of hot button social issue advocates to form organized movements for change.

Overall, changes in FBI hate crime totals from year to year are not significant. Too many problems exist in the FBI's data gathering and reporting process. Reliability of the ultimate numbers is further complicated because the number of police departments that actually submit data to the FBI changes every year.

Table 2: FBI Hate Crime Statistics 2008 to 2017

["Criminal incidents" include crimes proved to be motivated by hate; "Related offenses" include incidents that were committed in the context of a previously reported hate crime.]

FBI Hate Crime Statistics 2008 to 2017			
Year	Date of FBI News Release	Hate Crime "Incidents"	"Related Offenses"
2008	Nov 29, 2009	7,783	9,168
2009	Nov 22, 2010	6,604	7,789
2010	Nov 14, 2011	6,628	7,699
2011	Dec 10, 2012	6,222	7,254
2012	Nov 25, 2013	5,796	6,718
2013	Dec 8, 2014	5,928	6,933
2014	Nov 16, 2015	5,479	6,418
2015	Nov 14, 2016	5,850	6,885
2016	Nov 13, 2017	6,121	7,321
2017	Nov 13, 2018	7,175	8,437

Given the FBI's statistical unreliability as documented in the previous chapter, the agency's data are shrouded in uncertainty. Further, most government agencies, universities, and nonprofits that investigate and report on hate groups and hate crimes do so independently.

No *coordinated* effort is in place for law enforcement agencies and other researchers to share data and collaborate on a strategic approach to reduce hate crimes. No known government mission is articulated with objectives to manage or stop hate crimes within a given time frame. In the meantime, intragovernmental clashes result in conflicting statistics, complicated by inconsistent policies and protocols to investigate bias-oriented crimes and bring perpetrators to justice.

While BJS says a high number of hate crimes victims do not report incidents to police, up to 54 percent, and police departments do not always submit reliable accounts of such offenses, determining an accurate number of hate crimes each year is impractical at best, or worse, a statistical impossibility. This is not an acceptable approach to solve a growing national problem.

Whatever is currently being done to stop the hate movement is ineffective, as evidenced by the stabilized and frequently increasing numbers of both hate groups and hate crimes. The government's effort is somewhat analogous to homeowners with garden hoses dousing a building engulfed in flames while the fire department can't find its way to the blaze. In its defense, the FBI does pursue hate criminals, actively tracks behaviors of known or suspected extremists and is known to prevent major hate crimes. Overall, however, the Bureau's funding is inadequate, other federal departments are not always on the same page, reports to the public are unreliable, and no solid mission is articulated to stop hate crimes rather than count them.

In contrast, the vision of the hate movement is focused on a very simple two-part mission: perpetuate the white race and maintain white superiority.

While exploring the true power of hate groups, a chilling reality was voiced by senior hate crime investigators at both the SPLC and the ADL. That is, "Hate groups today are insignificant." The highest estimate of hate crimes committed by members of hate groups is under 10 percent, while many agree the rate is more likely between three percent and five percent. What makes these statistics worrisome is that because individuals rather than groups are committing the vast majority of hate crimes, there is great unpredictability in what and whom we're dealing with.

Also, because the latest generation of radical right extremists are not always affiliated with a known entity that resides in a specific area, attempts to harness the effects of hatred are more difficult to control. That dynamic may not be accidental. It is another underlying issue to confront so that the hate crimes data we receive each year leads the federal government to set a realistic goal, ideally to slow, if not stop, the consequences of hate crimes on innocent people.

Precious few Americans know how individual extremists and hate groups operate, where they are located, what techniques they employ, or the full extent of the damage they cause. Nor is it known how effectively the hate movement is being contained. Instead, public and private sector agencies compete for funding and are often at odds with one another while the public is largely clueless about their work. Clashing reports result in conflicting data complicated by inconsistent policies. Weak protocols are in place to investigate, quantify, and reduce malicious harassment.

The effort must start with a bold mission equal to that of NASA's assignment to rocket Americans to the moon and Mars. Without clear goals, deadlines, standards of accountability, and evidence of measurable progress, no mission can ever be accomplished. Nor will we know how close we are to achieving it.

None of that can happen without a clear understanding of the hate movement, well-defined terms that don't require a law degree to interpret, and a coordinated and well-managed effort to ensure ALL Americans are protected equally.

Not All Victims Are Protected Equally: Confusing Definitions

WHAT EXACTLY IS A HATE GROUP or a hate crime?

A hate **group** is the easier term to define. The Southern Poverty Law Center defines a hate group as "an organization that – based on its official statements or principles, the statements of its leaders, or its activities – has beliefs or practices that attack or malign an entire class of people, typically for their immutable characteristics." The SPLC definition is consistent with the FBI definition.

Defining a hate **crime** presents a more tangled knot to untie. Broadly speaking, a hate crime (aka bias crime, bias-motivated crime, or malicious harassment) is a criminal offense motivated by bias. A hate crime occurs when a perpetrator targets a victim because of that person's membership or *perceived membership* in a specific racial, social, or religious group. As explained in a previous chapter (Faulty Information), the FBI defines a hate crime as "a criminal offense committed against a person, property, or society that is motivated, in whole or in part, by the offender's bias against a race, religion, disability, sexual orientation, or ethnicity/national origin." This definition is consistent with many other sources.

In essence, what qualifies as a hate crime is defined in federal and state laws. Although the FBI, the largest law enforcement agency in the U.S., enforces the federal Matthew Shepard and James Byrd, Jr. Hate

Crimes Prevention Act (HCPA) on a national level, not all states protect the same categories embraced by the HCPA. That is, while the HCPA is a sweeping and inclusive law, not all states define hate crimes the same. Differences are based on the way state laws specifically articulate which groups are protected and which are not.

What makes the definition of a hate crime troubling is that distinctions regarding what is or is not a crime hinge on an interpretation of specific incidents, the charge against an alleged perpetrator, police and prosecutorial discretion, all under a veil of subjectivity.

A police officer writing a charge of malicious harassment may be influenced by personal feelings or opinions, as well as the need to obtain evidence that substantiates the charge. Defense attorneys will try every legal trick to prove the perpetrator is not guilty or to convert a hate crime charge into an offense likely to end in a lighter sentence.

Prosecutors have a degree of flexibility while preparing a victim's case for trial, including the possibility of a plea bargain that may reduce a hate crime to qualify as a non-bias crime in return for information from the offender. In most but not all cases, by the time the accused reaches a judge, the cast of characters will have determined whether the crime met the state's definition of malicious harassment and that the offense was indeed motivated by hate.

A huge difference in the definition also depends on the state in which a hate crime occurs. More confounding for those of us without a law degree, nailing down specific criteria required to meet one global definition of a hate crime can be an exercise in semantic gymnastics.

By virtue of the First Amendment to the U.S. Constitution, hate itself is not a crime, nor is speech that condemns specific groups, including threats of violence against ALL people in any category. That Constitutional protection is relinquished when the condemnation targets a specific person by name. When charges of malicious harassment are raised, however, the alleged perpetrator's language and behaviors form the backdrop to define it as a hate crime.

A threat becomes a crime only when it is judged to have been a "true threat" rather than bar talk or a threat not really meant to cause harm. To show the difference, courts often impose a "reasonable third party" standard, that is, if a reasonable third party would take what the offender said as a real threat to do violence, as opposed to just talk, that is a punishable "true threat." The most reasonable third party listeners to impress will be sitting in the jury box.

It is paramount that law enforcement authorities, elected officials, and community leaders know what constitutes a hate crime so that victims are protected. It is equally important that legislative action focus on ways to ease the process of reporting offenses to police. In turn, change is also needed so that police accurately include a count of all incidents in the FBI's annual hate crimes analysis. Seattle University Criminology professor William Parkin highlights the complexity of defining a hate crime by saying, "If we can't define it, we can't legislate it; if we can't legislate it, we can't prosecute offenders."

As every defector's comments suggest, laws and definitions never even crossed their mind while they were immersed in the movement. Bolstered by a raging fury behind every swing of a fist, every threat with a weapon, every destroyed landmark, and every hateful image marked on the wall of a sacred place, perpetrators are guided by thoughtless hatred.

Unpacking the issues and dynamics that make the hate movement tick requires an understanding of both hate crimes and the groups that commit them. How the movement started, what keeps it going, and what makes it so muddled and confounding to study and manage have baffled social scientists for decades.

Hate groups tend to lump all marginalized populations into one big target. The tendency to combine various constituencies into one amorphous group is a consequence of shifting populations. Factors that enrage extremists include increasing numbers of interracial and inter-religious relationships, increasing Latino and mixed-race populations, greater religious tolerance of sexual minorities, and an influx of refugees from various parts of the world, among others. The focus of white power rests on exclusion rather than inclusion.

Along the same lines, hate *groups* fall into one big confused lump of titles and sub-movements. White Supremacists. White Nationalists. Neo-Nazis. The Alt-Right. The Christian Identity Movement. The Creativity Movement. Making distinctions between any of these groups is far less important than recognizing the big picture. The core mission they all share is to perpetuate the white race and maintain white superiority; more specifically, Christian whites, heteronormative whites, American-born whites, able-bodied whites.

No matter how actively or robust their actions may be, individual groups generally target one category of people to harass. Yet, to an extremist steeped in the mission of the movement, deciphering one targeted group from another is inconsequential.

The hate movement has managed to elude most fair-minded people capable of critical thinking. Given the ability of extremists to stifle government agencies through the use of social media and whites-only websites, illegal ways to obtain funding, lobbying for the election or appointment of radical right wing candidates to high level public positions, and other below-the-radar techniques – the public consciousness has not yet reached the tipping point between a demand for change and the government's ability to make it happen.

Change is further hampered by localized issues such as inconsistent or weak media coverage of hate crimes, widespread fear of white supremacist groups, and legal standards regarding what categories of people are protected in hate crimes laws from one state to another.

Ask any American how many hate groups are active in their state or how many hate crimes are committed there in a single year and you're very likely to get a blank stare. Based on a poll of over 2,500 workshop participants across the U.S. between 2014 and 2019, most from marginalized populations, not one was able to answer either question correctly.

Most Americans are largely unaware of the hate movement or how deeply it affects their city or state, much less who is protected in their state's hate crimes law. Not even the federal government is fully capable of keeping up with what the hate movement is doing or reliably tracking the rate at which hate crimes are committed. What federal and state agencies do today is better than it was 20 years ago, but not adequate to stop the rising tide of bias crimes or to make solid predictions about where to concentrate the most effective actions.

With all the annual studies of hate groups and hate crimes conducted by government agencies, universities, research institutions, and social justice groups, accuracy on the number of hate crimes committed in the U.S. falls roughly between an educated guess and a collective hunch.

Types of Hate Groups

Knowing the motivations of various hate groups helps to understand the laws designed to protect the categories of people they target. Hate groups are organized into three main categories: Ideological, Religious, and Nationalist/Nativist. These groupings can be fluid and tend to overlap, depending on the group's leadership and mission.

Ideological groups are organized around an extremist point of view. The largest in this category are the Ku Klux Klan, White Nationalists, neo-Nazis, and racist skinheads. The KKK is the most infamous and most enduring of American hate groups. Although its ideology has focused primarily on African Americans and people of African descent, the Klan also has attacked Jews, immigrants, LGBTQ Americans and, until recently, Catholics. Within the same category, the alt-right movement, a creation of the ultra-conservative National Policy Institute popularized after the election of Donald Trump, operates on the basis of far-right ideologies, with the conviction that white people and their culture are being undermined by population changes, political sensitivity, and demands for social justice.

Religious-oriented hate groups espouse a fundamentalist perspective, most frequently Christian, based on strict biblical interpretations and religious dogma. They are most likely to target Jews, Muslims, Sikhs, Hindus and other religious minorities, as well as LGBTQ people. The Creativity movement, formerly known as World Church of the Creator, and Christian Identity groups like the now-defunct group Kerry Noble was a part of (CSA), fall into this category, along with the anti-gay Westboro Baptist Church. Some ideological and nationalist groups slide into the religious category because of disagreements over biblical interpretations.

Nationalist or *Nativist* groups are primarily anti-immigrant. Ironically, indigenous Americans have been a favorite target of such groups and, in fact, have been the target of government oppression going back to the first colonialist settlers. This category includes such groups as the Federation for American Immigration Reform, American

Immigration Control Foundation, and National Organization for European American Rights, to name a few. In the context of nativist thinking, immigrant populations may be targeted whenever they are perceived to cross into the white majority's belief of entitlement.

Although it's been active for decades, American nationalism got a boost in recognition after a series of coordinated terrorist attacks that killed 130 people in Paris in November 2015. The Islamic State (ISIS) claimed responsibility for the murders, saying they were in retaliation for French airstrikes on ISIS targets in Syria and Iraq. Soon after the Paris murders, the U.S. Congress voted overwhelmingly to halt the resettlement of Syrian and Iraqi refugees in the U.S. This decision eerily recalls past efforts to deny immigrants entry into the U.S.

Nativism was clearly behind President Donald Trump's 2017 executive order banning U.S. entry to refugees and foreign nationals from some Muslim countries.

Federal Hate Crime Versus State Hate Crime

Currently, the Matthew Shepard and James Byrd, Jr. Hate Crimes Prevention Act, passed by Congress in 2009, defines a nationwide standard of protected categories. The federal law was passed after two horrendous murders in 1998, and honors both victims, Matthew Shepard, a 22-year old gay university student murdered in Wyoming, and James Byrd, Jr., a 49-year old African-American killed in Jasper, Texas. Enacted in 2009 after both crimes received national media attention, the HCPA is the most comprehensive law to date, including categories previously unprotected by federal law. As a result, federal law now includes bias crimes based on nine categories, including a victim's *perceived* **race, color, religion, national origin, ethnicity, disability, gender, sexual orientation, and gender identity.**

By including "perceived" in the identification of protected groups, the law addresses the most common conflict many humans are unable to avoid: assumptions and stereotypes. Suspicions or judgments based on an individual's appearance, clothing, mannerisms, or behaviors do not always reflect reality. Because hate crime perpetrators often target victims based on their own presumptions, the law provides that a victim who does not fit into a protected category, *but looks like someone who does*, is equally protected by the law.

As extremists evolve, the laws against their hateful language and behaviors evolve as well, along with strategies to pursue offenders. In 1968, Congress passed the first federal hate crimes statute which made it a crime "to use, or threaten to use, force to willfully interfere with any person because of **race, color, religion, or national origin**." That law was followed by the 1990 Hate Crime Statistics Act[33], which requires the Attorney General to collect data on crimes, at least in theory. Congress subsequently passed the Church Arson Prevention Act[34] (1996), criminalizing damages or incidents that interfere with a person's religious practice. In 1994, the Violent Crime Control and Law Enforcement Act expanded the federal law to include crimes based on disability.

When Congress approved the Federal HCPA in 2009, the law provided more than newly protected categories. It also gave federal authorities greater ability to engage in local or regional investigations and facilitate prosecutions when local authorities are unwilling or unable to proceed. This provision is a saving grace for bias crime victims in states with hate crimes laws that **exclude** specific categories such as disabilities, sexual orientation, gender identity.

Despite the broad provisions of the HCPA, the overwhelming majority of hate crime cases are prosecuted at the state level. Federal authority is rarely exercised and the HCPA is not a substitute for state laws. What makes the distinction between state and federal standards problematic is that not all states protect the same categories of people covered under the HCPA's umbrella. In states with restrictive protections, how and when federal prosecutors get involved requires a process.

Federal, state and municipal police departments have the discretion to pick and choose which criminal charges to pursue and which do not warrant further investigation, based on the laws that govern their jurisdiction. Government strategies to contain hate crimes, which differ from one jurisdiction to another, are often as unstructured as they are difficult to comprehend. This is not necessarily bad. It does suggest, however, that neither society nor technology have advanced to a point at which humans are capable of objectively and accurately measuring or stopping hate crimes. To attorneys who defend extremist clients, this is an advantage.

Officer Mike Ghuneim, Hate Crimes Investigator with the Chicago Police Department's Civil Rights Unit, explained that navigating around state and federal laws is less ambiguous in states like Illinois, in which comprehensive hate crime statutes are compatible with the federal law. "Protected classes do differ nationally, but the HCPA helps ensure that offenses do not get overlooked. In Chicago, we have established sound partnerships with the Cook County Attorney's Office, FBI, and other agencies that support streamlining the process," Ghuneim said. When to involve a federal prosecutor is another issue.

Jurisdictional connections are common between law enforcement agencies in order to enforce the laws, ensure that hate crime victims are protected, and to secure justice for offenders. Two prosecutors who work separately in Washington State described the differences between a malicious harassment charge prosecuted by the federal government, based on the federal law, and one prosecuted according to state law. Bruce Miyake is Assistant U.S. Attorney for the Western District of Washington State, and Michael Hogan is Deputy Prosecuting Attorney for King County.

Miyake explained how and when federal prosecutors get involved. He said that in states that have no hate crimes statute or states without a law as inclusive as the HCPA, "The feds get involved only if a state doesn't want to pursue a case or if an evidentiary issue arises that prevents them from pursuing it. Under those circumstances the federal government will get involved and prosecute the case." Ultimately, Miyake said, "The HCPA exists to ensure justice is done."

Perhaps the most damning evidence needed to confer federal jurisdiction is that the crime must implicate interstate commerce, a concept that has been used to effectuate a wide range of federal and state regulations. The legal requirement to involve interstate commerce is that a free flow of merchandise between states must not be impeded in the act of committing a crime.

To explain how interstate commerce applies, Miyake sketched the background of a Washington State case in which a gay man was attacked by a perpetrator using offensive language. The crime grew to meet federal standards when the offender drew a knife on the victim. "We discovered that the knife was made in Oregon. If the knife was made in Washington, the feds could not pursue [the case]." In order for an offense like this one to be prosecuted as a violation of federal law, the weapon would have had to first cross state lines before the crime was committed. Miyake added that trying the case federally allowed for a more severe punishment. He also described an added benefit for the offender and the state; the accused was able to get help for the treatment of mental issues, a factor in the incident.

When Washington State's law was written to mirror the provisions of the federal HCPA, state lawmakers wanted to make a statement to the community regarding such categories as sexual orientation and gender identity. Miyake explained, "If we don't call a hate crime what it is, [citizens in protected communities] don't feel supported or protected. It is important to prosecute for the crime committed. Doing so sends a message that the behavior will not be tolerated." At least not in Washington State.

The key difference in trying the same crime under Washington State law, is that Prosecutor Hogan in King County, Washington, would not have to consider interstate commerce as a condition because that is not a state requirement.

To explain how he pursues a hate crime, Hogan first pointed out the need for police and prosecutor sensitivity in talking with victims to determine if they were subjected to a hate crime. Accurately categorizing the offense as a hate crime is essential because the sentence for a bias crimes is often greater than a sentence for an offense not motivated by bias. Over more than 25 years of prosecuting hate crime offenders, Hogan says *how* questions are asked is exceedingly important to the case. "We don't want to suggest answers from the way the question is asked. We want to determine the mental state of the perpetrator and whether or not the crime can be prosecuted as a hate crime."

For example, Hogan said, questions for victims may include: "What language was used?" "What was the perpetrator's tone of voice?" "Were personal injuries or damages to property part of the crime?" He also underscored the thin line between vulgar, offensive, and reprehensible language, which may be constitutionally protected, and clearly articulated hate speech, which is not. [More information about hate speech is covered in subsequent chapters.]

Specific words used during hate crimes often include targeted threats. Hogan said the prosecutor has to determine whether the crime was premeditated or opportunistic, which can influence how it is prosecuted. Plus, Hogan explained, in order to prevail in court, the fear a victim describes must include words an *average person* would find fearful. Even when the conditions stack up against an offender, Hogan said that every case is tried on a case-by-case basis. Each one involves different human variables, such as cultural background, emotions, context, and the mental state of both the victim and the offender, all of which are critical to substantiate the crime. "I have to convince the jury that a suspect's language was *subjectively fearful* as opposed to angry words. The evidence has to be admissible in court," Hogan said, adding, "One frustrating part of prosecuting a malicious harassment case is insufficient evidence for the case to hold up in court."

Like other prosecutors, Hogan disagrees that one monolithic definition of a hate crime is the panacea to end all doubts. Discovering accurate information, he said, "is inherent in the constitutional protections we enjoy under the First Amendment. It is supposed to be this way. It is not a flaw of systems. Since we have these protected rights, and only threats are prohibited, a case-by-case analysis is required to see if the words and conduct arise to a level of a targeted threat."

Subjectivity

Not all states are as aggressive against hate crimes as Washington or Illinois. As such, not all hate crimes victims are protected equally across the U.S., nor are they treated with the full brunt of the *federal* law.

The most commonly overlooked categories in state hate crimes laws are sexual orientation, gender identity, disabilities, and homelessness. Under the best of circumstances, without clearly articulated legal specificity, individual police officers make spontaneous decisions based on the facts they learn at the scene of the crime, with room for judgment and subjectivity. The lack of exact conditions to define a hate crime also leads to disagreements and confusion between law enforcement agencies, thereby undermining legal cases and giving more credence to the defense.

If proven to be motivated by bias, such offenses *may* qualify as a bias crime. Following a hate crime charge from incident to trial can be an emotional rollercoaster for victims and is another reason victims may opt out of the process by not reporting the crime to police. Even though a state law may include a specific category, the law does not ensure all police officers will charge an offender with a hate crime, nor does it ensure that all prosecutors will treat victims sensitively or pursue the case aggressively.

By trying a suspect for an offense that does not qualify as malicious harassment, the offender is likely to receive a less stringent sentence, notably a shorter prison term. That is why criminal defense attorneys who represent suspects facing hate crime charges attempt to reduce the charge to a non-bias-oriented offense such as assault, aggravated assault, battery, criminal trespass.

Also, at the time of an arrest, a police officer can put an unintended spin on a hate crime charge for such reasons as a lack of an appropriate investigation or the officer's own bias. Subjectivity can skew a case based on the testimony of eyewitnesses, judgment by the prosecutor and views presented by the judge hearing the case.

The HCPA criminalizes attempts to inflict bodily injury by the use of fire, firearms, explosives and incendiary devices, or other dangerous weapons. The U.S. Department of Justice website notes that hate crimes may include the use of "explosives, arson, weapons, vandalism, physical violence, and verbal threats of violence to instill fear in their victims." The federal law, however, does not specifically prohibit the most easily accessible weapons used in malicious harassment: fists and feet.

Since beating a victim with the use of the offender's body parts is not likely to affect interstate commerce, in the hate crimes described by the vast majority of the defectors I talked to, the federal HCPA is effectively neutered. In states with no hate crimes law or states that do not specifically protect certain categories, restrictive laws are equally useless against offenders who physically attack victims in unprotected groups. As a result, violators in many of the most routine hate crime incidents cannot be tried for committing a hate crime. It is up to a savvy prosecutor to determine charges that warrant a penalty commensurate to the offense.

Malicious harassment may also include racial, homophobic, or anti-Semitic slurs, or comments referencing a specific protected category. Such language may be verbal or appear as symbolic messages on walls and public or personal property. Cross burnings or swastikas are generally a product of criminal bias. The same is true for vandalizing sacred sites, including hateful language spray-painted on houses of worship or destroying or defacing gravestones or memorials in a cemetery. Hate crimes may also include sexual assault and destruction of property.

Even while enforcing the federal law, with its wide protections, subjectivity plays a role in a perpetrator's guilt or innocence. In the FBI's 2015 *Hate Crime Data Collection Guidelines and Training Manual*, the agency outlines 14 specific criteria to define a hate crime. The 62-page document notes, "The mere fact the offender is biased against the victim's actual or perceived race, religion, disability, sexual orientation, ethnicity, gender, and/or gender identity does not mean that a hate crime was involved. Rather, the offender's criminal act must have been motivated, in whole or in part, by his or her bias. Motivation is subjective; therefore, it is difficult to know with certainty whether a crime was the result of the offender's bias." Such a hefty set of rules does not guarantee all police, prosecutors, and judges are aware of it.

Aside from the specificity of federal laws, states write their own statutes and have the power to include – or exclude – whomever they like. When hate crimes are prosecuted at the state level, as most are, federal laws may nonetheless apply, that is, if a federal jurisdiction is involved. For example, the federal HCPA, like any other federal law, requires federal enforcement, unless a state is specifically authorized to rely on its own (state) power. That power would be part of what the legal establishment calls "co-equal sovereignty," a system in which states and the federal government each remain supreme within their own spheres of influence. The doctrine looks on the nation and states as co-equal sovereign powers. In short, that means states and the federal government should not be interfering in each other's legal business.

Given the subjective nature of what constitutes a hate crime, leaving critical decisions, such as what qualifies as a hate crime, in the hands of law enforcement agents can be a tricky proposition. That's why it is critical that the victim of a hate crime be given every opportunity to describe the incident with such specific detail that a "reasonable person" would be terrified in the same situation. In court, the jury needs to know what that terror feels like.

If the hate crimes law in the state in which an incident occurs does specify legal protection on the basis of the victim's identity and the federal government is not able to pursue the case, the offender may be charged for a generalized offense not motivated by bias. Examples may include assault, aggravated assault, battery, criminal trespass, arson, murder, attempted murder, and other felonies or misdemeanors. In such a situation, the offense would not meet FBI Hate Crime Data Collection Guidelines and would not be counted in the FBI's annual hate crime data. Potential targets within the victim's same category and other marginalized people may never know the depth of hate in their own community.

After Dylann Roof was indicted by a federal grand jury for murdering nine African Americans at a Bible study session at a black church in Charleston in 2015, U.S. Attorney General Loretta Lynch told reporters, "It is important to note that South Carolina does not have a hate crimes statute and as a result, the state charges do not reflect the alleged hate crime offenses presented in the federal indictment . . . "

Roof was charged with violating the *federal* Hate Crimes Prevention Act. The AG said the State of South Carolina was *also* prosecuting Roof for murder, attempted murder, and firearms offenses. Lynch's comments underscore that, unlike other states, South Carolina makes no distinction relating those offenses to a hate crime.

Each state's hate crimes law is as selective as liberal and conservative lawmakers are able to finesse. Pursuing extremists is no less selective. Similarly, police departments may be influenced by the same political persuasions.

As noted previously, in 2017, for various reasons only 12.6 percent of law enforcement agencies nationwide – 2,040 out of 16,149 jurisdictions – reported hate crimes statistics to the FBI. To be fair, many of the other 14,109 police departments that did not submit data to the FBI may have had a justifiable reason for not doing so. Many would have experienced zero hate crimes, in which case the

FBI report reflects no incidents within that jurisdiction. Leeway may also be warranted for police departments in which a handful of overworked officers are employed. Yet, the public deserves to know which agencies are fulfilling their obligation to provide data, which are unable to for forgivable reasons, and which are delinquent. Otherwise, agencies that simply opt out of a process required in the federal Hate Crimes Statistics Act reduce the law to little more than a symbolic gesture.

It is noteworthy that even the comprehensive and inclusive HCPA does not include specific protocols or strategies to investigate or prosecute offenders. How state prosecutors choose to address hate crime cases varies as widely as the laws themselves.

Not All Victims Are Protected Equally: A Political Choice

LEGAL COMPLEXITY AND THE EXCLUSION OF some protected categories from many states' hate crimes laws means some Americans are protected in some states while the same categories of people in other states are not.

The absence of a universal agreement over which specific categories of people should be included in every state's hate crimes statute is another reason white supremacists feel justified in their hateful actions. Extremist logic leads to the conclusion: If any state legislature believes a certain group of people doesn't deserve to be protected in its hate crime law, it's okay for us to harass them.

Decisions about whom to protect in hate crimes laws rests with the U.S. Congress at the federal level and each state's legislature. The federal Hate Crimes Prevention Act (HCPA), passed by Congress, is an all-inclusive law. State-by-state decisions regarding protected categories is the domain of state legislators. This is where laws go sideways.

When any one group believes it needs legal protection and a state government believes it does not, the issue is cursed to an unresolved political quagmire that can take years to remedy, if ever.

The federal law is not a surrogate for state law. That is, when a state's hate crimes law does not protect a specific category of citizens, federal law may apply only under certain circumstances, e.g. when interstate commerce is involved, and not as a substitute for a state that chooses not to protect all of its residents equally.

In an era when the hate movement is emboldened by some of the most powerful voices in U.S. government, including the President, his advisors, and members of his cabinet, some state hate crimes laws remain restrictive – or are nonexistent.

Today, five states have no hate crimes laws at all: Arkansas, Georgia[36]**, Indiana, South Carolina, and Wyoming.** In these states, it is particularly important to monitor offenses that qualify as hate crimes under federal law in order to assure citizens that police are truly empowered to protect them. It is strangely ironic that the comprehensive federal Hate Crimes Prevention Act was named in part to recognize the violent hate-motivated murder of a Wyoming resident, Matthew Shepard, yet Shepard's own state has failed to write a hate crimes law of its own.

Today, 19 states do not include protection for people with disabilities and 15 states do not include sexual orientation or gender identity in their hate crimes law. Currently, proposed revisions to hate crimes laws are pending in at least five states: Alabama, Louisiana, New Jersey, Ohio, and Utah. According to the UCLA Law School's Hugh and Darling Law Library, a bill was proposed in the Mississippi legislature that would expand certain portions of its statutes to include sexual orientation. The same source reports that New Mexico's laws provide enhanced penalties for crimes "motivated by hate," but that state's hate crimes law does not identify specific protected categories.

On the positive side, in 2018 both the Human Rights Campaign and the National LGBTQ Task Force identified **18 states that include sexual orientation *and* gender identity in their hate crimes laws**: California, Colorado, Connecticut, Delaware, Hawaii, Illinois, Maryland, Massachusetts, Minnesota, Missouri, Nevada, New Hampshire, New Jersey, New Mexico, New York, Oregon, Rhode Island, and Washington. The District of Columbia also includes sexual orientation and gender identity in its state statute.

On the not-so-positive side, in addition to the five states with no hate crimes law, another **15 states *do not* include either sexual orientation *or* gender identity in their hate crime laws**: Alabama,

Alaska, Idaho, Michigan, Mississippi, Montana, North Carolina, North Dakota, Ohio, Oklahoma, Pennsylvania, South Dakota, Utah, Virginia and West Virginia.

Laws in 12 states protect on the basis of sexual orientation *but not gender identity*: Arizona, Florida, Iowa, Kansas, Kentucky, Louisiana, Maine, Nebraska, Tennessee, Texas, Vermont, and Wisconsin. Lambda Legal, a national organization that defends the rights of LGBTQ people, identifies two additional states, Indiana and Michigan, that protect employees of state and local governments from discrimination on the basis of sexual orientation, but do not include the same legal protection for employees in the private sector. In those states, hate crimes against LGBTQ victims must be prosecuted as an offense under a general state criminal law provision rather than under a state hate crimes statute.

Making decisions over who is to be protected by law is a common legislative practice. Historically, federal laws were also passed to restrict or *deny* rights to some categories of Americans. Exclusionary laws were adopted by all three branches of government at the federal, state, and municipal levels. As a result of the civil rights movement, laws passed since the 1960s tend to reflect a greater concern for social justice, although many have fallen remarkably short of their goal.

The most profound of such laws are the Civil Rights Act of 1964, which aimed to end segregation in public places and ban employment discrimination on the basis of race, color, religion, sex or national origin, and the Voting Rights Act of 1965, which prohibits discrimination in voting practices or procedures because of race and color.

Corporate Leadership

Considered one of the crowning achievements of the civil rights movement, after 55 years the Civil Rights Act has failed to significantly change the racial profile at many of the nation's most venerable public and private institutions, most importantly at the leadership level. Among Fortune 500 corporations at the end of 2018, three had black CEOs (Merck, TIAA, and J.C. Penney) and six had Asian leaders (Google, Microsoft, Adobe and Blackberry, and PepsiCo). Nine large companies were led by Latinos and 25 by women. Only one U.S. corporation had a gay CEO (Apple). Not a single Fortune 500 company at that time had a Muslim CEO. The Civil Rights Act will be closer to its target when the boards of directors and senior management teams at public and private institutions match the ethnic and gender composition of their workforce.

Similarly, after 28 years, the 1990 Americans with Disabilities Act (ADA), another revolutionary change in governmental policy regarding employment, has garnered 15 CEOs with learning disabilities; however, no corporate leader today is known to be physically disabled.

By the 1980s, when businesses attempted to be more deliberate in recruiting and hiring from a diversified pool of candidates, white employees called the practice reverse discrimination. Yet, today the ethnic profile at many businesses and institutions doesn't come close to matching the nation's population. And the nation's unemployment rate in 2018, 3.9 percent, is at the lowest point since 1969, with the exception of 2000 when it also dipped to 3.9 percent. What is the explanation for a high job availability and low rates of employment among people protected in federal laws passed over the past 55 years? Simple. It's all about racism and bigotry, the same forces that drive the hate movement.

In order for communities to change the social dynamics around protecting people against hate crimes, businesses have to model the way. Employment opportunities available to individuals in certain categories – women and men who are educated, skilled, and willing and available to work in their field – are often passed over in favor of white candidates. A common explanation offered by managers is, "the applicant wouldn't fit with our team…"

Most human resources professionals rely on the Civil Rights Act to achieve the law's intended purpose, that is, to end segregation in public places and ban employment discrimination. At corporations, small businesses, government agencies, and nonprofits where new employees are expected to fit into the culture of predominantly white male teams, with no effort to train or inspire the entire workforce to succeed, or where hiring goals are not achieved while applicants are available, those entities are either not serious about hiring a diverse workforce or their lofty goals amount to morally bankrupt window dressing.

On a larger scale, efforts to maintain communities in which all residents are expected to fit into the neighborhood are more likely to fit into the rubric of white supremacy. When expectations turn to practices in which residents of any community are subjected to malicious harassment, the Hate Crimes Prevention Act is the protector.

In pursuing hate crime charges, the federal HCPA *may* be followed by states that have not adopted their own law, although it doesn't always work that way. According to hate crimes investigator Mark Potok, "FBI Guidelines instruct police departments to report according to standards provided in the federal Hate Crimes Prevention Act, irrelevant of state statutes. For example, Alabama doesn't name sexual orientation as a protected category, but if Alabama police officers do their job the way the FBI is asking them to, they would nevertheless follow the national standards and report anti-gay offenses as hate crimes. They don't do it much." Potok added that although the FBI trains local police to follow federal criteria, some do not.

Most Americans are convinced that state and federal laws protect ALL citizens equally and that all police abide by the law. That is a fallacy.

Trying to identify which categories are protected in the hate crimes laws of all 50 states and the District of Columbia is a frustrating exercise. Not all websites that identify which categories are protected in each state are accurate. This may be because hate crime laws are subject to changes and not all websites are updated frequently. Websites of otherwise reputable and trustworthy organizations and institutions often include conflicting citations. Information in this chapter came from an analysis of listings on websites for the ADL, NAACP, and the UCLA Law School. **The most definitive source to confirm who is protected in the hate crime law for any state is the State Attorney General's Office.**

Ultimately, each state's decisions about who is protected under its hate crimes law are made by members of that state's Senate and House of Representatives. When and how state lawmakers decide whom to protect is a messy process often based on which constituents have the loudest voices and who makes the biggest political contributions. Although candidates in both camps rely on funding from Political Action Committees to get elected and support social and other issues, conservatives have a fundraising edge over liberals, according to the Center for Public Integrity, an independent, nonprofit investigative journalism organization.

Some of the most conservative lobbyists and PACs use covert strategies to appear inclusive and to get what they want from elected officials. One common trick is hiding under the cover of family-oriented or patriotic-sounding names like the Family Research Council or We The People, organizations that double as radical right wing hate groups. In addition to knowing who wants to represent a state legislative district or serve in the U.S. Congress, it is useful that voters also be aware of who is funding their election and reelection campaigns.

Perhaps it is because the categories most commonly excluded from state hate crimes laws are sexual orientation, gender identity, disabilities, and homelessness, that people in those groups are subjected to high rates of hate crime victimizations. What is alarming about *any* group being excluded is that people in commonly overlooked categories often experience the highest rates of malicious harassment. Further, people in these categories and others have reasons to not report hate crimes to police.

Sexual Orientation and Gender Identity

Hate crimes against LGBTQ victims are difficult to quantify because many choose to not report the incident to police. Some have a concern nothing will be done to change homophobic behaviors in public settings ("Why bother?"). Others dislike the thought of being interrogated by police and prosecutors. Closeted victims may fear being outed if they are identified by name in news reports.

According to the SPLC, LGBTQ people are among the favorite targets lone extremists and members of white supremacist groups choose to harass, beat up, or murder. Most of the defectors interviewed for this book acknowledged committing hate crimes against gay men, lesbians, gender non-conforming or transgender people. According to the Human Rights Campaign, 1,130 (15.7 percent) of all hate crimes reported nationwide by the FBI in 2017 were based on sexual orientation bias; 119 (1.6 percent) on gender identity bias. What data like these cannot tell us is how many anti-LGBTQ crimes are not reported to police.

Despite high numbers of bias crimes against LGBTQ people, sexual orientation and gender identity are two categories that some states and municipalities choose not to protect. In recent years, according to FBI data, malicious harassment based on sexual orientation fluctuated from a high of 20.8 percent of all U.S. hate crimes in 2013, to a low of 17.7 percent in 2015 and 2016.

Gender Identity represents a constantly rising number of hate crime victimizations, from a low of .5 percent in 2013 to a high of 2.0 percent in 2016, an increase of 300 percent. The FBI reported 46 offenses in 2017 were based on gender identity. Before 2012, the FBI didn't even account for gender identity offenses. Over the past five years, anti-transgender hate has intensified. The HRC reports that at least 23 transgender people were victims of fatal violence in the U.S. in 2016, more than in any other year on record.

Muslims, Sikhs, Hindus, and Arabs

Most hate crimes against Sikhs, Hindus, and to some extent, Arabs as well, are primarily anti-Muslim offenses committed by Islamophobic extremists unable to distinguish one group from another. The Muslim population in the U.S. is nonetheless a central target of white supremacists.

In 2018, the Council on American-Islamic Relations (CAIR), the nation's largest Muslim civil rights and advocacy organization, reported that during the second quarter of that year, it received 1,006 reports of "potential bias incidents," with 431 of the reports determined to contain an identifiable element of anti-Muslim bias. Not all of these crimes will be included in the FBI's annual report because some offenses are not reported to police and those that are reported may not be prosecuted as hate crimes, but as non-bias-oriented offenses.

Sikhs practice a completely separate religion from Muslims or Hindus, yet since 9/11, followers of all three religions have felt the ire of many Americans for no justifiable reason other than their appearance, often based on assumptions about head coverings. Although the religious practice of head coverings has been an integral part of Christianity, Judaism, and Islam dating back to the 13th century BC, more American Muslims, Sikhs, and Hindu men and women wear head coverings in public today than ever before. White nationalists, neo-Nazis, and other extremists lump any person that doesn't look like them into one more threat opposing their image of white supremacy. Their rationale for harassing people in all three categories boils down the common and blissfully ignorant condemnation: "They all look alike."

In 2012, what were then called "anti-Islamic" hate crimes accounted for 130 of the 5,796 hate crimes reported nationwide. That year, bias crimes against Sikhs or Hindus were not yet even recognized by the FBI. In 2014, the FBI modified the category that accounts for anti-Islamic malicious harassment, specifically adding "Muslims" as a group in the Bureau's annual hate crimes count. That year, 154 of 5,479 hate crimes nationwide targeted Muslims and other anti-Islamic groups.

Until 2015, although the federal HCPA included religion as a protected category, the law did not specifically include Sikhs, Hindus, or Arabs. As a result, hate crimes against individuals in those three groups were listed as anti-Muslim hate crimes or as other categories, even though the victims were not Muslims. That year, Congress made the political choice to authorize a change in the FBI's Hate Crime Data Collection Guidelines to specifically include all three categories.

In 2015, the first year Sikhs were added to the FBI count of hate crimes, six anti-Sikh hate crimes were counted. In the months following the 9/11 attacks, more than 300 hate crime incidents against Sikhs were reported, according to The Sikh Coalition. As with crimes reported by CAIR, not all of those offenses were reflected in the FBI annual report. CAIR was founded by volunteers on the night of September 11, 2001 in response to a torrent of violent attacks against Muslim Americans throughout the United States. Two years later, 20 anti-Sikh crimes were reported nationwide, along with 11 anti-Hindu offenses. It took 14 years to include Sikhs and Hindus in the HCPA.

FBI data do not include the carnage in Christchurch, New Zealand, where 49 people were killed in shootings at two mosques in 2019, one more indicator of religious conflict on a global scale.

Between 2012 and 2017, the number of anti-religious hate crimes ballooned by 44 percent. Between 2017 and 2019, the most horrific mass murders and attacks were hate crimes against Jewish people and committed inside their own places of worship by lone gunmen. This includes the 11 murdered and seven injured at the Tree of Life Synagogue in Pittsburg (2018) and the death of one and three injured at the Chabad of Poway, California (2019).

People with Disabilities

Malicious harassment against people with disabilities (PWD) is often referred to as the invisible hate crime, mostly because PWDs are frequently not reported to police. Including five states with no hate crimes laws, an analysis by the ADL identifies the 19 states with hate crime statutes that do not protect on the basis of disabilities: Arkansas, Georgia, Idaho, Indiana, Kansas, Kentucky, Michigan, Mississippi, Montana, North Carolina, North Dakota, Ohio, Pennsylvania, South Carolina, South Dakota, Utah, Virginia, West Virginia, and Wyoming.

Not protecting PWD victims is a significant omission. A 2010 study by the U.S. Census Bureau found that 19 percent of Americans have a disability, half of which were identified as severe.

Defector Floyd Cochran told me he was forced to absorb a tough reality in 1992. After serving as the fifth-ranking member of the Idaho-based Aryan Nations, Cochran told me he abandoned the movement after a senior leader of the group refused to let him leave a Hitler Youth Festival to be with his four-year-old son during an emergency operation to correct the boy's cleft palate. When Cochran asked the group's head of security if he could leave the event, he was told, his son's ailment "…is a genetic defect. When we come to power, he'll have to be euthanized."

American neo-Nazi groups adhere to the barbaric Hitlerian doctrine that "the purity of [German] blood requires the elimination of the weakest and most defenseless." More than 112 of the 1,020 hate groups identified by SPLC in 2019 are distinctly committed to neo-Nazi ideology. From their narrow perspective, people with disabilities are an apt target.

In addition to being excluded from many states' hate crimes laws, PWDs are often omitted from the FBI's annual hate crimes count. For example, let's say a person in a wheelchair is verbally attacked and threatened in a state that does not protect on the basis of disabilities in its hate crimes law. Now say the incident escalates and the offender pushes the chair down a flight of stairs, leaving the victim critically injured. Unless the wheelchair was manufactured in another state (activating the interstate commerce protection), the case cannot be prosecuted as a federal offense because it doesn't meet HCPA requirements. Nor can the case be pursued under the state's hate crimes law because the law does not protect people with disabilities. The offender could be accused of a crime with less severe sentencing requirements, but not of a hate crime. Plus, that state would omit such a brutal attack from its hate crimes count for the year, as if it didn't happen.

In 2017, 116 of 7,175 (1.6 percent) hate crime victims were people with disabilities, according to the FBI, 32 with physical disabilities and 84 with mental disabilities. Unlike incidents against victims in other categories, the number of bias-oriented crimes against people with disabilities stays fairly constant. In 2012, the FBI reported 92 of 5,928 (1.55) percent faced a similar fate.

This constituency is used to being oh-so-politely ignored in certain environments, such as restaurants and other public and private venues. Many are routinely challenged by a lack of access to public or private accommodations. Being unsure whether an act of openly hostile bigotry against them qualifies as a hate crime is not only humiliating and hard to fathom, it is also a key reason crimes against them are underreported.

Homelessness

The FBI's hate crimes analysis does not identify offenses committed against homeless victims.

Currently, only three states, Florida, Maine, and Maryland, and the District of Columbia include homelessness or homeless status as a protected category in their hate crimes law. Several defectors talked specifically about physically harassing, assaulting, or beating up homeless people during their time in the movement. For example, Julie Miller said her first husband would go out on "bum rolls" to beat up gays and homeless men.

Homelessness is one of the most widely overlooked categories and one of growing concern as many municipalities report increasing numbers of homeless people. It is also a difficult category to track because a victim' homeless status may not be identifiable by the offender. Also, offenders may avoid using specific anti-homelessness language while committing a bias crime. For those reasons, the number of hate crimes based on an individual's homeless status is extremely difficult to quantify with any degree of certainty.

Prisons

Political choice has little to do with assigning a convicted hate criminal to a federal or a state institution. However, where a prisoner is assigned is based on whether the offense was prosecuted as a federal crime or a state crime. State legislators may choose to protect more categories as a way of maintaining state control over offenders under their own sovereignty, but have little motivation to do so.

In general, hate crime offenders convicted of a federal offense are assigned to a federal facility; those found guilty of a state offense are assigned to a state prison. The Federal Bureau of Prisons attempts to send inmates to facilities commensurate with the offender's security and program needs and within a 500-mile radius of their residence.

Sentencing a prisoner to a federal or a state institution makes a world of difference. Federal and state prisons are completely separate institutions, funded differently and with different rules. Federal prisons are recognized for allowing inmates better food, quarters, and amenities than are permitted in state institutions. State prison budgets are tighter and allow fewer comforts. They are also more numerous and have higher levels of security than federal institutions.

In any prison, good behavior is relative, especially for those convicted of a hate crime. How one is visually evaluated and treated by prison staff and fellow cellmates is even more critical for those with neo-Nazi or white supremacist tattoos, the most common way to identify an incarcerated extremist.

Many defectors said that how cellmates treated them in the general prison population during their incarceration often made their life a living hell. In cases where hate-prone inmates are harassed because of their tattoos, federal prison officials are more responsive to requests for protection than their counterparts in state facilities. For example, when Angela King first entered a federal prison, she was immediately put in solitary confinement. The concern was not related to her crime; the isolation was imposed for Angela's own safety and protection because her tattoos may have incited violence against her.

At a federal prison, prisoners may be reassigned to another cell or moved to another facility to shield inmates from racial violence or negative interactions at the hands of other inmates. This practice is often used as a mechanism to protect prisoners of color from malicious harassment by white supremacist prison gangs. In contrast, at many state prisons, moving a cellmate for such a reason is against internal policy. Consequently, inmate-on-inmate crimes are higher in state facilities.

Cellmates have an uncanny ability to discern whether other prisoners are allies or adversaries. White supremacists generally rely on tattoos and a covert network to communicate who they are to the rest of the prison population. This is particularly useful to the whites-only prison group known as the Aryan Brotherhood (aka the Brotherhood), who broadcast their identity via tattoos such as the words "The Aryan Brotherhood," AB, 666, and Nazi or Celtic symbols. The initial purpose of the Brotherhood was to protect white inmates from being physically attacked by blacks and Hispanics. The group's focus today is on white domination inside any prison's walls.

Inmates have been known to use the prison environment to recruit likely supporters and harass those they oppose. The Brotherhood started at San Quentin State Prison in the 1960s. By the 1980s, its tactical maneuvers had progressed from personal protection to extortion, sometimes dealing in narcotics, weapons, and murder-for-hire, all inside the confines of a prison. The estimated 10,000 members of the Brotherhood nationwide comprise less than 0.1 percent of the total prison population. Yet, according to the FBI, the Brotherhood is responsible for up to 20 percent of murders in federal prisons.

According to the ADL, "Driven by a belief in their superiority, white supremacist prison gangs contribute to increased racial tensions and violence in American penitentiaries. Not only do their activities undermine prison security, but their extreme rhetoric and animosity toward other races often stay with gang members long after their release."

Legal Exclusions:
The Roots of American Extremism

FOR ALL OF ITS PROGRESS AS A NATION, America has a sordid past, tainted by laws and policies that allowed some to prosper while others were denied the same rights or forced to work in servitude. The practices of the past continue to haunt certain specific populations.

When Hiram Revels was elected to the U.S. Senate in 1870, the first African-American in Congress broke the mold of what had been an all-white brotherhood. Until the appointment of Thurgood Marshall in 1967, the U.S. Supreme Court was also exclusively white, as was the Office of the President before the election of Barack Obama in 2008. People of color were arbitrarily denied access to the loftiest ranks of government in the early days of the nation's founding, leaving the rights of all Americans under the selective control of white decision makers.

The pattern of exclusion at the highest levels of government rolled downhill to anyone who didn't conform to the nation's expectations of exemplary Americans. That history is slowly changing with the election of Congressmembers who come closer to matching the nation's increasingly diverse population. With those changes comes a greater likelihood that "freedom and justice for all" will eventually embrace every American equally.

Throughout the nation's history, the white male-dominated political power structure has, from time to time, approved heavy-handed
laws written to deny or limit citizenship to hopeful immigrants from
Africa, Asia, and Spanish-speaking countries who came to the states
expecting what most Europeans received when they arrived. Even some
European countries have had limits imposed on the number of immigrants allowed to enter the U.S. Other groups have been marginalized
and denied the same Constitutional freedoms afforded the majority of
Americans, only because of their skin color, ethnicity, country of origin, religion, sexual orientation, gender identity, or some other variable
deemed "inferior" by lawmakers. Yet, no other population has suffered
more than the indigenous people who occupied the land before white
settlers arrived and their ancestors.

Over time, the most egregious laws, policies, and practices were
reversed or rescinded by elected officials who value the Constitution
and the Bill of Rights as drivers of the nation's conscience. As a result
of the civil rights movement through the 1960s, inclusive laws like the
Civil Rights Act and the Voting Rights Act were adopted to prohibit
discriminatory practices in public and private institutions and in the
voting booth.

But, even those laws did not erase the physical and psychological scars in their wake. And, as the nation tried to heal the wounds
from restrictions that later proved to be discriminatory, new ones were
imposed to coincide with the latest political conflicts.

**It is no coincidence that the groups white supremacists target
as "inferior" today are the very same populations that have been
disenfranchised and discriminated against by their government
throughout the country's history.**

Since the earliest days of the Republic, many Americans have been
stripped of their civil rights, ostracized into segregated ghettos, barrios,
or reservations; forced to live only where white men and bankers said
they could live; and attend schools separated by racial barriers and
economic status. Hopeful immigrants were sent back to their original
homeland or suffered more dire fates. Laws that denied basic human
rights, now recognized as blatantly discriminatory, established a proto-
type that validated white superiority.

Those who were able to rise above selectively negative treatment in schools, colleges, the armed services, and elsewhere, had to prove themselves by working harder, longer, and with fewer luxuries than their predominantly white, male, Christian, straight, or able-bodied colleagues and coworkers.

America was born out of the passion of religious radicals. In 1620, after years of religious persecution, Protestant separatists came to what is now New England to sever ties with the Church of England. As they colonized and expanded, they built homes and farms on land that had been cultivated for generations by indigenous people. After some early bargaining to borrow and use Indian land and farming grounds, the pioneers wanted more. Want begat demand.

Treaties and settlements were negotiated between government agencies and indigenous tribal leaders to manage native land. By 1830, the colonies had branched so far into the Westward Expansion that Congress saw fit to enact the Indian Removal Act, ushering Indians to federal territories west of the Mississippi River in exchange for the ancestral homelands they inhabited before the birth of Christ. Much of the expansion was in the name of American enterprise and to support a growing economy.

But that didn't stop the government from trampling over well-crafted treaties and court decisions. A recent publication issued by the U.S. State Department's Office of the Historian commented on past agreements and the Indian Removal Act, "The government sometimes violated both treaties and Supreme Court rulings to facilitate the spread of European Americans westward across the continent." This was not new information to generations of Native Americans.

As Army troops and early citizen militias began the mass genocide of Native populations, European-Americans turned the concept of Manifest Destiny into entitlement, proprietary rights, and public domain. Over time, the national focus shifted from controlling and murdering native people to obtaining free labor from *any* group that could be manipulated by the dominant culture. Starting in the 1400s, the slave trade brought shiploads of black workers from Africa to the Americas against their will, a move that gained momentum in the cotton and tobacco fields of the South and split the nation into civil war.

Today, public commentary from the Office of the President legitimizes white supremacist thinking with a not-so-subtle seal of approval and the use of unsubstantiated accusations and derogatory epithets to demean women, people of color, Muslims, journalists, and anyone he doesn't see in his own image. Although the nation's elected officials have always determined which groups can benefit from the country's largess, such Presidential hubris hasn't been experienced to such an extent in post-Civil War history.

The following list demonstrates how laws, policies, and practices imposed by Presidents, Congress, or the U.S. Supreme Court have fostered the modern-day hate movement.

A Sampling of Exclusionary Laws and Legal Actions

All branches of American government played a role in a structural and institutional system created to deny or curtail rights to some, based on standards predominantly defined by white, Christian, heteronormative men. These policies, almost all of which have since been abolished, formed a foundation upon which hate groups have continued the practice of extremist ideologies. One remaining active policy is Executive Order 13780, the Muslim Ban signed by President Donald Trump in 2017.

When they were passed, these directives were not considered to have been motivated by malice or by beliefs deemed extreme at the time. Yet, they became law, written with the distinct intent to prevent citizenship or to deny civil rights to segments of the American population. Today, discrimination that was once legal and later ruled unconstitutional continues in the form of institutional racism as reflected in disparities regarding wealth, income, criminal justice, employment, housing, health care, political power and education, among other factors.

The laws, court decisions, and presidential orders listed below provide a backdrop to the mindset of legal exclusion. **This list offers only a sampling of laws and policies adopted or enacted to eliminate or restrict the civil liberties of specific populations and is not intended to include all such actions.**

Such regulations show no signs of stopping.

Commonwealth of Virginia Defines Who is Black (1705-1924)

In 1705, the Commonwealth of Virginia defined any child, grandchild, or great grandchild of a Negro as "mulatto." In 1866, the state decreed that every person having one fourth or more Negro blood shall be deemed a "colored person." In 1910, the percentage was changed to one sixteenth. In 1924, The Virginia Racial Purity Act defined black persons as those having *any* trace of African ancestry – creating the "one-drop" rule. Because other states defined African Americans differently at the time, historian James Horton notes in the PBS series *RACE – the Power of An Illusion*, that "one could cross a state line and, literally, legally change race."

The Naturalization Act of 1790

The Naturalization Act of 1790 allowed citizenship *for whites only*. African Americans were not guaranteed citizenship until 1868, when the Fourteenth Amendment to the Constitution was ratified. In the early 20th century, many immigrants petitioned the courts to be legally designated white to gain citizenship. Before the Indian Citizenship Act was passed in 1924, Native Americans became citizens only through individual treaties and intermarriage.

Indian Removal Act of 1830

The Indian Removal Act, signed by President Andrew Jackson, was created to "relocate" Native American tribes living east of the Mississippi River, moving them to lands west of the river.

The Mexican-American War (1846-1848)

This war against Mexico was influenced by the administration of U.S. President James K. Polk, who believed the United States had a "Manifest Destiny" to spread across the continent to the Pacific Ocean. The war ended with the Treaty of Guadalupe Hidalgo (1848). By signing the treaty, Mexico recognized the U.S. annexation of Texas (1845) and agreed to sell California and the rest of its territory north of the Rio Grande.

Through the mid-to-late 1800s and early 1900s, the U.S. "obtained" from Mexico, generally by force, land that encompassed California, New Mexico, Arizona, Nevada, Utah, Texas, and parts of Wyoming and Colorado. Since then, generations of former Mexican families (now Americans) whose ancestors were born in those and other border states before they became U.S. territories, have faced ridicule and rejection, including being identified as immigrants. As many American ancestors of Mexican families say, "We didn't cross the border, the border crossed us."

The People v. Hall *(1854)*

In The People v. Hall, the California Supreme Court established that Chinese Americans and Chinese immigrants had no rights to testify against white citizens. The Court reversed the murder conviction of a white man, ruling that the testimony of key Chinese witnesses was inadmissible because "no Black or mulatto person, or Indian, shall be allowed to give evidence in favor of, or against a white man." Chief Justice Charles J. Murray remarked: "The Chinese are a race of people whom nature has marked as inferior . . . The same rule, which would admit them to testify, would admit them to all the equal rights of citizenship, and we might soon see them at the polls, in the jury box, upon the bench, and in our legislative halls. This is not a speculation . . . but an actual and present danger."

The Homestead Act of 1862

This law encouraged a flood of squatters to invade Native American land in the Midwest. Already suffering from decimation of the American buffalo, their most critical resource for food, clothing, and shelter, nomadic American Indian tribes were forced to relocate to government reservations.

Chinese Exclusion Act of 1882

The Chinese Exclusion Act was the first major law restricting immigration to the U.S. It was enacted in response to economic fears, especially on the West Coast, where native-born Americans attributed unemployment and declining wages to Chinese workers whom they viewed as racially inferior. Signed into law by President Chester A. Arthur, the act effectively halted Chinese immigration for ten years and prohibited Chinese people from becoming U.S. citizens. Ten years later, **The Geary Act of 1892** extended the Chinese exclusion for another ten years before becoming permanent in 1902. The Chinese Exclusion Act fostered other immigration laws through the 1920s, extending its restrictions over 60 years. The law was repealed by Congress in 1943.

The Dawes Act of 1887

The Dawes Act, also known as the General Allotment Act, authorized the President to survey American Indian tribal land and divide it into allotments for individual Indians. The policy focused specifically on breaking up reservations by granting land allotments to individual tribal groups. Purportedly adopted to protect Indian property rights, particularly during the land rushes of the 1890s, land designated for Indians included desert or near-desert lands unsuitable for farming, creating other complications. Many Indians weren't interested in agriculture or couldn't afford the tools, animals, seed, and other resources necessary to get started.

Jim Crow Segregation (1887)

Jim Crow was the name of the racial caste system which operated primarily, but not exclusively, in southern and border states, between 1877 and the mid-1960s. Beginning in the late 19th century, southern states codified a system of anti-black laws and practices that, in essence, separated African Americans into an "inferior" class in which whites were deemed superior and entitled to certain services and amenities. The laws were named after a fictional slave in a song and dance routine performed by a white entertainer in the 1830's and 1840s.

The new social order, reinforced through violence and intimidation, affected schools, public transportation, jobs, housing, voting rights, and private life. During the Jim Crow era, poor and wealthy whites were united, while African Americans were denied freedom of assembly and movement, as well as equality in the courts or full participation as citizens.

Alien Land Laws (1889-1946)

Alien land laws were generally associated with attempts by western states to limit the presence and permanence of Japanese immigrants from the late 1880s through the end of World War II. For example, in 1889 the Washington State Constitution banned selling land to "aliens not eligible for citizenship," which at the time exclusively meant immigrants from Asian countries. In California, the **Alien Land Law of 1913** (also known as **the Webb-Haney Act**) permitted leases lasting up to three years, but prohibited "aliens" from owning agricultural land or possessing long-term leases over such property.

Plessy v. Ferguson (1896)

This 1896 U.S. Supreme Court decision (7-1) upheld the constitutionality of state laws requiring racial segregation in private businesses, particularly railroads. Under the "separate but equal" doctrine, the ruling held that laws intended to achieve racial segregation through separate but equal facilities, a concept generally defined by white men, and did not violate the 14th Amendment to the Constitution. The Plessy decision was overturned in 1954 by the landmark Brown v. Board of Education of Topeka, Kansas, a unanimous decision of the U.S. Supreme Court. The ruling found that state-sanctioned segregation of public schools was a violation of the 14th amendment and was therefore unconstitutional.

United States v. Wong Kim Ark (1898)

In a more inclusive move, the U.S. Supreme Court case of United States v. Wong Kim Ark first established the precedent of birthright in 1898. The Court ruled that a Chinese man born in America to immigrant parents is a citizen even though his parents are *not* eligible for citizenship. Conversely, throughout the 19th and 20th centuries, Asians consistently fought for, and were denied, the same inclusion extended to European immigrants.

Takao Ozawa v. United States (1922)

In Takao Ozawa v. United States, the U.S. Supreme Court ruled unanimously that native Japanese are not white. Ozawa petitioned the court to be identified as a naturalized citizen. The Court concluded that Ozawa, a Japanese-American who was born in Japan but had lived in the United States for 20 years, was ineligible for naturalization because white meant "Caucasian." The court deemed Ozawa to be part of the Mongolian people based on the scientific description of Mongolian," an "unassimilable race." The Court further held that Japanese were not "free white persons" within the meaning of the law.

United States v. Bhagat Singh Thind, (1923)

Less than a year after the Ozawa case, in U.S. v. Bhagat Singh Thind, the Supreme Court ruled unanimously that Asian Indians were ineligible for citizenship because U.S. law allowed only "free whites" to become naturalized citizens. The case resulted in the exclusion of all Asians from obtaining naturalized citizenship. Thind, a Sikh immigrant from Punjab, India, enlisted in the U.S. Army before the end of World War I. In 1918, he received his citizenship certificate. The Immigration and Naturalization Service did not agree with the district court's granting citizenship and revoked it on the grounds that Thind was not a "free white man."

Although anthropologists had defined the East Indian population as part of the Caucasian race, which made Thind "scientifically white," the court argued science is "too subjective" to be used as a way to identify race, concluding, "The average man knows perfectly well that there are unmistakable and profound differences" between races. In short, the Court found that, like Japanese [in the Ozawa case], East Indians were not "free white persons" and, therefore, racially ineligible for citizenship. The Court declared whiteness should be based on "the common understanding of the white man."

Historians and others believe that in the seemingly contradictory Ozawa and Thind decisions, the Court failed to specify what race is and instead argued what race is not.

Immigration Act of 1924 (aka The Johnson-Reed Act)

Congress passed the Immigration Act of 1924 to limit the number of immigrants allowed entry into the United States through a national origins quota. This law ended further immigration from Japan, while restricting the number of immigrants to the U.S. from southern and eastern Europe. The law meant that even Asians not previously prevented from immigrating – Japanese in particular – would no longer be admitted to the United States. It also targeted Japanese, whose entry had already been controlled through non-legislative regulations. The law was also aimed at Jews, Italians, Slavs, and Greeks, who had immigrated in large numbers after 1890.

The Immigration and Nationality Act of 1952 modified the national origins quota system introduced by the Immigration Act, rescinding the earlier law's prohibition on Asian immigration. The national origins quota system was eliminated in 1965 with the passage of the Immigration and Naturalization Act.

The National Origins Act of 1929

This law capped overall immigration to the U.S. at 150,000 per year and barred Asian immigration. The law was repealed by **the Magnuson Act in 1943** during World War II, when China was an ally in the war against imperial Japan. The Magnuson Act limited Chinese immigrants to an annual quota of 105 new entry visas per year. This "national-origin only policy" was not eliminated until passage of the **Immigration Act of 1965**, which allowed Chinese immigration to the U.S. to resume – after 80 years of exclusion.

Also, in the 40 years between 1889 and passage of the National Origins Act, immigration to the U.S. from southern and eastern Europe skyrocketed. Many new arrivals were labeled "ethnics," employed in undesirable low-wage jobs, and forced to live in urban ghettos. European ethnic groups, notably Irish, Germans, and Italians, were deemed "*inferior*," because they were believed to be "not fully white."

Executive Order 9066 (1942)
Korematsu v. United States (1944)
Trump v. Hawaii (2018)

Less than three months after the Japanese attack on Pearl Harbor, President Franklin D. Roosevelt signed **Executive Order**

9066. The order forced the relocation and internment of between 110,000 and 120,000 people of Japanese ancestry who lived in designated areas in the western U.S. The internment was applied to all people of Japanese descent, regardless of their citizenship or loyalty to the U.S. The order was in effect until the end of World War II. The same executive order and other war-time restrictions were applied to smaller numbers of U.S. residents of Italian or German descent. Some 3,200 Italian immigrants were arrested and more than 300 of them placed in internment camps. About 11,000 German residents – including some naturalized citizens – were arrested and more than 5,000 interned.

In 1944, in **Korematsu v. United States**, the U.S. Supreme Court, in a 6-3 decision, upheld the constitutionality of Executive Order 9066, and ruled that the forced relocation and internment of *all* people of Japanese origin did not violate the Constitution. The plaintiff, Fred Korematsu, was a 23-year-old Japanese American citizen who refused the order to go to one of the Japanese camps in 1942. He was convicted of violating the order and the Court upheld his conviction. The Court held that it was within the power of Congress and the Executive to exclude all those of Japanese ancestry from the West Coast war area at the time they did.

The Court's Korematsu decision has long been reviled by legal scholars and others, and in 1998, Korematsu received the Presidential Medal of Freedom, the nation's highest civilian honor, from President Bill Clinton. The decision was finally repudiated by the U.S. Supreme Court in 2018 in **Trump v. Hawaii**, which involved the constitutionality of a Muslim travel ban to the U.S. issued by President Trump by Proclamation. The Court's majority stated that the *Korematsu* case "was gravely wrong the day it was decided, has been overruled in the court of history, and – to be clear – 'has no place in law under the Constitution.'"

The repudiation of *Korematsu*, however, did not help the plaintiffs in Trump v. Hawaii. The Court, in a 5-4 decision, reversed a preliminary injunction against the ban while the case worked its way through the lower courts. The plaintiffs argued that the ban was unconstitutionally discriminatory, based solely on animus against

Muslims, and that the ban should not be enforced while it was being pursued in the lower courts. The Court refused to uphold the lower courts' injunction against the ban while the case was being heard in the lower courts.

Post-World War II FHA Restrictions/Redlining

After World War II, when veterans returned from the battle lines, the Federal Housing Authority (FHA) created the GI Bill to help veterans find affordable housing. During the post-war era, both the FHA and banks began to restrict subsidies for African Americans, that is, FHA housing benefits did not extend to black veterans. In a practice now known as redlining, FHA and banks denied housing and other services, either directly or by selectively raising prices to residents within certain areas, based on the racial or ethnic makeup. The most affected neighborhoods, circled by a red line on local maps, were largely populated by African Americans. At the same time the FHA and banks were controlling GI Bill funding, property owners started to add restrictive covenants that prevented other ethnic minorities and Jews from owning property.

Anti-LGBT Army Regulations (1942-2010)
DOD Directive 1332.14 (1982)

Beginning in 1942, Army mobilization regulations were put into effect so that homosexuals were routinely discharged, regardless of whether they had engaged in sexual conduct while serving. In 1982 the Department of Defense issued DOD Directive 1332.14, stating, "Homosexuality is incompatible with military service."

Don't Ask/Don't Tell (DADT, 1993)

In theory, Defense Directive 1304.26, more commonly known as Don't Ask/Don't Tell, ordered that military applicants not be asked about their sexual orientation. The mandate also barred gay, lesbian, or bisexual persons from disclosing their sexual orientation or speaking about such relationships. The policy was instituted by President Bill Clinton and became effective in

February 1994. Despite public opposition, DADT was upheld five times in federal court, and in one Supreme Court case. Congress rescinded the law and President Barack Obama signed the repeal in 2010.

Defense of Marriage Act (DOMA, 1996)
United States v. Windsor (2013)
Windsor Obergefell v. Hodges (2015)

Passed in 1996, DOMA defined marriage for federal purposes as "the union of one man and one woman," and allowed states to refuse to recognize same-sex marriages granted under the laws of other states. The law selectively deprived LGBTQ couples of some 1,138 protections and responsibilities that marriage provides at the federal level.

Originally proposed as a Constitutional Amendment, the law passed both chambers with significant majorities [85-14 in the Senate; 342-67 in the House of Representatives]. President Clinton signed the legislation into law in September 1996.

DOMA was later reversed in two landmark decisions by the United States Supreme Court. In a 2013 case, **United States v. Windsor**, the court ruled (5-4), that restricting marriage to only opposite-sex unions was unconstitutional.

In 2015, the court ruled in **Obergefell v. Hodges** (5-4) that state-level bans on same-sex marriage were unconstitutional, making marriage equality legal in all 50 states.

Transgender Military Ban (2019)

In 2017, President Trump announced via Twitter a policy to ban transgender service members. The move blocked individuals who have been diagnosed with a condition known as gender dysphoria from serving with limited exceptions. It also specifies that individuals without the condition can serve, but only if they do so according to the sex they were assigned at birth.

In January 2019, the U.S. Supreme Court allowed the Trump transgender ban to go into effect while lower courts continue to hear arguments against it.

Executive Orders 13769 and 13780 (The Muslim Ban, 2017)

Executive Order 13769, titled **Protecting the Nation from Foreign Terrorist Entry into the United States,** often referred to as the Muslim ban or the travel ban, was signed by President Donald Trump in 2017. The order was in effect from January 27, 2017, until March 16, 2017, before being blocked as unconstitutional by various courts. Executive Order 13769 lowered the number of refugees to be admitted into the U.S. in 2017 to 50,000, suspended the U.S. Refugee Admissions Program (USRAP) for 120 days, and suspended the entry of Syrian refugees indefinitely. The countries most affected were Iran, Iraq, Libya, Somalia, Sudan, Syria, and Yemen. More than 700 travelers were detained, and tens of thousands of visas were revoked.

Executive Order 13769 was superseded by **Executive Order 13780** when President Trump signed a revised order with the same title on March 6, 2017. The order limits travel to the U.S. from certain countries, and bars entry for all refugees who do not possess either a visa or valid travel documents. The order was subsequently revised by two presidential proclamations. As of the most recent revision of Executive Order 13780, travel is banned on tourist or business visas for nationals from Libya and Yemen, some government officials of Venezuela; and all except student and exchange visitor visas for nationals from Iran. The order also bans immigrant visas for nationals from Somalia, North Korea, and Syria. In the **Trump v. Hawaii** decision (cited above), the U.S. Supreme Court upheld the most recent version of Executive Order 13780 in June 2018.

Resources for this chapter include the ACLU, SPLC, ADL, *Washington Post, New York Times,* CNN, and other media, as well as various law libraries and online references.

The following list of online resources can provide more information about additional laws, policies, and governmental actions instituted to deny legal entry into the U.S., to restrict or eliminate freedoms to specific Americans, and to separate Americans from one another:

• American Civil Liberties Union https://www.aclu.org/cases/lesbian-and-gay-rights/windsor-v-united-states
• *Race – The power of an Illusion*, PBS http://www.pbs.org/race/000_General/000_00-Home.htm
• History.com http://www.history.com/topics/mexican-american-war
• History Matters http://historymatters.gmu.edu/d/5076/
• Densho Encyclopedia http://encyclopedia.densho.org/Alien_land_laws/
• Library of Congress http://www.loc.gov/exhibits/civil-rights-act/segregation-era.html
• Ourdocuments.gov http://www.ourdocuments.gov/doc.php?flash=true&doc=50
• SCOTUSblog https://www.scotusblog.com/
• Thealamo.org http://thealamo.org/history/the-1836-battle/index.html

Reshaping the Dominant Culture

LAWS AND NATIONAL POLICIES INFLUENCE HOW the dominant culture perceives categories of people based on skin color, gender, religion, and other variables. The U.S. culture is rooted in a semblance of political, social, and economic practices in which sub-groups, sometimes called co-cultures, are also present. The dominant population merges together a variety of co-cultures into a set of languages, religions, social values, and customs that guide behaviors and social norms of both majority and minority groups.

But, lingering in the background are projections from the U.S. Census Bureau that show the American population is shifting and the dominant culture is shifting along with it, thereby challenging the notion of "majorities" and "minorities."

At its core, culture is the way we do things; how we conduct ourselves, with degrees of flexibility within the context of a specific environment. The culture in a workplace is not the same as in our home. We are expected to behave differently in a house of worship than we would at a bar. In certain cities, local districts such as Broadway or Chinatown, each has its own unique subculture; Broadway in New York City has a different character than Broadway in Seattle. Chinatown in San Francisco is not the same as Chinatown in Boston.

A subculture or co-culture is a cultural group within a larger culture, often having beliefs or interests at variance with those of the larger culture. Subcultures and co-cultures form a subset of values and norms practiced by others within any cultural grouping. Subcultures often do not conform with the dominant culture, which can make members feel subservient, unless or until they adopt the beliefs and norms of the majority. This dynamic has strengthened the development of distinctive communities and neighborhoods in which inhabitants feel comfortable with others who look like, talk like, and act like themselves.

Over time, cross-cultural collaborations form so that subcultures can exist within the dominant group. For the most part, people from different races, religions, sexual orientations, and others learn to coexist with one another without violating another person's values or beliefs. When any group is not accepted by the dominant culture, conflicts too often escalate from rejection to violence.

To a significant degree, the dominant American culture is largely responsible for the rise and continuity of the hate movement. Populations unable or unwilling to conform to mainstream American social values and behaviors are put on the defensive and pressured to adapt – or suffer the consequences of a rejective majority.

In a nation primarily comprised of immigrants, some of whom look very different from one another, practice diverse religions and have conflicting lifestyles, the hate movement's principal aim is to ensure the dominant culture survives. Although the American culture has been maturing over centuries, rising birth rates among certain racial groups, increases in bi-racial families, immigration changes, and other population variables translate to a menacing threat extremists are unwilling to accept.

Recent U.S. Census Bureau predictions forecast significant demographic changes. The dominant culture is rapidly being subsumed by groups otherwise called "minorities." By 2043, according to USCB projections, whites will no longer make up the majority of Americans. At that point, the dominant culture is *destined* to become more inclusive.

As the nation grows and transforms, one option is to accept the norms of emerging population groups that prefer to maintain much of their own culture, learn from one another's traditions, and live harmoniously. That vision was first established in 1787 when the framers of the U.S. Constitution set the new nation's goals . . . *"to form a more perfect union, establish justice, insure domestic tranquility, provide for the common defense, promote the general welfare, and secure the blessings of liberty to ourselves and our posterity . . . "*

Over the nation's history, as immigrants from continents beyond Europe increased, domestic tranquility and blessings of liberty started to fall by the wayside. As the population shifts, self-appointed groups have formed to enforce their own rules with their own weapons and their own vision of a more perfect union, all under the banner of what we now call the hate movement.

Today, the dominant U.S. culture is comprised largely of white, Christian, straight men and women. The nation's lawmakers have much the same profile, which makes the prospect of stopping the hate movement more difficult. But cultural domination is going into a tailspin.

Will the vision of liberty and prosperity for all be accomplished when the dominant culture is no longer dominant?

U.S. Congress

Lest we think otherwise, the composition of the U.S. Congress is firmly in the hands of the dominant culture and is unlikely to change dramatically any time soon. In 2018, the Congressional Research Service found, " . . . the overwhelming majority of Members of Congress have a college education. Dominant professions are public service/politics, business, and law. Most identify as Christians. Protestants collectively constitute the majority religious affiliation. Roman Catholics account for the largest single religious denomination."

Following the 2018 midterm elections, the composition of the 116th Congress represents an uptick in representation by "minorities," including the first Native American Congresswoman and the youngest woman ever elected to Congress at age 29. The first two Muslim women ever to serve in the House of Representatives caused the body to alter a 181-year-old rule in order to allow Muslim representatives to wear a headscarf on the House floor.

In 2019, the incoming class of 100 Senators and 435 Representatives is younger, bluer and more diverse than ever, with more women,

women of color, openly LGBT members, and millennials serving in the House than ever before. These demographics are relative. According to *Politico*, even though this is the youngest freshman class since 2011, the 116th Congress will be, on average, 58.6 years old, the same as the last Congress, and about a year older than the 114th. In 2019, the five oldest members of Congress have an average age of 89. The average age of the five youngest members is 32.

Although the average age of Congress members in 2019 is lower than previous years, in 2016, the average age of House members was 57; of Senators, 61. According to a Google poll in 2015, the average age of Americans was 37.8 years. Although the point may be arguable, based on the age, gender, ethnicity, race, religion, sexual orientation, and economic status of its members, Congress is making policy decisions for a population that does not look like, talk like, or act like them.

By 2019, many of the most egregious laws and policies established in the past were repealed, rescinded, or amended. Some have been replaced by new ones. Protected categories are subjected to bureaucracies that bounce from left to right on the whim of voters. Under one administration some groups are extended freedoms, while under another those rights are curtailed or cancelled.

The dominant culture is less likely to know what it feels like to be harassed, beat up, or have their property destroyed. That's changing.

Although anti-white hate crimes by lone wolf *black* extremists are less common than the reverse, with the rising numbers of black nationalist and black separatist groups in many states over recent years, the dominant population is increasingly becoming the hate movement's latest target. This issue is detailed in the chapter Black Separatists/Black Nationalists.

Through the Trump administration, Muslims, immigrants (primarily from Mexico, Central America and the Middle East) and transgender people have been targeted for systematic exclusions. Those groups, along with Jews, gay men and lesbians, and people of color are under attack at home and places where they play and pray. As with previous presidents, groups targeted by the Trump administration are among the prime targets of hate groups.

In general, Americans that do not identify as "minorities" are less aware and less concerned about the effects of hate. The dominant culture is less likely to know what it feels like to be harassed, beat up, or have their property destroyed. That underlying dynamic changing.

With the rising numbers of black nationalist and black separatist groups in many states over recent years, the dominant population is increasingly becoming the hate movement's latest target, although anti-white hate crimes by black extremists are less common than the reverse. This issue is detailed in the chapter Black Separatists/Black Nationalists.

Obstacles

Key points covered in subsequent chapters examine the obstacles undermining why what most Americans know or believe about hate groups and hate crimes is not necessarily true. First, Americans tend to stay isolated within their own cultural group. Without deeply meaningful relationships outside of our own cultural sphere, the mold of historical racial and religious friction will never be broken. Until that happens, the dominant culture is not likely to fully understand the consequences of communities that deal with fear more often than the current majority population is aware.

Second, we can help to manage the hate movement by understanding how they run their day-to-day operations, including how and where their resources are obtained. Although we are unlikely to change the flow of dollars to any specific hate group, if we know which corporations give them financial support, we can make better choices about whether to invest in those companies or purchase their products and services. We can also make better decisions about which nonprofits are worthy of our contributions. Only when we know which radical extremist organizations are funding the campaigns of candidates running for public office can we make sound voting chooses or pressure elected officials who fail to support all Americans.

Third, reports in print, broadcast, and social media tend to focus on the most heinous of bias-oriented offenses, with routine beatings and terrorizing threats often unworthy of in-depth reporting, or any coverage at all. Over recent years, the news industry has made enormous changes that affect perceptions of current events. Moreover, social media have created an avenue that is making some mainstream media obsolete.

Building Meaningful Relationships

WHITE SUPREMACISTS SHUN DEEPLY MEANINGFUL relationships with people considered different from themselves. One thing defectors teach us is that as they gained friends from a variety of cultural backgrounds during their time in the movement, they began to recognize their own rigid perceptions and assumptions as misguided or false.

One close friendship could jeopardize a narrow view of others and convert ignorance into understanding and acceptance. Defectors eventually learned that knowing someone who faces routine oppression and harassment leads to compassion and knowing what it feels like to be hated.

Extremists know they are peripherally connected to people they hate – at work, in the neighborhood, through extended family, or in some unavoidable social setting. Those they talk to may even be considered likable, an "exception," or a "good" member of whatever group they otherwise detest. But, chances are, they wouldn't invite that person to their home for dinner.

To neo-Nazis and white supremacists, venturing into a friendship with anyone in a category of people they hate gets dangerously close to fraternizing with the enemy.

Self-segregating from those we see as different is not necessarily a choice. Many regions of the U.S. are well known for a staggering lack of diversity. Cities such as Scottsdale, Arizona, Boise, Idaho, and Lincoln, Nebraska are known for inordinately low percentages of people of color. Conversely, Atlanta, Memphis, Washington DC, and a growing number of other cities are known for fewer white residents.

As defectors attest, a lack of exposure to and understanding of human differences allows otherwise loving people to construct barriers that prohibit direct connections with others who share their beliefs and values. This dynamic doesn't only apply to members of hate groups and individual extremists. Avoiding differences is a basic human tendency.

Because the fundamental mission of white supremacists is to keep the majority population in a psychological position of superiority and control, leaders of such groups realize, along with lone extremists who have no connection to an organized group, that their goal is increasingly in peril. Traditional roles are reversing. Ethnic populations in the U.S. that have been numerically lower than whites are beginning to outnumber them. As that trend continues, personal connections with the dreaded "other" will become inevitable.

Defectors prove that deeply personal friendships with friends and coworkers outside their own circle shatters stereotypes and negative perceptions.

Belonging

Defectors talk about being attracted to the movement after a period in which they felt detached and disconnected from their peers and sometimes from their family. To them, the movement became a substitute household.

Researchers who study sociological patterns of extremists agree that no matter how fragile, faulty, or insecure the ties that bind members of hate groups together, the movement survives because it is solidly built on a foundation of belonging. The movement endures because it offers followers a bond so enticing that they are willing to give up their own values in submission to a leader's credo, no matter how abstract or absurd, and commit to the cause. Such unity is often foreign to those who share characteristics of angry loneliness and an inability to form enduring friendships. The sense of belonging breeds comfort and safety.

But that belongingness is grounded on a false premise. In a hateful environment, alliances are tenuous at best and companionships can be temporary. Adherence to the ideology often reaches a point of entrapment. When a follower begins to doubt the leader, the cause, the group, or its tactics, kinships start to unravel.

"What goes on in hate groups is magical thinking," says Pete Simi, co-author of *American Swastika: Inside the White Power Movement's Hidden Spaces of Hate.* "When the magic is gone and a member decides to leave," Simi maintains, "defectors discover a quick reversal of that belonging."

Stress multiplies as members start thinking about how to escape with their morals and their skin intact. Once they leave, defectors are forced to be on guard against the fury of one-time colleagues who feel betrayed. Every one of the defectors in Part One experienced that U-turn from former compatriots.

Defectors know the reversal from feeling detached and "out of sync" with peers then falling prey to the pitch of a persuasive recruiter and finding themselves in a new arena. Yet, they all agree that what got them out of the hate movement was gaining a close association with someone in a group they previously resisted or hated, someone who was able to show them their perceptions were being manipulated. As Arno Michaelis learned, it can happen in as few words as, "I know you're a better person."

Breaking through hatred can cause even the hardest of hearts to melt.

Where Hate Groups Get
Their Resources

LIKE ANY OTHER ORGANIZATION, HATE GROUPS require funds to cover basic expenses. Some larger groups may need to pay for an administrative space, even if it's in a person's home, as well as utilities, communications, promotional materials, a newsletter, a website and other operational needs.

Most hate groups are comprised of volunteers. Smaller groups, like a skinhead crew, may occupy a common living space, requiring rent and overhead costs to maintain the operation. Members may work full- or part-time jobs to pay their own way. Operating funds come from various means: membership dues, online product sales (music CDs, books, t-shirts), and internal and external fundraising.

Internal money conflicts are a common concern. Bryon Widner lamented that financial friction at his group, Vinlanders Social Club, occasionally led to serious disagreements, including fistfights between members.

Major Funding Source: Hate Rock Music

Most Americans unfamiliar with the inner workings of the hate movement are equally unaware of one of the most powerful tools white power groups use to spread their ideology to young people: hate rock music.

Hate rock, also referred to as white power music, is a loud, heavy metal or punk rock sound that promotes white nationalism. Lyrics often advocate race war and include explicit racial or ethnic slurs, anti-Semitic language, stereotypes, foul language, and graphic threats of violence. The dynamic is magnified by loud voices and sounds believed to provoke violent behavior. Hate rock audiences have reportedly stomped on other concertgoers with boots and beat others with baseball bats and hammers.

White power music is a multi-million-dollar industry performed on a worldwide stage, with lyrics that promote white supremacy and capitalize on racist and homophobic language. Music sales, marketed online and through international vendors, serve as a key revenue stream for many groups and provide a core vehicle for promoting aggressive racism and oppression against specific "minorities." In Europe alone, the hate rock music business was reportedly valued at $3.4 million in 1999.

Income from hate rock is a carefully kept secret and difficult to determine. One hate rock label, Resistance Records, was reportedly selling up to 70,000 hate rock CDs per year in the early 2000s, netting hundreds of thousands of dollars in profits. In 1999, the National Alliance (NA), then the premier neo-Nazi group in the U.S., bought out the Resistance Records. No longer active, in its heyday the NA network cleared as much as $1 million a year from music, books, magazines, video games, and other products featuring content specifically created for a "whites-only" audience. Today, hate rock distributors are located all over the world. Two of them, Diehard Records and ISD Records, are based in the U.S.

Hate rock lyrics were first written in the 1980s, in opposition to civil rights and human rights activists who are often identified by name. Despite legal restraints abroad or calls for the end of such themes within the U.S., white power music maintains its popularity online and through underground channels. In the U.S., hate rock lyrics are protected by the First Amendment. Many European nations have banned such tunes.

Portland State University sociologist Randy Blazak, who spent nearly a year gathering research undercover in a skinhead group, points out a contradictory twist of hate rock music in a report titled *Hate Rock 101.* "The white supremacist subculture whips its members into a frenzied state of paranoia, and then calls this a legitimate expression of white culture. Then, when someone starts acting out the subculture's rhetoric, they deny playing any role in the mayhem."

White power music embraces a variety of styles from pop and country to rap and folk. Specific genres include Nazi punk and National Socialist black metal. Confrontational lyrics and the wildly shrieking voices of hate rockers showcase the genre as powerful ways to aggrandize the white supremacist ideology.

An added resource hate rock contributes to the movement is that white power concerts and music events attract extremists *and their friends.* New listeners form a body of prospective new members, making hate rock one of the major recruitment mechanisms of the hate movement, as well as a tool to motivate individual extremists into action. The Anti-Defamation League website calls white power music "one of the most significant ways neo-Nazis attempt to attract young people into their movement."

Hate music began to lose its luster in the late 1990s. In their 2014 book *Beyond Hate: White Power and Popular Culture (The Cultural Politics of Media and Popular Culture)*[37], co-authors C. Richard King and David J. Leonard write, " . . . while white power engages with and appropriates pop music for its own ends, [the genre] remains wildly unpopular, as evidenced by market share, public outrage and condemnation, and the reaction to it . . . "

Protests by anti-fascist groups have contributed to the decline of the genre and have taken a toll on the ability of white power bands to secure gigs and plan tours. Music critics say another cause of a weak market is the low quality of the music. One former hate rock musician said that when he first started performing, the lyrics were the only attraction for the few audiences he played for, not the quality of the performance.

But, while white power music may have its setbacks, it is not dead. Sold overtly or covertly, white power music is still performed on stage in venues across the U.S. Combined with online product sales, hate rock music is one of the most effective revenue generating resources and propaganda techniques for the movement.

Corporate Support

Corporate giving to hate groups and radical right wing causes is seldom in the forefront of a business plan. However, multiple online news reports[38] reveal how corporate contributions support extremist ideologies. In one example, the Chick-fil-A tax-exempt foundation bankrolled more than $1.4 million in donations to anti-LGBTQ organizations. The company also funds Eagle Forum, a socially conservative "pro-family" organization that opposes immigration, the legalization of abortion, and same sex marriage. Chick-fil-A also funded other identified hate groups, including . . .

- Exodus International, a now-defunct group that opposed hate crime legislation on Capitol Hill and was dedicated to "helping" gay Christians become straight
- The Family Research Council, a conservative Christian organization that opposes and lobbies against, abortion, divorce, embryonic stem-cell research, same-sex marriage, and LGBTQ adoption
- Focus on the Family, one of the most well-funded anti-LGBT organizations in America, which opposes abortion, divorce, gambling, pornography, pre-marital sex, substance abuse, LGBT adoption, and same-sex marriage.

Individuals may give up to $2,500 per election to a political campaign, up to $5,000 a year to a PAC, and up to $30,800 a year to a national party committee, according to a 2019 article in the *Wall Street Journal.* "None of these contributions is tax-deductible, and they aren't reported to the IRS," the WSJ noted, adding that public charities such as the Heritage Foundation (a staunchly right-wing group) and the Nature Conservancy (a more left-leaning nonprofit) "can't support or oppose candidates, but they can work to educate the public and can take positions on ballot initiatives. Contributions to them are usually tax-deductible as charitable gifts by individuals."

The *Washington Post* reported in 2017 that the Internal Revenue Service benefits white-nationalist groups by putting their fundraising into the same legal category as zoos, colleges, museums, orchestras and planetariums, allowing them to avoid paying taxes. The tax status also allows supporters to write off their donations.

The IRS tax benefit is a huge boost to white supremacy coffers. According to an analysis by the *Associated Press*, four well-known organizations associated with white nationalism – the National Policy Institute, the New Century Foundation, the Charles Martel Society and VDare Foundation – have raised $7.8 million in tax-free donations over the last decade. Corporate giving to organizations like these is not always made public.

On a smaller scale, Major League Baseball donated $1,000 in 2017 to Minnesota Republican Congressman Jason Lewis, who has a history of making racist and misogynistic remarks. According to the *Washington Post*, Lewis suggested that abolishing slavery was an overreach by the federal government. Lewis also reportedly said white Americans are not reproducing at the same rate as Latinos, and female voters who care about abortion and same-sex marriage are "nonthinking" (sic).

In addition to being a tax write-off, corporate and other contributions to radical right political action committees (PACs) help members of hate groups collaborate with people, organizations, and federal or state institutions in an effort to garner support of ultra-conservative causes. The same criticism may be voiced against liberal PACs. Among the strongest conservative supporters are elected officials and senior managers in some of America's most powerful public offices, many of whose beliefs are invisible to voters because they hide behind campaign finance rules put in place to protect them.

In Citizens United v. Federal Election Commission (2010), the U.S. Supreme Court held, by a 5-4 margin, that political spending is a form of protected speech under the First Amendment and the government may not keep corporations or unions from spending money to support or oppose individual candidates in elections. The decision opened the floodgates for unlimited election spending by individuals and corporations. Big businesses and unions were given a green light to spend unlimited sums on ads and other political tools, calling for the election or defeat of individual candidates. Since 2010 when the Citizens United case was decided, at least 16 states and more than 680 municipalities have called on Congress to pass a constitutional amendment to overturn the decision. In 2014, the Democracy For All amendment, which would have effectively overturned Citizens United, came within six votes of passing in the Senate.

In a more positive trend, many corporations are giving funds to stop white supremacist actions. MSNBC reported in early 2017 that JPMorgan Chase chairman and chief executive, Jamie Dimon, joined other business leaders condemning President Donald Trump's response to the deadly violence in Charlottesville, Virginia, by pledging up to two million dollars to anti-hate groups. After the 2017 white nationalist rally in Charlottesville, Trump commented on the "egregious display of hatred, bigotry and violence on many sides, on many sides," not exactly a condemnation of the murder and dozens of injuries committed by white nationalists at that event. The MSNBC report also noted that Apple CEO Tim Cook pledged one million dollars each to the SPLC and ADL and said the company would match employee donations; James Murdoch, head of 21st Century Fox, also pledged one million to the ADL, according to MSNBC.

Online Fund Transfers

Many hate groups rely on online businesses to obtain and transfer funding into their accounts, often beneath public awareness. Funds may include income from product sales or direct transfers through online companies like Amazon or PayPal. According to SPLC, administrators at Counter-Currents Publishing, a white nationalist book-selling website, earned nearly $20,000 through its referrals to Amazon.

PayPal, however, is a major money-juggling source. Although PayPal policy bans the promotion of hate, violence and racial intolerance in its terms of service, SPLC reported that PayPal, among the largest online payment processors in the world, " . . . was an integral tool" in raising money for Unite the Right rally in Charlottesville orchestrated by alt-right organizers. In addition to the violence during the event, two Virginia State Patrol troopers were killed in a helicopter crash while assisting public safety efforts there. According to SPLC, organizers, speakers, and individual attendees relied on PayPal to move funds in the run-up to the event, supporting at least eight leaders of identified hate groups.

In 2014, SPLC also found that at least 69 hate groups relied on PayPal during that year alone to help finance their activities. SPLC added that PayPal specifically disallows the sale of items that contain

Nazi, SS, or Ku Klux Klan symbols, including authentic German WWII memorabilia. To its credit, PayPal banned Stormfront.com, one of the largest white nationalist websites online.

The SPLC also discovered that hate groups have found other creative ways to facilitate online transfers of money. For example, a Tennessee-based white supremacist radio show called *The Political Cesspool,* uses Authorize. net as its internet gateway. SPLC also found that Sons of Aesir Motorcycle Club, a pro-white motorcycle club dedicated to the preservation and advancement of the white race, uses miiduu.com, which also accepts PayPal accounts. According to SPCL, the anti-gay organization You Can Run But You Cannot Hide, is powered by the online E-commerce site Volusion.com. The Center also notes North East White Pride and a separate group of New England neo-Nazis uses the website Merchant One, a credit card processing firm, to funnel money into its coffers.

Illicit Financial Gain

Through its plotline, *The Turner Diaries* advocates that larceny as a way to fund racist causes. The story unfolds in the year 2099 after the federal government confiscates all civilian firearms under a fictional federal law. The book is structured on the diary of a white revolutionary named Earl Turner who leads an apocalyptic overthrow of the U.S. federal government and a global race war. Following the mythical Earl Turner, hate groups often resort to crime as a funding stream.

The Turner Diaries has inspired hate groups and individual extremists since the day it was published, from Timothy McVeigh's plan to bomb the federal building in Oklahoma City to defectors profiled in this book.

Ill-gotten funds also often find their way into members' pockets. Robberies are common, especially at businesses catering to activities their members consider to be in opposition to the group's values. Angela King described how she and a boyfriend pocketed cash taken during the armed robbery of a video store. A black separatist talked about robbing white men.

Funding the operations of hate groups is not isolated to video store heists and on-the-street larceny. When compared to more violent crimes undertaken by larger hate groups, the net gain is small potatoes.

In December 1997, five members of the Aryan Republican Army, a white supremacist group, were indicted by a federal grand jury over federal bank-robbery charges. The ARA had been linked to as many as 22 bank robberies in the Midwest from late 1992 through the mid 1990s. In 1985, David Tate, a 22-year-old neo-Nazi, and 23 other purported members of The Order were indicted after being implicated in some 50 crimes, including murder, counterfeiting, and armed robberies totaling over four million dollars. The Order, no longer in operation, was a white supremacist revolutionary terrorist organization active in the early to mid 1980s.

Media

THE NEWS MEDIA HEAVILY INFLUENCE PUBLIC perceptions of religion, gender, sexuality, ancestry, immigration, and other hot button issues that affect community cohesiveness. Weak media coverage of hate groups and hate crimes is one of the central reasons Americans are misinformed or uninformed about the hate movement.

Also, over the past two decades Americans have witnessed significant changes in journalistic standards as big media pursue larger audiences and advertising dollars. As a consequence, stories about bias-related incidents that were once worthy of coverage are often relegated to brief tidbits taken directly from the daily police blotter or given no attention at all. This trend is most apparent in suburban and rural locations.

Cover stories and in-depth reports often focus on the most heinous hate incidents, with the more numerous incidents of malicious harassment getting far less coverage. Truncated, unbalanced, and half-true news stories play a role in American apathy toward the hate movement and create another tier to a false sense of security. Another concern is news guided by a right wing conservative editorial agenda. In the end, news consumers are unlikely to know they're forfeiting full disclosure of what's happening around them. Instead, they learn what media moguls want them to learn.

In most cases, any deficit in reporting is not because highly skilled investigative journalists are uninspired or lacking intellectual curiosity.

While that may be true at small community print and broadcast outlets with tight budgets and few reporters, media in larger cities are more responsive to the needs of a more diverse consumer base.

Two additional factors working against deeper coverage are a wave of media consolidations and the impact of social media.

Media Consolidations

Another contributor to the public malaise is that while white nationalism is evolving and growing, the media world is evolving and *shrinking*.

Over the past 30 years, mega-media corporations have been dominating the industry. Readers of traditional newspapers have seen the reporting staff at their favorite sources downsized. In many cases, the entire medium has disappeared, mostly due to the emergence of online news choices and social media. Major U.S. cities that once enjoyed competitive morning and evening newspapers now have one – or none. In broadcast media, the rush is on to consolidate markets via mergers and buyouts.

According to a 2019 article in the *New Yorker*, between January 2017, and April 2018, a third of the nation's largest newspapers reported layoffs. The same article reported that between 1970 and 2016 "500 or so dailies went out of business; the rest cut news coverage, or shrank the paper's size, or stopped producing a print edition, or did all of that, and it still wasn't enough." Those media were unable to stay profitable.

The push to merge media giants has created a new threat to journalism: the rise of a media oligopoly in which news outlets are owned by fewer providers. The trend fosters a blend of more restricted programming and limited competition. Such a paradigm leads to the prospect of overtly politicizing news and works against the most common targets of hate groups.

One of the most powerful media oligarchs is the Australian-born American media giant, Rupert Murdoch, creator of Fox News. Murdoch hired former Republican Party media consultant and CNBC executive Roger Ailes as its founding CEO. Under Ailes' direction, Fox became notorious for unabashedly biased reporting, espousing radical right wing points of view with little attempt at objectivity. After Ailes resigned from Fox amid allegations of sexual misconduct, he became an adviser to the 2016 Trump campaign.

The direction of Fox News is partially responsible for a counter-point of biased reporting from liberal-oriented and moderate media such as MSNBC and CNN. The decline of media objectivity means Americans are not getting an accurate picture of white extremists or, more important, reasonable exposure to the crimes they commit.

While nonprofit media like National Public Radio and public television stations rely on member fundraising campaigns to finance commercial-free news analysis, many profit-driven media focus more on advertising sales than providing wide-ranging news angles. Big media consume one another in trades that translate to a net loss of staff and a cutback of in-depth reporting. As coverage declines, the public is less informed. More politicized reporting risks legitimizing shady political perspectives in a cycle that damages media credibility and erodes trust.

Conservative thinkers prefer conservative news and progressive thinkers prefer progressive news. To further chip away at the concept of journalistic integrity, cash-flush media conglomerates swoop in to buy economically fraught and generally smaller news outlets. Their reporting replaces independent editorial content with more traditional interpretations of politics, the economy, and controversial social issues, as opposed to a contemporary perspective on current events.

In late 2018, Nexstar Media Group agreed to acquire the Tribune Media Company in a deal that, if approved by the Federal Communication Commission (FCC), would elevate Nexstar to become the largest local television station owner in the country, just behind Sinclair Broadcast Group. The proposed $4.1 billion purchase would put a combined total of 216 stations in into Nexstar's hands.

Approval of such gargantuan shifts in media dominance could change the future of broadcast news. The FCC has already rejected a bid by Sinclair Broadcast Group to buy Tribune Media. As of this writing, the Nexstar deal is pending before the FCC. Sinclair owns 192 stations, reaching 39 percent of American viewers. Journalists are cautious about Sinclair for its penchant to report news with a heavy conservative spin.

In 2018, *The New Yorker* reported that Sinclair's executive chairman, David Smith, is "a conservative whose views combine a suspicion of government, an aversion to political correctness, and strong libertarian leanings." Sinclair's fiercest competitor is Fox News. With market leaders like Sinclair and Fox News dominating broadcast media, scrutiny of the hate movement is more likely to be pegged *down* in importance rather than up.

Sinclair itself hit headlines across the country in 2018 when other media sources revealed the company forced news anchors, once regarded for their independent perspectives on current affairs, to read from scripts prepared by the conglomerate. *The New Yorker* article repeated a Twitter post from Dan Rather, former anchor of CBS Evening News. Rather wrote, "News anchors looking into camera and reading a script handed down by a corporate overlord, words meant to obscure the truth not elucidate it, isn't journalism. It's propaganda."

Propaganda is putty in the hands of white nationalists. Neo-Nazis rely on disinformation to downplay their destructive intent on people and property. The concept of manipulating media was one of Hitler's favorite techniques to influence the acceptance of Nazi ideology during the rise of the Third Reich.

Seasoned reporters are trained to look for controversy and public conflict. For readers and listeners, controversy is a double-edged sword. As editors choose any medium's direction, consumers get pithy newsbreaks about the puzzle of the day. But, between staff cuts, spin, and the profit-over-content polemic, the public may never be able to put all the pieces together.

Kerry Noble discovered the power of editorial choices after the 1985 siege at his former group. He asked reporters why so few covered the CSA takedown. At the time, Kerry was the organization's spokesperson and number two in command. After he and the compound's leader surrendered to the FBI and were eventually released from prison, he asked reporters why so few covered the story. One reporter from a national newspaper was blunt: "Because nobody died."

Journalists quickly learn the editor's refrain, "If it doesn't bleed, it doesn't lead." The CSA takedown followed a three-day standoff with all the same overtones as the FBI's siege of the Branch Davidian compound in Waco (TX) eight years later. The CSA barricade involved hundreds of forces from multi-government agencies meeting face-to-face with a heavily armed militia of Christian Identity extremists trained in guerrilla warfare. Yet, the event was not newsworthy enough for all but a handful of major media outlets to bother assigning a reporter and informing the public.

The cost of the CSA siege was no doubt huge, but inestimable, including the financial costs. Taxpayers deserve to know about potential threats in their states and cities, including the financial costs. The media's editorial blunder in failing to more widely cover the CSA siege cost national news consumers a critical opening to understand the hidden dimensions of one of the most meticulously organized hate groups in America.

Since its demise, CSA remains virtually unknown, its lessons rarely discussed. As a result of journalistic failures like this, few Americans are aware of the Christian Identity (CI) movement or the 20 CI hate groups located throughout the U.S. in 2017[39]. The Anti-Defamation League estimates CI adherents at between 25,000 and 50,000 nationwide. And that's only one sliver of the hate movement.

Consumers are being unwittingly drawn into non-stop media wars in which the casualties are news coverage, fairness, and objectivity. Today, rather than relying on traditional media, a growing number of news consumers gravitate to sources that deliver what they want to hear, when they want to hear it. Increasingly, the preferred choices are online news and social media.

Social Media

The evolution of social media as a principal news source, especially for millennials and younger audiences, is a big part of why so many print media and broadcast stations are altering their news model or folding the tent. The potential market for online news distribution is exhilarating for consumers who want punchy, up-to-the-second news hits tailored to their own political taste, not so much for those who prefer in-depth news analysis.

But even online news outlets are vulnerable to the profit motive. One source reported that between 2017 and 2019, an estimated 25 percent of digital news sites cut their staff.

In 2018, *The Daily Beast* signaled the extent of the social media marketplace when it reported President Barack Obama's Twitter feeds totaled more than 101 million followers, adding that Obama was the third most-followed person on the site, a few million behind singers

Katy Perry and Justin Bieber. That's encouraging for those interested in a more politically moderate or liberal point of view. In the same year, the *Washington Post* reported that President Trump's Twitter followers amounted to just over half of Obama's, 53 million in all.

Any news consumer who fails to see the political power and persuasion of diametrically opposed presidents is asleep at the screen. Progressives and centrists turn to President Obama's Tweets whenever they like. They hear balanced or liberal concepts from the former President of the Harvard Law Review and U.S. senator from Illinois, a fierce fighter for the underdog.

Since 2017, many conservatives get their news directly from President Donald Trump, one of the most fabled Twitterers of all time; a white, self-described "nationalist" who soft pedals comments from or about white supremacists and avoids criticism of their antics.

Another dubious practice among television news outlets today is repeatedly broadcasting President Trump at public events in which he is surrounded by Republican voters and right wing conservative supporters who applaud every line. Because this president refuses to face the media at White House press conferences – and media go along with it – Trump has effectively seized control of news in order to present himself only in situations where audiences agree with his every word.

When the President of the United States relies on propaganda and a Twitter account to disseminate decisions delivered by previous presidents speaking on primetime news from the Oval Office, journalism is reduced to commenting on staged hype and spontaneous Tweets – and presidential decorum is reduced to whimsey.

Thomas Jefferson famously said, "Were it left to me to decide whether we should have a government without newspapers, or newspapers without a government, I should not hesitate a moment to prefer the latter."

Whites-Only Websites
The rise of whites-only websites is a troubling development. While such sites generally identify themselves as exclusively for white viewers, they are accessible for anyone who cares to read their content.

Under the protection of the First Amendment right to free speech, the internet provides an electronic cover to protect hate-filled fanatics as nameless, faceless, seemingly innocent consumers of information. Supremacist websites give dues-paying members and guests unlimited access to a constant flow of ideological hype that augments their rigid view of white superiority. When a member of those sites uses its ideology or posted messages in the context of a hate crime, the website or its administrators may be clear of any offense, depending on specific circumstances of the charge.

The Daily Stormer (dailystormer.com) is the most widely known neo-Nazi/white supremacist news and commentary website today. The site was founded in 2013 by Andrew Anglin, a Holocaust denier, who continues to manage the site and write most of its posts. With strings to the alt-right movement, the Daily Stormer advocates for the genocide of Jews. It has a political base that supports candidates and elected officials who agree with its reactionary ideology.

When The Daily Stormer replaced a former website, Total Fascism, it quickly became the most popular hate site online. The platform is known for posting vicious anti-Semitic images. The site was bumped from several servers and ultimately shut down after it ran a series of venomous remarks about Heather Heyer, the 32-year-old woman .killed by alt-right neo-Nazis during the 2017 white nationalist rally in Charlottesville, Virginia. The Daily Stormer is now active online, referring to itself as "The Most Censored Publication in History."

The first major racial hate site on the internet was Stormfront (stormfront.org), the most popular online platform for biased news feeds until it was outpaced by the Daily Stormer. The site was created to espouse white nationalist, white supremacist, and neo-Nazi beliefs under the motto "White Pride World Wide." Many Stormfront followers are holocaust deniers. The site was established in 1996 by Don Black, a nationally recognized white supremacist and former Grand Wizard of the Ku Klux Klan in Alabama. Black is believed to have been a member of the American Nazi Party in the 1970s, which later became the National Socialist White People's Party.

Another online white supremacist resource, NewSaxon.org connects whites-only users, touting itself as "The Viking Rage Network." NewSaxon is a social medium, a kind of Facebook for racists, which promotes itself with the phrase, "You could either go through life with the philosophy that if you are the nail that sticks out you will get hammered down or you could be the hammer!" The pledge is an odd choice for a whites-only organization. The phrasing is an ironic rip-off of a Japanese proverb, "The nail that sticks out gets hammered down."

Online hate sites have so proliferated that an Australian website, the Online Hate Prevention Institute (ohpi.org.au), was formed in 2012 with a vision to "change online culture so hate in all its forms becomes as socially unacceptable online as it is 'in real life.'"

Sites like Facebook, YouTube, Instagram, Myspace, and Twitter provide a convenient platform to view hateful material not otherwise available in the more conventional mainstream. These sources have the added benefit of sending faster broadcasts with links to other stories.

Social media are mostly comprised of messages from individuals rather than companies or non-profit organizations. Personalized news feeds can also be a crime-dodging haven for radical extremists. "Social media can negate the First Amendment," says Dr. Caitlin Carlson, Assistant Professor of Strategic Communication at Seattle University. Carlson learned about the inside dynamics of hate group communications by joining an online neo-Nazi group as part of a graduate school research project. Her doctoral dissertation examined hate speech on social media.

Carlson explained, "In an essentially private space, the First Amendment does not apply. In that case, users can speak freely without fear of breaking the law. That freedom and flexibility also gives validation to the movement. Social media help support mainstream thinking by bringing extremists together online, rather than having to go to a place where a hate group congregates to talk or hang out. Social media provide a platform for these individuals to virtually meet and discuss things they can't talk about anywhere else."

Carlson clarified recent U.S. Supreme Court decisions that examined statements in which the speaker meant to communicate a serious intent to commit an act of unlawful violence to a particular individual or group of individuals. In a Seattle Times op-ed piece, Carlson wrote, "Saying 'I'm going to my Muslim neighbor's house on Sherman Avenue tonight at 8 p.m. to hurt her' might constitute a punishable threat. But saying, 'I'm going to kill all Muslims' would not."

While explaining hate speech may be an intellectual exercise for academics and judicial experts, most Americans are left scratching their heads trying to distinguish a chest-thumping forethought from a diabolical threat. To highlight the root of misunderstandings over what is or is not hate speech, Carlson commented, "Although many of us associate the phrase 'hate speech' with racist, homophobic, or misogynistic slurs, U.S. courts have never actually defined the term."

When journalists cover malicious harassment incidents in detail and with accuracy, they educate the public about hate activities in their area, language and behaviors to be on guard against, and, with hope, the importance of reporting hate crimes to police. By covering and explaining the latest techniques law enforcement is using to fight hate, community groups can act more responsibly to support effective policing and insist on clearer standards of accountability for convicted hate criminals.

Respond to Inadequate Media Coverage

With media competition as intense and as tenuous as it is today, it is important for news consumers to speak up about coverage of hate groups and hate crimes. First, commend journalists for well-detailed news stories. Reporters thrive on feedback. That's why most print media and online outlets include the reporter's email address at the end of most news entries.

Similarly, when news stories don't measure up to expectations, sending an email to the reporter or editor can make a difference.

Should one choose the more dramatic response to cancel a subscription to a medium that fails to adequately cover hate groups and hate crimes, management needs to know the reasons for your dissatisfaction. To say nothing empowers editors to believe their strategy to beat the competition is working.

Fear

THE HATE MOVEMENT RUNS ON FEAR. To a person, defectors said they became so defined by the vision of their leader and peers that their own ability to think and reason independently disappeared. Yet, at the core of their being, perpetrators of hate crimes often feel the same fears their victims experience, although the former rarely acknowledge the emotion, much less how deeply it drives their behavior.

Arno Michaelis says, "It's important to understand that living with this racist mindset, you're in fear of the world around you *constantly* – all day, every day."

Fear conflates the mission of the movement with individual choice. Extremists, whether alone or a member of group, are not likely to acknowledge the fear they feel, especially to colleagues. As a baseline emotion, fear fuels the hate movement from the inside out and from the outside in.

Internal Fear

Defectors rarely talk directly about the anxiety they experienced inside a hate group. What they talk about is the *effects* of fear on their ability to act independently; the limitations of being surrounded by people who think alike, an inability to express differing opinions or to make deeply personal choices, the expectation that family time is secondary to group time.

One fear defectors describe in detail is how they felt when they finally realized, "I can't do this anymore." They define the decisions they faced at the time: Do I just stop showing up? Do I share my inner turmoil with others? Do I announce I've decided to leave the group, knowing that once the word is out, my family and I will risk serious consequences? The fear of being ostracized or hurt by former comrades locks them in a kind of hate group handcuffs, acting on an ideology that violates their own core values, yet unable to do anything about it.

White supremacists are expected to display the superiority of their race, or in their own vernacular, "Man up." White power is the common denominator of all white extremists. Ironically, that power also means following a course set by a powerful leader rather than being responsible for their own decisions. If they are conflicted by the directions they're given, they are limited in how to raise opposing points of view without being seen as usurping someone else's power.

After the birth of his son, Bryon Widner wanted to spend more time with his family and less time with the group he co-founded, Vinlanders Social Club. He fretted over what would happen when his neo-Nazi followers realized they were no longer his top priority. When he finally renounced his connection to the movement, he dreaded the impending retaliation against him, his wife, and their children. He also grappled with the fear of looking in the mirror and seeing a face covered with threatening tattoos, suddenly realizing the images were blocking his chances of finding a job. That same fear affected Julie, his wife at the time, who was in the process of leaving the National Alliance.

Arno Michaelis said that members of his Wisconsin-based skinhead crew secretly loved to watch the Green Bay Packers. But, being a Packers fan was not wise because most of the team's players are black. He didn't talk with other skinheads about watching Packers games at home – until he discovered other closeted skinhead Packers supporters. Each was afraid of disclosing a commitment to the team they were secretly rooting for.

The fear Frank Meeink felt when he was raped with a gun barrel on his head kept him from telling his white supremacist buddies about the trauma. Instead he went out and mercilessly brutalized a gay man.

Apparent to them or not, internalized fears are just as damaging to extremists as they are to their victims. Most humans know what it's like to be afraid, but not as many know what it's like to be responsible for creating fear. The stories defectors share supply ample reasons to believe that terrorizing innocent people to fear for their lives was exhilarating, but wore them down emotionally and psychologically.

Fear allows otherwise rational human beings to lose control of their better judgment and lash out indiscriminately. Groupthink and positive reinforcement for hateful conduct obscures thinking about core values like compassion or empathy in deference to the group's distorted moral judgments.

The fear of loneliness and detachment lures hurt people to a place where they belong to a new family, one with little interest in truly loving them. Like quicksand, the environment is a trap for other socially disconnected souls. Fear is implied in every white supremacist website online and in every manifesto written by an extremist on the edge of a complete emotional breakdown.

No matter how unreasonable, irrational, or detestable such thinking may sound to an emotionally secure person, white extremists are driven by the existential threat of losing their power and privilege. Not only do white supremacists see their own livelihood at stake, they fret over the expectation their children and grandchildren will face even deeper peril.

The fear of being surrounded by same-thinking people with reinforced, lock-step values and irrational social views can be an overwhelming betrayal of self-respect. Like any other animal in fear, extremists respond to emotional danger with the fight or flight instinct. Afraid of losing the entitlement they enjoy, white supremacists are more compelled to entrench themselves in a fight for the survival of the white race than to abandon their extremism and live a life of dignified self-determination.

In the meantime, the fear they cause victims compensates for their own.

External Fear

Outside of the movement, fear galvanizes victims so devastated from biased acts of violence that they become immobilized to rise against the hatred. Fear scores a victory whenever a victim chooses to keep the crime private rather than report it to police. The movement gets another boost every time a government agency fails to fully investigate a hate crime or report one (or more) to the FBI, and yet another when hate criminals end up getting tried for less serious offenses with lighter sentences.

On a larger scale, fear overrules good governance whenever elected officials fail to adopt aggressive policies designed to stop hateful behaviors and protect the lives of the people in their district. The threat of losing an election makes the intoxicating appeal of campaign funding from radical right wing supporters and bigoted political action committees an exceedingly difficult choice – even when a politician's heart tells them what they're doing is not in the best interest of their constituents.

Because of political fear, the U.S. government has failed to enforce the Hate Crime Statistics Act that *requires* the Attorney General to collect data on crimes.

Federal and state legislators are also subject to the fear of violating the wishes of radical right wing conservative funders by supporting bills to strengthen their state's hate crimes law or by imposing restrictions on the sale of guns and other weapons that empower extremists to commit acts of extreme violence.

Fear and Police

Two reasons hate crime victims say they do not report an offense to police are: one, the feeling that nothing will be done; and two, fear of being revictimized by police who discount or disregard the incident. Distrust of police officers is strongest in populations targeted for hate crimes, specifically, ethnic, religious, and sexual minorities, immigrants, people with disabilities, and the homeless. These populations have a long history of unfair treatment by law enforcement.

That history continues. According to a 2015 Gallup Poll, overall confidence in police in the U.S. that year was the lowest in 22 years. As a specific category, African Americans have experienced some of the worst effects of organized hate. The Gallup study found that, between 2013 and 2015, African Americans' confidence in police averaged 30 percent, "well below the national average of 53 percent and much lower than for any other subgroup."

Cultivating trust between police and communities where cynicism over police officers' use of force is high is a source of heated public debate. Police guilds and internal management associations are almost universally averse to police-community relations programs for fear officers will be set up for further public scrutiny as bad guys.

Good guy police who treat victims with sensitivity and immediate action deserve to be recognized for their service to the people in the jurisdiction they serve. "Minority" officers who strive to be fair in their work often experience internal pushback from bigoted peers as a frustrating rebuff to their professionalism.

Lest false impressions be made, white supremacist cops do exist. One police officer with a misguided moral compass can be enough to tarnish an entire department's public image and destroy public confidence that hate crime victims will be treated humanely.

Dispel the Fear

William Parkin, professor of criminology at Seattle University, says the culture of a police department or a prosecutor's office can impact hate crimes laws and how they are enforced. Parkin asked, "How likely are police to file a report if they believe the local prosecutor will do nothing about it? In that kind of an environment, how likely is it that the police culture will follow up on hate crime victimizations?"

Parkin also questioned if a community cares more about crime victimization or *the perception* of crime victimization. The difference, he said, may be reflected in how local police departments interact with citizens. Communities, Parkin said, need to know the extent to which police are concerned about hate crimes – and how the fear of crimes affects them.

With rare exceptions[40], even if police do not agree with a victim's account of a hate crime, the recipient of an offender's malicious harassment will have experienced the fear and terror of being victimized. If victims can't go to police, where do they go?

In order for a prosecutor to pursue a hate crime in court, the victim must be identified by name. That requirement does not bar victims from talking about harassment experiences with members of their own community organizations and empowering others to report similar crimes to police.

If police fail to respond according to a community's expectations, the public must be informed. In such a situation, local and regional media can be among the most useful allies. Editors generally listen when highly regarded community leaders show up at their desk demanding changes in the way police treat their people.

It is essential that individuals, community groups and coalitions band together to protect themselves against hate. Such groups can provide a place for bias crime victims to discuss what happened to them and to get support. That protection may include designating someone to escort a victim to their local police department to ensure the report is taken seriously and the person is treated sensitively.

It is equally important that nonprofit community groups, particularly those that receive public funding, promote specific services that protect hate crime victims. Providing such services is part of the group's fiduciary responsibility to the people who fund their operations. Cities known to harbor one or more recognized hate groups benefit the most from such services.

Some cities and neighborhoods have instituted "Safe Place" sites, havens for anyone who feels bullied or threatened because of their cultural identity. Such systems include small businesses that agree to post prominent signs in their window that alert potential victims they will be protected inside. With the victim's permission, "Safe Place" participating businesses call police and do their best to provide comfort until an officer arrives.

Those who are not part of a "minority" group or in a protected category need to know such programs exist so they can inform their friends and neighbors where to go and how to get help when they need it. Without such programs, communities risk not being aware of a lurking threat. Worse yet, residents may walk along streets and through parks, going about their business assuming extremists are nowhere near them.

Research and Help

Several nonprofit organizations have been created to help study the hate movement and offer ways to help victims.

The Matthew Shepard Foundation is a nonpartisan nonprofit with a mission to erase hate by replacing it with understanding, compassion and acceptance. Through local, regional and national outreach, the Foundation empowers individuals to find their voice to create change and challenge communities to identify and address hate that lives within their schools, neighborhoods and homes. The nonprofit was formed after the brutal hate-motivated murder of 21-year-old Matthew Shepard in 1998 outside of Laramie, Wyoming.

The Lawyers' Committee for Civil Rights Under Law was created in 1963 at the request of President John F. Kennedy to enlist leadership and resources to combat racial discrimination and the inequality of opportunity and to secure equal justice for all through the rule of law. The organization has its own Stop Hate Project which offers prevention strategies and legal advice to victims of hate crimes.

The Center for the Study of Hate and Extremism at California State University, San Bernardino, examines the ways bigotry, advocacy of extreme methods, or terrorism, deny civil or human rights to people on the basis of race, ethnicity, religion, gender, sexual orientation, disability or other relevant status characteristics. The nonpartisan center seeks to aid scholars, community activists, government officials, law enforcement, the media and others with objective information to aid them in their examination and implementation of law, education and policy.

Asian Americans Advancing Justice advocates for an America in which all Americans can benefit equally from, and contribute to, the American dream – "fighting for our civil rights through education, litigation, and public policy advocacy."

These organizations join countless others throughout the U.S. created to support and defend the civil rights of all Americans.

Christianity and Hate

EXTREMISTS ARE OFTEN SO MOTIVATED BY THEIR devotion to religious beliefs they truly expect that if others don't follow the same beliefs, the world order will collapse. To that end, Christian-oriented white supremacist leaders are committed to forcing others into submission – to their God, their theology, their dogma, their values, and their more-often-than-not implausible ideologies. This overview barely scratches the surface, yet exposes a part of the hate movement that seldom gets the scrutiny it warrants.

Despite the Constitutional separation of church and state, God and Christianity have always been a dominant influence on the American culture and its government. Religious beliefs have also been a central force behind many hate groups.

Christian Identity and The Creativity Movement

Two main categories of hate groups fall under the Christian umbrella, each with a coordinated movement of interconnected groups in their camp. To separate the two, the Christian Identity (CI) Movement is more anti-Semitic, although CI adherents do not restrict their abominations to Jewish people alone. This assessment is subject to dispute by some who believe CI is not a Christian organization.

Creativity groups are anti-Semitic *and* anti-Christian. The Southern Poverty Law Center classifies the Creativity Movement, formerly known as World Church of the Creator, as a neo-Nazi organization and is primarily motivated by white supremacist values. Both organizations confuse mainstream Christians into thinking they are all on the same theological page as mainstream denominations. They are not.

Some Christian-based hate groups choose names that add another layer of confusion about who they represent. In name alone, they sound more pious than exclusionary. For example, America's Promise Ministries, National Prayer Network, Christian Anti-Defamation Commission, and Christian Guardians are among hundreds of organizations identified as hate groups by the SPLC.

The confusion is deliberate. Christian-oriented groups represent a significant percentage of the American hate movement. Every year they change, sometimes in name, sometimes in number, sometimes both. In 2014, for example, of 784 hate groups listed on the SPLC Hate Map that year, 30 groups called themselves a "church," 29 used "Creativity" in their name, another 16 included "Christian" in their title, seven called themselves "ministries," and two included "Christianity" in their name. Four specifically "Baptist" and two "Catholic" organizations were also identified as hate groups.

Such groups do not focus their hatred only on pro-Christian or anti-Christian themes. They also manipulate unique ideologies to justify harassment and attacks on non-whites, LGBTQ people, Jews, Muslims, immigrants, and others.

In 2019, SPLC identified 17 CI groups nationwide and another 11 hate groups listed under the umbrella of Radical Traditional Catholicism, an ideology that is rejected by the Vatican.

At its core, the Christian Identity movement believes non-Christians have no spirit and that members of other religions cannot be saved and are not worthy of divine redemption. Indeed, to followers of the Christian Identity movement, Jews are not recognized as human. Kerry Noble, a one-time Baptist preacher and later CI leader, said that the CI movement considers Jews "demonic children of the devil."

In the Pacific Northwest, Our Place Fellowship, a CI group established in Colville, Washington in 2000, is one example of Christianity gone awry. According to its website, the group follows a theology based on Albert Einstein's breakthrough discovery. The site says the group follows "the Theory of Relativity applied to spiritual things; a new revelation of Christian thought and purpose."

Our Place Fellowship boasts "an entirely new approach to Christianity, which flows from a new perspective . . . founded upon a fresh model of God's plan for the earth." Similar groups demonstrate how the Bible can be – not just interpreted – but reinvented to mean whatever a leader wants it to mean. Were he alive today, Einstein, an avowed and unapologetic atheist, would surely object to Our Place Fellowship's cavalier appropriation of his name.

Creativity groups are rooted in the beliefs committed to the survival and advancement of the white race. Members believe in a racial holy war between white and non-white races. Adherents believe non-whites include Jews and people of mixed races. Followers of Creativity call themselves "Creators," a term that refers to adherents of the ideology. Membership is restricted to European Americans whose genetic heritage is white.

Separate from the anti-Semitic CI Movement, the Creativity Movement follows a rationale unique to the hate movement consciousness: Theology is anything a group's leader wants it to be. The Anti-Defamation League identifies the Creativity Movement as one of the most violent hate groups on the radical right. Before it became World Church of the Creator, the original COTC was founded in 1973 by Ben Klassen, who proudly called himself a white supremacist. Klassen is cited as popularizing the term racial holy war (RaHoWa). In 1993, after the death of his wife and the decline of his church, Klassen committed suicide.

To demonstrate the wisdom of the Creativity Movement, the following passage is from a 1987 philosophy statement Klassen wrote for COTC followers to absorb:

> *"We gird for total war against the Jews and the rest of the goddamned mud races of the world – politically, militantly, financially, morally and religiously. In fact, we regard it as the heart of our religious creed, and as the most sacred credo of all. We regard it as a holy war to the finish – a racial holy war.*

*RaHoWa [Racial Holy War] is inevitable. No longer can the
mud races and the White Race live on the same planet."*

Racial Holy War

Threats of an imminent "race war" or "Racial Holy War" (aka
RaHoWa) are common drumbeats of the hate movement and espoused
by many groups that do not conform with either the CI or the Creativity
credo. As American cultural standards relax over such issues as marriage
equality, advances in reproductive rights, and others, followers of CI
and Creativity groups predict the erosion of long-cherished religious
and cultural values that benefit white people.

Race war rhetoric is largely related to distress over increases of non-
white populations in the U.S., perceptions of rising immigration rates
and changing cultural norms. Much of Christian-oriented hate is based
on the belief that increasing numbers in Jewish, Muslim and other
faith-based communities translates to the demise of Christianity.

Arguably, one can say a race war has been raging since before Custer's
Last Stand at Little Big Horn, where Native American tribes were trying
to preserve their way of life. What we read about in daily newspapers,
broadcasts and online today may not be the all-out Armageddon envisioned by radical extremists, yet it is a race war nonetheless. Its worst
form is an insidious and destructive failure to understand and embrace
anyone who appears in any way different from the white supremacist
ideal image of humanity.

Most of the defectors interviewed for this book were well aware of
a foreseeable racial holy war during their time in the hate movement.

Kerry Noble, said that in the early 1980s, he believed his destruction of a gay church would be a sign to the rest of the hate movement
that the race war had started. His group (CSA) described conflicts in
the U.S. at the time as a race war, even if it didn't include race and
included other target groups like LGBTQ people.

In 1998, when Angela King met her boyfriend Ray Leone, both
were active in WCOTC (now the Creativity Movement). By then, some
of WCOTC's leading figures had been convicted of serious hate crimes,
including first degree murder, weapons possession, and other bias-motivated offenses. George Burdi, whose profile was deleted from this book

just prior to publication after evidence revealed he never really left the hate movement, purposefully named his hate rock band RaHoWa and included lyrics advocating racism and race war.

Race war has been conspicuous in historical inequities such as redlining and is evident at the top of the power structure, where white men rule in business, in government, and in the nonprofit world, with few exceptions.

Today, telltale signs of a race war are inherent in school districts creating ways to close the opportunity gap between white students and students of color so that all can graduate with the same degree of proficiency. The signs of race war include an embarrassingly low number of students of color and young women studying the so-called STEM subjects (Science, Technology, Engineering, and Math) required to fill future jobs in the high technology industry.

Race war is part of programs that try in vain to correct the school-to-prison pipeline in which black men are incarcerated at absurdly higher rates than white men who are able to afford a legal defense or who police overlook in their rush to pursue criminals that fit a negative stereotype. The imprisonment of African Americans is researched and carefully outlined in Michelle Alexander's monumental 2012 opus, *The New Jim Crow: Mass Incarceration in the Age of Colorblindness.*

According to a 2009 U.S. Department of Justice report, "Approximately twelve to thirteen percent of the American population is African-American, but they make up 60 percent of the almost 2.1 million male inmates in jail or prison." Numbers like these raise, or should raise, red flags about who gets incarcerated and who does not.

The threat of a race war, in combination with the distorted Christian values of the Creativity movement and CI groups across the U.S., is more of an all-out culture war, a conflict against anyone who doesn't conform with some idealized American avatar in which whiteness, religion, sexuality, and an able body are seen as God-give birthrights.

Domestic extremists go to extraordinary lengths to maintain their domination over anyone deemed inferior to their image of an ideal human. Extremists with weapons make the threat even more real. Those familiar with the tyranny of being victimized may also arm themselves, not because they feel weapons are the answer, but for self-protection against irrational hatred.

Not knowing how hate groups operate and which populations are among the most victimized is not so much ignorance as it is the product of inaccurate or false reporting by law enforcement agencies, misleading and incomplete news reports, legislative disinterest among elected officials who can correct historic wrongs, and an epidemic of public apathy.

In the midst of race war, real or imagined, everyone has a reason to live in fear. That fear is increasingly troublesome to peace-loving African Americans who, in addition to the wrath of white supremacists, are now coping with the rise of black nationalist and black separatist hate groups, further stigmatizing their own cultural identity.

Black Separatists/Black Nationalists

BLACK EXTREMISTS HAVE AT LEAST ONE IDEOLOGICAL element in common with white extremists: at the core of their existence, both would prefer a world without the other.

Black hate groups fall into two categories: separatists and nationalists. In 2018, the Southern Poverty Center re-categorized black separatists under the umbrella of black nationalists. The term black nationalist has come to embrace black separatists as part of a single social movement, with some distinctions.

Black separatists are motivated to create their own "place." The overall intent of the black separatist movement is to develop economic, cultural, and social standards for African Americans and people of African descent. Ultimately, their mission is to form a "state" or an environment where black people can live free of the domination of a white government, white norms, and white people.

Black nationalists base their ideology on social or religious issues, often with a strong focus on anti-Semitic and anti-LGBTQ values, in addition to an underlying loathing of white people. A rise in black nationalism, starting in the early 2000s, emerged as a response to increasing numbers of white nationalist groups. In essence, black nationalists mirror white nationalists, albeit with reversed perspectives.

Fine-tuned differences between the two factions are not particularly crucial to understand their motivations. Some experts see black separatists and black nationalists as a single category. As such, both are occasionally referred to as black *supremacists*. As with white hate groups, no ideology is absolute; some separatists may share nationalist values and vice versa. Both adhere to an anti-white sentiment.

Some do not agree with the concept of categorizing all anti-white black groups as hate groups, saying that if any racial group had a reason to disdain another, blacks have a sufficient excuse to justify their discontent, not necessarily their outright hatred, of whites – due to America's history of slavery, anti-black discrimination, and institutionalized racism.

"James"

A former Muslim and Nation of Islam activist described his experience as a hate group operative over five 90-minute interviews in 2016. He asked not to be identified by name. Through the 1960s and into the early 1970s, "James" was a black separatist. He has since disowned the hate movement and returned to his original Christian faith. His story involves a series of violent crimes, including attempted murder with a handgun modified to be untraceable. None of his offenses were prosecuted as hate crimes. The circumstances of his life experience demonstrate the conflicts of being black in a white-dominated culture and why anti-white hatred is so prevalent today.

James grew up in the Watts neighborhood of Los Angeles, an environment where racialized street gangs were common. At age 15, he watched the infamous Watts riots explode through six days of bombs, fires, and flaming crosses on lawns around black homes. Still in his teens, he was convicted of armed robbery, one of several offenses for which he served time in prison. His robberies did not target whites as a racial statement. Instead, he said, he didn't rob black people "because they didn't have anything to take."

In prison, James saw guards support the Aryan Brotherhood and treat Muslims and other African American inmates with contempt. In a steady upbeat voice, James portrayed a lifetime of opposing indignities from classmates, cellmates, and police. He said that during his years in the hate movement, all he wanted was a place where blacks didn't have to fight whites for their humanity.

James reiterated that African Americans who choose to be part of an organized anti-white group do not necessarily intend to cause harm or grief to white people – they just want to get away from them.

Black Nationalist Hatred

The SPLC takes the same hardline view of black hate groups as it does of white supremacists. On its website, SPLC explains that "White groups espousing beliefs similar to black separatists would be considered clearly racist. The same criterion should be applied to all groups regardless of their color. If we seek to expose white hate groups, we cannot be in the business of explaining away the black ones." The Anti-Defamation League expresses a similar viewpoint about organized black extremists, also identifying them as hate groups.

Out of the 1,020 hate groups SPLC identified in 2019, more than 25 percent (264 in all), were black nationalist groups. The combined category pivots on the understanding that anti-white groups are opposed to living in a white dominated culture.

The SPLC started listing black separatist groups in the 1990s. Heidi Beirich, SPLC Director of Intelligence, explains the distinction this way: "At the time, those groups argued for a separate state or country for black people. Today the groups are more diverse, including for example, Israel United in Christ and the Israelite School of Universal Practical Knowledge, which are primarily anti-Semitic, not separatist."

The SPLC points out a potential limitation confronting black nationalists: "Black hate groups have made virtually no inroads into the mainstream political realm and have virtually no supporters among elected officials." Radical right wing voices, meanwhile, have permeated the political establishment, with headliners like David Duke, former Ku Klux Klan Grand Wizard during the 1970s, at the forefront. Duke was elected to the Louisiana House of Representatives in 1989 and later ran unsuccessful campaigns for the U.S. Senate and President (1992). That was before he was convicted of defrauding political supporters by obtaining funds for personal expenses.

Not alone in his political quest for white power at the highest levels of government, Duke's style is among the most overt.

Black Nationalist Hate Speech

Hate speech is defined as the use of words that offend, threaten, or insult groups, based on race, color, religion, national origin, sexual orientation, disability, or other traits. Some experts say such language can be as detrimental as the actual commission of a crime, while others call hate speech just another name for words the listener doesn't like.

Black extremists have a reputation for using compelling oratory to inspire large audiences on a scale white supremacist's envy. Rancorous anti-white diatribes by black nationalist leaders are a key reason watchdog organizations like the SPLC and ADL identify them as hate groups and censure their actions.

Oren Segal, Director of the ADL Center on Extremism, cautions, "Hate speech is inherently a threat and leads to acting on the ideology." Segal calls Nation of Islam (NOI) the largest anti-Semitic organization in the U.S. He said NOI followers will believe in the group's ideology and act on what their leader urges them to do. "If a group calls for violence, that group may be more of a public threat than others," Segal said. As the epitome of black nationalist leadership, Segal pointed to the charisma of NOI national leader Louis Farrakhan. "Farrakhan will fill 18,000 seats at a speaking event. No white supremacist group could attract that many people."

As the leader of the most familiar black separatist group in the U.S., Farrakhan's rousing public lectures inspire African American sentiment against whites, often promoting and encouraging violence. The 82-year old NOI torchbearer is known for making statements against whites, Jews, women, and gays and for praising Hitler as "a great man." Among the biggest concerns about anti-white hate speech is that such hostile talk provokes members of recognized black nationalist hate groups and lone extremists to commit violent acts independently.

Farrakhan's pernicious demagoguery is mild compared to the more inflammatory rhetoric of Malik Zulu Shabazz, former National Chair of the New Black Panther Party (NBPP), not to be confused with the far less aggressive original Black Panther Party. SPLC identifies the NBPP as a black nationalist group. While speaking at the international headquarters of B'nai B'rith in Washington, D.C., a Jewish community organization dedicated advancing human rights, Shabazz urged lethal action. "Kill every goddamn Zionist in Israel! Goddamn little babies, goddamn old ladies! Blow up Zionist supermarkets!" Shabazz's statement is posted on the SPLC website, which also quotes the late Khalid Abdul Muhammad, former chair of the New Black Panther Party (NBPP) as saying, "There are no good crackers, and if you find one, kill him before he changes."

Despite the most sinister commentary from recognized black separatist *leaders*, no news report specifically links a hate crime directly to any one of them. That's because their legally acceptable hate speech arouses followers to act for them. Moreover, as a mark of the nation's poor hate crimes record keeping, no analytical methodology available today is able to detect the total number of hate crimes motivated by loners who listen to Farrakhan, Shabazz, or any other black extremist. The same is true of individuals who follow white supremacist leaders.

It is difficult for peace-loving people to absorb that, short of naming a specific individual target, hate speech is a Constitutional right. Yet, while black Americans face an extraordinary burden to gain the same religious and constitutional freedoms as whites, organized black hate groups are no more justified in their hate speech or actions than white supremacists.

Anti-White Hate Crime Data

SPLC's Heidi Beirich commented, "Of all the white people convicted of hate crimes, less than 10 percent are members of hate groups. They may have sucked up the ideology, but they're not card-carrying members." On the issue of race differences, Beirich added, "Based on FBI data, the number of black people arrested as perpetrators of anti-white bias crimes, roughly 18 percent, is much higher than the 13 percent of African Americans in the population."

Looking at the differences in the number of hate crimes committed by black offenders against white victims and whites against African Americans, over the seven years between 2010 and 2017, FBI data show that the percentage of anti-white hate crimes fluctuated only slightly. Yet, with few exceptions, white offenders always outpace anti-white African American extremists. During those seven years, the widest disparity was a more than two-to-one difference in 2011, when the FBI reported "59 percent of 5,731 known offenders were white and 20.9 percent were black." In 2016, the Bureau reported 5,770 known [hate crime] offenders, specifying "46 percent were white and 26.1 percent were black."

While quantifying hate crimes based on FBI annual statistics is far from perfect, numbers from the Bureau of Justice Statistics reflect a conflict with FBI data. According to the BJS 2004-2015 Hate Crime Victimization Report, "More than half (53.4 percent) of hate crime victimizations were against whites," while 14.5 percent were anti-black offenses.

Because BJS statistics originate from surveys completed by individuals as opposed to numbers furnished by police departments, these data suggest whites may *feel* more victimized by blacks. The *feeling* of victimization is difficult to separate from reality. That sentiment was voiced by several defectors who talked about being bullied by black classmates at school and in their neighborhoods.

Incompatible numbers from the FBI and BJS suggest that, based on the best data at our disposal, the reliability of statistical breakdowns separating bias-oriented offenses by racial category falls somewhere between elusive and tenuous. This open discrepancy should alert Americans, and the elected officials who represent them, that the information we get does not always measure up to an acceptable level of credibility.

As noted earlier, three critical flaws in the FBI's data collection process render its analysis unreliable. These discrepancies may contribute to a belief that black extremists are more prevalent than they are in reality. First, the astronomical number of police departments that report zero hate crimes in their jurisdiction every year; second, the number of city police and county sheriff's departments (roughly 18.2 percent) that fail to submit definitive hate crime data to the Bureau; and third, the inordinate number of hate crimes never reported to police.

Until government agencies can collect data that more convincingly reflects the number of hate crimes committed by and against any category of Americans, the numbers we do get will continue to weaken trust and raise even greater doubt.

Black nationalism is likely to become more widely known as a main element in the hate movement. According to SPLC, between 2013 and 2019, the number of organized black nationalist groups more than doubled, from 115 to 264. Before 2017, a previous surge flared between 2000 and 2003 when the number mushroomed from 48 to 136.

White Supremacist Fear Versus Black Nationalist Fear

A critical difference between white and black extremists is that the fears white supremacists feel are largely *perceived*, although nonetheless real *to them*. Without ever referring to a fear of losing privilege or power, white supremacists' concerns focus more on a false assumption of diminishing access and higher competition.

Perhaps the greatest fear white supremacists face today is the decline of the white population and increases in ethnic "minority" categories. Within the white power world, increasing numbers of immigrants and people of color translates to fewer jobs, greater difficulty getting into colleges and universities, competition for housing, and a distaste for having to share the planet with "inferior" humans. Race and nationality concerns are fundamentally rooted in a shared assumption of scarcity; a belief that more for "them" means less for "us."

According to a 2018 update from the U.S. Census Bureau (USCB), whites declined more than 9,000 between 2015 and 2016 and more than 31,000 between 2016 and 2017. In those same two years, "minorities" grew by 4.7 million, with gains of 2.4 million Latinos, 1.1 million Asians, and 1.2 million "other races," according to the USCB. The new data show that, for the first time in the nation's history, "minority" children under age 10 now outnumber whites.

For white supremacists, the latest USCB data may suggest a grim future, while for people of color, the numbers show hope. As the need for new workers expands to meet a constant consumer demand, corporate America and labor groups see opportunity in the numbers. The future is especially optimistic for companies trying to hire a more diverse workforce and meet the demands of an increasingly diverse marketplace.

Today, which groups qualify as minorities is shifting at a rate higher than previous USCB predictions. As the population changes, a contradictory term has evolved to describe the nation's population: the absurdly ambiguous "majority-minority" or "minority-majority" in which ethnic minorities make up a majority of the nation's population.

Black Hebrew Israelites

One group of black nationalists, Black Hebrew Israelites (also called Black Hebrews, African Hebrew Israelites, and Hebrew Israelites) are comprised of African Americans who believe they are descendants of the ancient Israelites. In varying degrees, adherents follow religious beliefs and practices of both Christianity and Judaism. The greater Jewish community, however, does not recognize Black Hebrew Israelites as Jews.

Black Hebrew Israelites are the second largest black nationalist organization nationwide, with 75 separate groups identified as hate groups by the SPLC in 2017, just behind Nation of Islam with a total of 81 groups.

Religious doctrine is implied in the names of many black nationalist groups. In 2017, 34 anti-white groups used the name Israel United in Christ; 19 called themselves Israelite Church of God in Jesus Christ; 10 went by the name Israelite School of Universal & Practical Knowledge; and 10 were titled All Eyes on Egipt [sic] Bookstore, a group that includes book sellers who self-identify as part of the Egyptian culture.

Black Israelite groups practice a theology that is fundamentally a race-reversed version of the Christian Identity movement. Yahweh ben Yahweh (born Hulon Mitchell Jr.), founder of Nation of Yahweh (also known as the Temple of Love), reportedly told his members that blacks were the "true Jews," proclaiming that God and the apostles were black. Mitchell told his followers he was the black messiah and he would lead them back to the promised land of Jerusalem to establish their kingdom. Yahweh was allegedly implicated in 14 murders, including several of white people (accused for the sin of being white) whose ears were cut off and brought back to show to Yahweh as evidence.

Black Nationalists and Prison

Whether in state or federal institutions, imprisoned African Americans face an uphill battle to be treated on a par with white inmates.

In 2014, African Americans constituted 2.3 million, or 34 percent of the total 6.8 million correctional population, according to a report by the National Association for the Advancement of Colored People (NAACP). The report also notes, "The imprisonment rate for African American women is twice that of white women." The NAACP study found that although African Americans and Hispanics make up approximately 32% of the US population, they comprised 56% of all incarcerated people in 2015." This issue is vividly detailed in Michelle Alexander's best seller, *The New Jim Crow: Mass Incarceration in the Age of Colorblindness*.

James, the former black separatist, told me he served time in both federal and state prisons for various offenses not tried as bias crimes. He said that the white supremacist Aryan Brotherhood had an ominous presence and always got priority over black inmates; "They were allowed to do whatever they wanted." Muslims and non-Muslim [black] inmates united for protection from the Aryans. In prison, members of groups are easily recognizable by such variables as tattoos, physical appearance, demeanor, and language. Skin color also plays a critical role in whom one associates with behind bars.

In a 2012 report titled *Bigotry Behind Bars: Racist Groups In U.S. Prisons*, the Anti-Defamation League made a chilling observation: "… prison officials and inmates have reported that prisoners identify themselves primarily along racial lines. Open identification makes it easier for racist prison gangs – with the help of white supremacist 'outreach' programs – to attract new members, especially those seeking protection from threats inside the prison." The report went on to predict that in such a racially charged environment, animosities can easily get out of control, a fact that can lead to prison riots and to race-based violence after black inmates are released. This makes prison gangs a problem not only for law enforcement, but also for society as a whole."

Neo-Nazi Tom Metzger, leader of White Aryan Resistance, not one to compliment African Americans lightly, is quoted as saying black supremacist groups, "are the black counterpart of White Aryans."

James, the former black separatist whose story is polarized against the lives of white supremacist defectors, said that during his time as an NOI activist, he stuck to the belief that black people were the chosen people. Similarly, Kerry Noble told me the Christian Identity movement is predicated on a belief that white people are God's chosen people.

Today, being identified as self-proclaimed chosen people is a hallmark of many hate groups vying for their ideology to be blessed by the

Almighty, most of which have absolutely nothing else in common and are perfectly content never having to interact with the others.

Black nationalists face much different threats, with the effects of white power and privilege at the vanguard. Black nationalists' fears are embedded in a long and undeniable history of systematic discrimination and institutional racism. Historically, in addition to constitutionally-imposed slavery from the colonial times until the end of the American Civil War, African Americans and people of African descent were forced to endure the use of separate restrooms and drinking fountains from those reserved for whites, and routinely inhumane treatment in public places through Jim Crow laws that enforced racial segregation in the Southern U.S. from the late 1800s until 1965. During those years, cross burnings and lynchings were a common occurrence.

Blacks were summarily denied the right to vote, then "red-lined" or barred from buying homes in middle class neighborhoods from the 1940s and up to the 1990s. They were shut out of jobs to pay for whatever housing they could find and still encountered more hurdles to secure health care, despite suffering health issues unique to their race.

Today, applying to colleges and universities is difficult for African Americans, who also face a persistent opportunity gap between blacks and whites in K-12 education. And despite a BJS report that the numerical difference between black and white prisoners is half as wide as it was in 2009 when America's prison population peaked, the mass incarceration of black men rages on.

Few whites have ever had to abide similar indignities or injustices. Against a backdrop of historical anti-black oppression, African Americans have a justifiable reason to be upset with the dominant white culture and a political establishment that has failed to support them on a par with whites. Despite the Declaration of Independence proposition that "all men are created equal," in practice, such a reality has never been self-evident.

9/11 in Slow Motion

THE INCREMENTAL IMPACT OF HATE CRIMES on the American psyche approximates a passively tortuous slow motion version of 9/11. According to the FBI's faulty hate crimes data, 135 hate crime murders have been accounted for since 9/11. Those deaths cannot compare with 2,996 lives lost from three misguided aircraft, even though the families and friends of all terrorized victims share a similar grief.

September 11, 2001 marks a turning point in how the nation copes with targeted violence. Since then, Americans have become all too aware of the threat of international terrorism. Aside from the inconvenience of heightened security checks at airports and government offices in the U.S., today the aftermath of 9/11 extends around the globe.

Some facts help to conceptualize the reach of malicious harassment by domestic terrorists inside U.S. borders and how the overall impact of crimes by American extremists relate to 9/11.

Less than a month after the 9/11 attacks, U.S. troops invaded Afghanistan to dismantle al-Qaeda.

During the first year American forces invaded Afghanistan, extremists were active throughout the U.S as members of 1,018 hate groups, some of whom were considered *domestic* terrorists. That year, 6,222 hate crimes were reported to law enforcement agencies across the U.S.

By mid 2018, the toll on American servicemembers in Afghanistan totaled 2,372 U.S. deaths and 20,320 injuries. While the war in Afghanistan ended three-years after it began, 8,000 American troops were still stationed there in 2018.

In 2017 alone, six American soldiers were killed and 11 injured in Afghanistan. **That same year, 15 Americans were murdered by extremists on American soil and 7,175 hate crimes were reported to law enforcement agencies nationwide.** The *New York Times* reported in 2015, "Since Sept. 11, 2001, nearly twice as many people have been killed by white supremacists, anti-government fanatics, and other non-Muslim extremists than by radical Muslims." To this day, Muslims continue to be a prime target of the hate movement.

Equating the power of Al Qaeda or ISIS in any way to American white nationalists is a stretch. The idea here is to unmask the combined force that hate groups and countless individuals who practice acts of terror wield against Americans every day, often with similar physical and emotional consequences on their victims.

Homeland Security

Since 9/11, 22 former federal departments were merged into a new super-agency, the Department of Homeland Security. Created to provide a coordinated federal response in the event of a terrorist attack, natural disasters or other emergencies, the DHS mission also aims to "prevent and deter terrorist attacks and protect against and respond to threats and hazards to the nation." The DHS budget has expanded from $38.2 billion in 2015 to $47.5 billion requested in the 2019 federal budget. Today, DHS is the third largest Cabinet department, after the Departments of Defense and Veterans Affairs.

White supremacists harass, threaten, harm, and in some cases, kill Americans they deem "inferior" to themselves. They act on their threats to destroy property and sacred sites. **Currently, in the absence of a specifically documented line item budget, it appears more government funding is allocated to *count* hate crimes than is committed to strategizing a coordinated plan to stop them.** This contradicts whatever the FBI agents do to thwart large-scale bias crimes before they can happen.

The overall U.S. cost for global intelligence and surveillance is unknown and largely inestimable. As reported in a 2018 *Washington Post* article, the best idea we have about funding the U.S. intelligence community is a 2013 budget of $52.6 billion for the operation of 16 spy agencies. That figure came from a document leaked by Edward Snowden, the former government contractor working in the Central Intelligence Agency. The main focus of those resources is a response to international terrorism against Americans – where it belongs.

Yet, since September 11, 2001, 135 Americans were murdered by domestic extremists and more than 89,000 hate crimes occurred in the U.S., nearly 15 times the 6,000 injured in the 9/11 attacks. Yet, no line item budget accounts for security against the threats and hazards from American-born terrorists. The extent of government funding designated to stop American extremism is a public mystery.

Between 9/11 and early 2018, the cumulative cost to fight terrorism abroad through 2017 amounts to $2.8 trillion, according to a report issued by the Stimson Center, a Washington DC-based nonpartisan policy think tank. The trouble with conclusions in reports like the Stimson Center study is that uncertainty is embedded into any such estimate.

Why? **Because no one knows how much of the federal budget goes to fight terrorism by American extremists against American citizens.**

At an ADL event in 2014, former FBI Director James Comey highlighted the effects of malicious harassment in one pithy statement. "Hate crimes are different from other crimes. They strike at the heart of one's identity. They strike at our sense of self, our sense of belonging. The end result is loss: loss of trust, loss of dignity and, in the worst case, loss of life."

Since then, a new trope has evolved to describe such an effect on people: Erasure, the practice of collective indifference that renders certain people and groups invisible.

Hate crime victims are too often unrecognized, their stories untold, their experience erased.

Psychological Effects

The American Psychological Association views hate crimes as "message crimes." In 1998, an APA report commented, "The perpetrator is sending a message to the members of a certain group that they are despised, devalued, or unwelcome in a particular neighborhood, community, school, or workplace."

Canada may be ahead of the U.S in the ways it addresses hate. The APA assessment was echoed in a 2011 report issued by the Canada Department of Justice titled *Understanding the Community Impact of Hate Crimes: A Case Study*. In 2017 alone, the research discovered hate crimes against Muslims, Jews, and black Canadians rose 47 percent over the previous year. A brochure circulated by the Edmonton (Canada) Police Hate and Bias Coordinators captures the psychological loss:

"Victims of hate crimes suffer more than just the physical and emotional effect of the crime. Hate crimes send a message to the victim and the victim's community that they are threatened, inferior, unwanted and less than human. This leads to victims and communities feeling anxiety, stress, fear and isolation. Attitudes can become hardened which may lead to distrust and retaliation. Peaceful coexistence is put in jeopardy, and *community fracture can occur.* If people who commit such crimes are not charged, they might believe that society agrees with them."

The Canada report concluded, that after a hate crime incident, "many people experienced increased levels of fear for their personal safety and for the safety of their family." For some, however, the case study offered a positive twist. Half of Canada's hate crime victims reported that the incident strengthened their relationship with other ethnic/cultural communities."

The psychological impact of hate crimes is difficult to measure. Even if a victim's injuries are not visible, that person is unlikely to return to work or home as if nothing happened. For many, the aftermath includes embarrassment, shame, and questions. Why did it happen? How could I have prevented it? Who can I (or should I) tell about it? When the effects are apparent and significant, colleagues and coworkers try to comfort the victim and one another, often at a cost in work productivity.

In the community, an emotional chain reaction affects family members, close friends, neighbors, and others in the victim's social network, especially those who share the minority status for which a victim was targeted. To those unwilling or unable to share their experience with others, the result is further internal agony.

Economic Effects

Hate crimes have a cumulative effect. Because more than half of all hate crimes may not be reported to police, law enforcement is unable to identify, investigate, or prosecute all offenders. Without rigorous standards of accountability, the total punch of American extremism on a community's economic vitality is impossible to fathom.

At work, hate crime victims may need time to recuperate before they can return to their full capacity. For those unable to tell their supervisor about an incident, or a boss who is unable to detect a possible trauma to their employee, the consequences can include low performance ratings or income losses. At home, relationships can be impaired, especially if family members and friends doubt the severity of an incident. The hidden costs pile up.

Reports assessing the costs of hate are rare. In December 2015, a single incident paralyzed schools in one of the most populous U.S. cities. After the Los Angeles Unified School District (LAUSD) received an email threat suggesting an act of violence was imminent, all public schools were shut down. Although the incident was called an act of public terrorism rather than a hate crime, the difference is indistinguishable. This is one of the rare examples in which the cost of the threat was even speculated.

Officials at the LAUSD estimated the cost of the shutdown at $29 million. The State Superintendent of Public Instruction later told reporters the cost could be closer to $50 million. Nearly 32,000 teachers were idled along with another 39,000 staff. Police, fire fighters, and other city personnel were taken away from other emergencies. The consequences of that single email do not account for the loss of business productivity as parents of 655,000 students rushed to comfort their children.

Financial costs left to pay after the biggest hate crimes in the U.S. have never been determined. We don't know the cost to Orlando, the State of Florida or the federal government after 49 people were murdered and 53 wounded at the Pulse, a gay nightclub. We don't know the cost to

Pittsburg, the State of Pennsylvania or the federal government after 11 Jewish members were gunned down and six injured at the Tree of Life Synagogue. We don't know the cost to Charleston, the State of South Carolina or the federal government after nine church members were killed and three injured at Emanuel First African Methodist Episcopal church. The unexpected cost to a city, county, or state, can also affect its ability to cover the costs of other and more urgent public commitments.

The Future

Over recent decades, the hate movement has merged into an amorphous, high-tech diaspora of terror. As some hate groups consolidate, lose members, or face a reluctant demise, no agency predicts a corresponding decline in the number of bias-motivated incidents. Despite periodic contractions in the number of extremist groups from one year to another, it is impossible to predict whether the number of hate groups or hate crimes will increase over the foreseeable future.

Based on U.S. Census Bureau (USCB) projections that by 2060 the overall "mixed race" population in the U.S. will more than triple and both the Latino/Hispanic and Asian/Pacific Island populations will more than double, white supremacists and domestic terrorists of all persuasions will feel more compelled than ever to act. [The USCB projects only a slight (1.6%) increase in the number of African-Americans over the next half century.] While many Americans see hope and progress in the predictions, white extremists see reason to protect their turf and fear for their future. To them, the survival of the species relies on a white majority.

One defector described his experience in a neo-Nazi group this way: "As the racial composition changed, we felt threatened. We felt that our culture and our birthright were being taken away from us."

What white extremists see as losses, U.S. employers see as gains. Businesses are recruiting like never before. From farming and building maintenance jobs to workers in high tech positions, health care, and the sciences, employers are deliberately wooing a skilled and more diverse workforce. In addition to increased profit, their goal is to show consumers their employees reflect, embrace, and serve the cultural needs of the entire marketplace. The absence of an inclusive work environment can cost a company its image.

Between 2018 and 2019, three major retailers joined a long history of companies facing public ridicule in the wake of embarrassing cultural goofs. Gucci, the highest selling Italian luxury brand of fashion and leather goods, found itself in a national controversy after it ran an ad for a $890 black-knit sweater that showed the product, including bright red lips ringing an opening for the mouth pulled up over the lower half of a woman's face. The photo was criticized for looking like blackface. Clothing retailer H&M hit a similar backlash after running an online ad that pictured a black child wearing a hooded sweatshirt that said "coolest monkey in the jungle." And Nivea, which calls itself "the World's #1 Skincare Brand," dumped a short-lived tagline, "White Is Purity." At a time when white supremacy is in the news every week, a slogan touting white purity did not go over well with consumers.

Perhaps these vendors could have avoided days of negative publicity and internal efforts to clean up their image if there were more people of color in their board rooms, on their executive teams, and in their advertising staff, and if all employees were encouraged to speak up when foolish errors jeopardize their company's brand.

It is not much of an exaggeration to compare these corporate errors to what happens when citizens fail to respond to hate in their communities.

In 1987 the Hudson Institute, a Washington, D.C.-based strategic management organization, issued the results of a landmark study titled *The Workforce 2000 Report*, predicting that over the ensuing decade, "The workforce will grow slowly, becoming older, more female, and more disadvantaged [and] new jobs in service industries will demand much higher skill levels." Among the Institute's recommendations at the time: "Stimulate balanced world growth, maintain the dynamism of an aging workforce; reconcile the conflicting needs of women, work, and families; integrate black and Hispanic workers fully into the economy; and improve the education preparation of all workers."

That future came faster than predicted and the Institute's recommendations provide a business imperative that is as insightful today as it was over 30 years ago.

The effort to rectify a history of shortcomings in the way the nation addresses the hate movement is filled with conflicts and contradictions: the total number of hate group members and lone wolf extremists-at-large is unknown and unpredictable; the FBI says hate crimes are decreasing while BJS estimates suggest the opposite; many Americans who insist they are not racist exhibit racist behaviors.

Without consistent protocols to prosecute bias-motivated crimes uniformly in every state, and as long as police departments fail to research and report every hate crime in its jurisdiction to the FBI, the public has no reliable or credible mechanism to know the extent to which extremists cause harm to people and communities.

The future requires a proactive strategy for rational, pragmatic, and ethical legal standards in order to trump ignorance, intolerance, and hatred. That strategy simply does not exist today. We have to start thinking more positively about change and answering some critical questions:

What if the U.S. Congress or some forward-thinking federal government agency saw the wisdom to allot an adequate budget and fund research that effectively leads to a measurable reduction in white supremacist harassment and the number of hate crimes?

What if people in communities targeted by hate groups were able to secure more government resources to stop further damages to their people? What if all communities of color, faith groups, LGBTQ and disability advocates worked together to defend themselves from the burgeoning undercurrent of bigotry and hate? What if more white allies came to their defense?

What if more American universities and private funders joined those already committing resources to study ways to prevent Americans from becoming radicalized, from entering organized hate groups, or plotting attacks on people in their own communities?

What if every victim of a bias crime felt safe and empowered to report the offense to police?

What if every police department trained every police officer to respond to a hate crime call with cultural sensitivity? What if all police officers who disregard the seriousness of a hate crime were disciplined, or better yet, terminated for their inability to live up to the requirements of their job?

The U.S. government's response to the hate movement is shameful and regrettable, although it is consistent with America's history of discrimination and oppression of marginalized people.

Despite government inaction, the failure to capture the public's attention to the impacts of hate relates to the Boiling Frog Fable. The premise of the tale is that a frog put into boiling water will jump out of the pot, but a frog put in tepid water – slowly brought to a boil – will not perceive the danger and be cooked to death.

On 9/11, the water boiled. For victims of hate crimes, the temperature is still rising.

The sacred ground of the 9/11 Memorial and Museum is an apt recognition of lives lost and injured. Walking through the somber exhibits helps visitors understand the scope and impact of terrorism, as well at it facilitates healing. No monument commemorates the victims of white supremacist violence.

Hate groups and their loner brethren operate within the same ideological and religious framework that motivated men to fly jets into iconic landmarks. Mercifully, the ingenuity of American extremists does not match the scale and scope of their international counterparts.

We have a long way to go to ensure that never happens.

Author's Note

When I interviewed Kerry Noble in 2006, the first defector I met in person, little did I suspect the journey would take me into the depths of American domestic terrorism and white supremacist thinking. Yet, with each meeting or phone call to other defectors, a picture came more clearly into focus of how perceptions of race and identity can lead from childhood innocence to a prison term. Through their stories, defectors explain how hateful ideologies, whites-only websites and social media can easily trick otherwise sensible, compassionate people into believing hypocritical diatribes and adopting distorted ideologies.

Two things are certain: (1) the hate movement is here to stay and (2) the white population is shrinking.

First, as hate progresses, it is possible that by uniting many diverse voices, the divisiveness that emboldens extremists and makes their hateful goal so much easier to attain can be reversed.

The only way to stop hate is by action. That action must include all categories of people targeted by hate groups working in tandem with their allies. From community support comes political support. Until a majority of elected officials understand the extent and absurdity of the hate movement, the tautological and hypocritical arguments and the vicious practices of white supremacists, white nationalists, black nationalists, and whites-only web sites will continue to sway the political establishment to either support them or do nothing to stop them.

Second, the U.S. population is slowly losing its white majority status. This is an infuriating reality to those who have hoped to maintain a white-dominated society. At the close of the 2010 census, the U.S. Census Bureau predicted that by the year 2043 whites will no longer make up the majority of Americans. The forecast was based on future projections of childbearing, mortality rates, and international migration. In 2018, the USCB updated its projections after data showed declines among whites and a counterbalancing increase in the number of "minority" populations, with unexpected increases in children age 10 and younger.

By the time those children reach voting age, they will think in much more inclusive ways than adult voters today. By the time those children receive their college degrees, they will understand the challenges marginalized populations and immigrant Americans have experienced in deeply personal and emotional ways. They will have walked down that path and heard stories from their families and loved ones. Their workplaces will be more diverse. And the aging traditionalists of today will no longer be around to stop them.

An influx of new immigrants arrives daily. Unless any of us is among the fewer than one percent of Americans born into a family of indigenous Americans or Alaska Natives, the newcomers are no different than our own earliest ancestors who emigrated here from another land. Chances are, it was not much easier for our families to settle here than it is for migrants in the 21st Century.

As the ethnic composition of Americans continues to change, any business entity that fails to include innovations devised and driven by the needs of a diverse population is doomed to produce products and services for a diminishing consumer base. The same is true for government agencies and nonprofits.

The more our neighborhoods, places we recreate, and the American workforce reflect the *entire* population, the more likely we are to build communities and commercial enterprises that appeal to and meet the needs of a broad marketplace. Contrary to the radical ideologies of fear-mongering white supremacists, neo-Nazis, white nationalists, the alt-right and any other faction of organized hate – this is a win-win strategy.

The threat of a American extremist-led 9/11-sized culture war is ever present. As population shifts continue, halting hate groups and hate crimes may become a little bit easier. Meanwhile, we've got our work cut out for us.

Seven Ways to Resist Hate

THESE SEVEN STRATEGIES SYNTHESIZE SUGGESTIONS from defectors, as well as the vision and guidance of professionals who commit their lives to understanding, deconstructing, and stopping hate. They offer an approach to gradually and deliberately rob the movement of its invasive power. Each point is based on the expectation and belief that we can – and must – embrace differences, rather than judge them and wish they didn't exist.

ONE: Vote. Choose a candidate in EVERY election.

In every election cycle, do your best to learn the platforms of your local elected officials and their challengers, as well as new candidates. Do they support fairness, immigration, equal access to jobs and pay equity?

If you can't attend debates or political forums, talk to like-minded friends who do.

For years, our government has been in an ideological crossfire, pitting extreme conservative thinking against sometimes unknown progressives. Trying to balance the playing field can be a full-time job. Politics today is like a spinning roulette wheel on which tax dollars are weighted to stop where the money benefits those placing the bets.

Be at the table. If you are unable to support a candidate financially or as a volunteer, let your friends know why you agree with that person's ideas. For years, the League of Women Voters used the slogan, "Vote and the choice is yours. Don't vote and the choice is theirs." That nails it.

TWO: Be involved in your community.

Community organizations are the main line of defense against hate. In recent years, trust in the political establishment, government agencies – including police – to protect the needs of vulnerable people has eroded to a low point. Opposing factions have yet to figure out a way to get beyond their differences and reconcile a history of white privilege and discrimination against any group identified as a "minority." This is where like-minded colleagues can – and must – unite with their cultural peers and rise above all the negativity they face every day in the mainstream.

Were it not for community leaders like the Rev. Dr. Martin Luther King Jr, Susan B. Anthony, Helen Keller, and Harvey Milk, or civil rights organizations such as the National Association for the Advancement of Colored People, the National Jewish Federation, Human Rights Campaign, the Council on American-Islamic Relations and their local and state chapters, to name a few of thousands of such leaders and community organizations, we would still be living in the darkest days of America's past.

For those who are unable to be politically active, or choose not to be, community groups can be your voice. Virtually every interest group has an organization to lobby political leaders and corporations on behalf of the constituencies they represent. Groups with an opposing viewpoint are just as likely to have their own lobbyists.

The goal is to have inclusion and fairness prevail over public perceptions of superiority and inferiority. The groups you believe in – and which believe in you – must have more members, raise more dollars, be more politically active, and refuse to accept the status quo. This means that only by attending local community meetings whenever possible, contributing when and how much you can, and articulating your concerns to people who share your life experience can you have a loud, unified voice that will not fall on deaf ears.

It is essential that nonprofit groups be empowered to monitor hate crime incidents within their population – even more aggressively than law enforcement agencies. Citizens who distrust police must have an alternative for reporting bias crimes and public harassment.

THREE: Empower victims of hate crimes to file a police report.

Encouraging victims to make themselves vulnerable to police requires trust. If police are not capable of treating victims of hate crimes fairly and with cultural sensitivity, talk to your elected officials, and local media.

When nonprofit organizations that represent "minority" populations monitor police reports of bias crimes in their communities, the number of stories they hear should match the number of hate crimes reported to police. If they do not, a dialogue will help to identify discrepancies and what can be done.

Expect pushback. Police do not like being told they're not protecting people in their jurisdiction. Be prepared to provide evidence to substantiate disparities.

At a time when the Bureau of Justice Statistics reports that more than half of U.S. hate crimes are never reported to police, we have to examine why. Another option is to ask editors and reporters at the most objective regional newspapers, broadcast stations, and online news services to examine the issue and report to the community.

FOUR: Teach children about differences at the earliest possible age.

Birth is not too early to expose children to a variety of people and cultural experiences. This advice requires family members to have a cadre of diverse friends who can welcome you and your children into their home, their house of worship, their community center, or some sacred space that represents their culture. Children pick up on the subtle messages of inclusion just as easily as they learn to exclude people.

Pre-school programs are only as strong as the faculty and curricula they employ. To whatever extent possible, question any program before and during your child's pre-kindergarten education. Does the faculty reflect the ethnic profile of the students it serves? Do activities allow children to feel confident about themselves? If not, demand change independently or with the help of local community groups.

FIVE: Know – and adhere to – your own core values.

A value without action to support it is meaningless. Every defector talked about violating their most cherished values in order to buy into the values of a group or its leader. One after another, they said that only when they realized they had lost track of their core principles were they sufficiently empowered to leave the movement and rely on their own moral barometer.

The old adage "If you don't stand for something, you'll fall for anything" doubles as a call to action. Taking a position to support or oppose something is one of the main reasons people join groups. Get involved in and support groups that support your values.

Try this: Take an inventory, a list or a tally of the values you cherish most. Which are you certain you will never violate? Be aware of the times a weighty value can be difficult to maintain. Honesty. Respect. Compassion. Love. At times, even the most cherished ethical and moral standards can pose a personal conflict. Be aware of the times your values are being tested or, more importantly, when they may no longer be valid.

It is worthy of note that the very same leadership dynamics that empower white supremacist leaders may also be used to unduly influence decisions regarding religion, education, health care, and other important personal choices.

ALWAYS be aware when persuasion is more focused on the speaker's choices rather than the listener's values and personal decision making.

SIX: Exercise curiosity and critical thinking.

The most unreasonable and irresponsible ideas evolve and endure when the people who create or believe them *insist* they are right – and lose their ability to accept reasonable feedback. Charismatic leaders rarely question their own logic. Don't be afraid to activate your BS detector. Under the best of circumstances, all information is filtered through biases and judgments that most of us are not aware we have.

Analyze and evaluate what you hear and see. Being a rational and disciplined thinker helps to distinguish what is relevant from what is not.

Insist on getting the facts. If something doesn't make sense, ask hard questions. Think like a journalist. Reporters are trained to ask the most critical questions: Who, What, Where, Why, When, and How? It's not necessary to be confrontational in an inquiry, but it is important to help yourself and others separate reality from nonsense.

SEVEN: Whenever possible, protest *politically*, not *physically*.

Be very cautious about attending rallies or events organized by known hate groups. Attend peace marches instead.

It is impossible to stop protesters who are emotionally prepared, equipped, and trained to withstand the taunts of hateful people. It is arguable whether their protests do more to reclaim community power or give more fuel to the movement. Those who carry weapons to such events merely increase the likelihood of someone getting hurt or worse.

Leave the confrontational actions to activists and community leaders who are trained and prepared to stand up to bullies.

The hate movement gets its power from being recognized for the fear it generates and by the opposition it engenders. The attention feeds egos and emboldens organizers to do more. A rally communicates a point, or in the case of a white power event, a threat. A robust showing by protestors can communicate a message to its organizers: We are not afraid. Similarly, when hateful people mobilize a march to provoke fear – and no one shows up – the same message is sent.

What happens if no opposing activists show up at a white supremacist rally? Extremists get visibility. Protesters may believe the hatemongers get their way. But by disregarding demonstrations promoted by organized hate groups, good guys don't get hurt. Media have less to report. And, in reality, not much changes.

Casting a vote is a more powerful action than screaming at the top of your lungs about injustices.

Additional Resources to Resist Hate . . .

A Google search for such key words as "Stop Hate," "Organizations that Oppose Hate," or "How to Resist the Hate Movement" will guide you to an abundance of helpful resources. Here are some of my favorites:

- The Southern Poverty Law Center's Teach Tolerance Program offers easy-to-use tools and guides for teachers and parents, including professional development and educational materials, classroom planners, film kits, webinars, and a resource-rich quarterly magazine and other publications. Another helpful SPLC tool: *Ten Ways to Fight Hate: A Community Response Guide.* https://www.splcenter.org/20100216/ ten-ways-fight-hate-community-response-guidel

- An article available on Character.org titled *19 Signs Your Child Is Being Bullied and What to Do about It* offers a quick and well-written guide for anyone who suspects a child is being bullied.

- The Mayo Clinic offers useful tips regarding the symptoms of child abuse. An online article is available at http://www.mayoclinic.org/diseases-conditions/child-abuse/basics/symptoms/con-20033789

- The National Crime Prevention Council lists Strategies for Preventing Hate Crime at http://www.ncpc.org/topics/hate-crime/strategies

- American Psychological Association features insights in an article titled Understanding and preventing Hate Crimes at http://www.apa.org/monitor/nov01/hatecrimes.aspx

Acknowledgments

My gratitude goes first to the brave women and men who trusted me and poured their souls out over hours, and in some cases days, of probing questions and spontaneous phone calls and emails: Kerry Noble, Bryon Widner, Julie Miller, Angela King, Arno Michaelis, and Frank Meeink. I extend equal thanks to the more than two dozen other defectors who agreed to telephone interviews.

I especially appreciate the support of my family, brothers Frank (and Ginny), Fred (and Joy), Roger (and Nanja), and my late sister Virginia, for always loving their gay brother, even when I believed they didn't.

I am also grateful to the content experts at the nonprofit organizations who so graciously gave their help: the American Civil Liberties Union, the Matthew Shepard Foundation, the Council on American-Islamic Relations, the Global Faith and Justice Project, and many others.

I thank my colleagues who gave me constant encouragement and support to continue writing this book: LueRachelle Brim-Atkins, Peggy Nagae, Cleo Molina, Alexandra Liggins, Donna Stringer and Andy Reynolds, to name a few.

I sincerely thank the staff at Southern Poverty Law Center, especially Mark Potok, former Editor of SPLC Intelligence Report, who gave me the first names of defectors and always returned my requests for information, as well as Mark's successor Heidi Beirich, and SPLC Public Affairs Director Booth Gunter. Same for the staff at the Anti-Defamation League, especially Oren Segal, Director of the ADL Center on Extremism. I also extend a huge thank you to Tim Wise for giving me the inspiration of another white guy challenging racism.

I appreciate the help of law enforcement professionals who responded to a litany of questions, especially my ever-patient friend Mike Hogan, as well as other federal and county prosecutors, lawyers, and police officers who helped me make sense of complex ways hate crimes laws work (in most cases) to bring hate criminals to justice.

My gratitude also goes to Bill Brummel, Bill Brummel Productions (producer of *Erasing Hate*); Danny Coulson, former FBI agent; Cooper Thompson, co-author of *White Men Challenging Racism:35 Personal Stories*; and all the authors, professors, and academics I interviewed and were eager to share their research on hate groups and hate crimes with me, especially Randy Blazak, Caitlin Carlson, William Parkin, Pete Simi, Corrie Wallace, and many others. I particularly appreciate the guidance and support from author friends who helped me navigate the publishing process: Geoff Bellman, Posy Gering, Kathleen O'Connor, Thom Speidel, Norm Stamper, Pat Vivian, and others.

I thank Jerry Paulukonis and Carole Glickfeld for editorial guidance, and Mary Pat DiLeva for proofreading; Lynn Hagerman who helped me focus on my writing, as well as the beta readers who previewed and commented on early drafts: Una Boyle, Nancy Burkhalter, Adam Kuglin, Lynn Lambie, Verda Lofton, Barbara McMichael, Barbara Olsen, Alec Stevens, and others. Big thanks also to Ed Parks and Deb Dollard who allowed me the use of their cabin for writing retreats.

I also thank the courageous souls who, during my 28 years as a cultural competency consultant, put their hearts on the line to share deeply personal histories of discriminatory behaviors by coworkers, colleagues, family members – as well as those who acknowledged making biased judgments about people from different backgrounds. I grew with them.

I also thank all my closest friends who gave me their candid opinions and moral support to keep writing: Michael Auch and Scott Carley, Deborah Balick, Phil Bereano, Tim Bradbury, Sylvia Fisher, Jordon Goldwarg, Derek Kiewatt, Vicki Legman, Jan Levy, Kimberly Reason, John McMichael, Bob Wood, Jeff White, Terri Zimmerman, and so many more – plus anyone who had the misfortune of istting next to me on an airplane, and asking, "What do you do?"

THANK YOU ALL

Endnotes

Kerry Noble

[1] *Tabernacle of Hate: Why They Bombed Oklahoma City*. Kerry Noble. 1st edition. Voyageur Publishing, 1998; 2nd edition published as *Tabernacle of Hate: Seduction Into Right-Wing Extremism*. Syracuse University Press. 2010.

[2] *Saved By My Enemies*. Copyright 1998-2004 Kerry Noble. This book is not available in bookstores. Kerry Kerry wrote the volume as a follow-up to *Tabernacle of Hate*.

[3] *Blood and Politics: The History of the White Nationalist Movement From the Margins to the Mainstream*. Leonard Zeskind. Copyright 2009 by Leonard Zeskind. Farrar, Straus and Giroux 2009.

[4] The Voice Stress Analyzer Test uses a panel of colored lights to measure physiological stress or agitation in a person's voice, as evidenced through micro-tremors and voice amplitude, indicating whether a person is telling the truth while responding to a series of questions. "We tested [the VSA] on all our men to judge their dedication to the group," Kerry writes in Saved By My Enemies. The test is highly controversial. According to a study funded by the National Institute of Justice (NIJ), two of the most popular VSA programs in use by police departments across the country are "no better than flipping a coin when it comes to detecting deception regarding recent drug use."

[5] *No Heroes: Inside the FBI's Secret Counter-Terror Force*. Danny O. Coulson and Elaine Shannon, Pocket Books, 1999.

[6] ibid.

[7] According to the ATF, "Binary explosives are pre-packaged products consisting of two separate components, usually an oxidizer like ammonium nitrate and a fuel such as aluminum or another metal. These components are not specified in ATF regulations as "Explosives" and the agency does not regulate their sale or distribution, even when sold together in binary "kits." However, when both components are combined, the mixture is an explosive material subject to ATF restrictions.

[8] C4 or Composition C-4 "plastic explosive" is a combustible material in flexible or elastic sheet form, made with one or more high explosives. C-4 is composed of explosives, a plastic binder, and usually a marker or odorizing chemical.

Bryon Widner and Julie Miller

[9] The Imperial Klans of America, Knights of the Ku Klux Klan is a white supremacist organization styled after the original KKK. In 2008, it was reported that the IKA had the nation's second largest KKK membership. Founded in 1997, the group is headquartered in Western Kentucky.

[10]StormFront.org is promoted as "a community of racial realists and idealists." It serves as a primary internet link to white nationalists, white supremacists, and neo-Nazi groups around the world.

[11]The Southern Poverty Law Center cites Blood & Honour, which was originally based in the United Kingdom, as "a shadowy international coalition of racist skinhead gangs. The SPLC also reports "two rival groups claim to be affiliated with Blood & Honour. One faction, in North America, is known as Blood & Honour America and includes skinheads, neo-Nazis and Christian Identity adherents. The other group, known as Blood & Honour Council USA, was affiliated until recently with the Vinlanders Social Club. The group is now represented by two skinheads who run a racist music label in Ohio and a racist video company in Texas.

[12] The name "Creativity Movement" evolved after a lawsuit in the year 2000, charging that the Church of the Creator infringed the trademark of a similarly-named church in Oregon that had no connection to a hate group. The anti-Semitic and anti-Christian group continued under the name World Church of the Creator. U.S, District Judge Joan Lifkow, who presided over the court case, later fined WCOTC $1,000 a day until it complied with the court's ruling to discontinue using COTC in its name. In 2003, the founder of the original COTC, Matthew Hale, was arrested for soliciting an undercover FBI informant to kill Judge Lefkow. In 2005, Hale was sentenced to a 40-year prison term. He later committed suicide. According to the ADL, the Creativity Movement has languished since Matt Hale's arrest in 2003, however some followers dispersed into other smaller groups.

[13] According to the Anti-Defamation League, Jason Tankersley, a former Hammerskin, created the Maryland Skinheads "as an offshoot of the Baltimore Eastern Hammerskins crew." Tankersley's vision was to unite skinheads throughout the State of Maryland and become more closely aligned with the Vinlander Social Club and Keystone State Skinheads (KSS) in Pennsylvania.

[14] The National Socialist Movement was founded in 1974 as the National Socialist American Workers Freedom Movement by Robert Brannen and Cliff Herrington, former members of the American Nazi Party before its decline. The group claims to be the largest and most active National Socialist organization in the United States.

[15] Erasing Hate. 2011. Bill Brummel Productions, Studio City (CA). Written, produced, and directed by Bill Brummel, the documentary first aired June 6, 2011 on MSNBC.

[16] Odinism is a type of Germanic neo-paganism, specifically focused on honoring Odin and other Norse deities in the pre-Christian religion of Scandinavia. The religion was favored in Nazi Germany. In 1998, SPLC reported in the *Intelligence Report* that an offshoot of Odinism was "drawing on images of fiercely proud, boar-hunting Norsemen and their white-skinned Aryan womenfolk (and) is increasingly taking root among skinheads, neo-Nazis and other white supremacists across the nation."

Angela King

[17] Non-racist skinheads or Skinheads Against Racial Prejudice (SHARPs) are popular and well-organized in many states, often with chapters in colleges and universities. Even though SHARPs follow a philosophy that opposes racism, their tactics can be as violent as racist skinheads.

[18] *The Turner Diaries: A Novel.* Andrew McDonald. 1978. Andrew McDonald is the pen name of William L Pierce, leader of the National Alliance. During the trial of Timothy McVeigh who was accused of bombing the Murrah Federal Building in Oklahoma City, evidence found that The Turner Diaries had provided the formula for making the explosives.

[19] Intelligence Report, Fall 2005.

[20] Pansexuality differs from bisexuality. Those who self-identify as pansexual may be attracted to men, women, or to other genders and sexual identities whether they fall within the male-female gender binary or not.

[21] The six founding members of Life After Hate are Sammy Rangel, Angela King, Arno Michaelis, Christian Picciolini, Tony McAleer, and Frank Meeink. The organization's website islifeafterhate.org.

Frank Meeink

[22] *Autobiography of a Recovering Skinhead.* The Frank Meeink Story as told to Jody M. Roy, Ph.D. 2009. Hawthorne Books & Literary Arts.

Arno Michaelis

[23] *My Life After Hate.* Arno Michaelis. La Prense De LAH. Copyright 2010 Arno Michaelis/ Life After Hate.

[24] Deathers are those who think the Obama administration is lying about Osama Bin Laden being killed on May 2, 2011 and that the announcement was concocted for political purposes.

[25] A townhaller is one who is easily turned against the establishment through fear mongering and partisan rhetoric, who attends political gatherings not for the purpose of discussion, but to disrupt the proceedings.

What Makes Defectors' Stories So Important

[26] *Leaving the World of Hate: Life-Course Transitions and Self-Change.* Bryan F. Bubolz and Pete Simi. Published in *American Behavioral Scientist, June 1, 2015.*

[27] *Out of Hatred: The Awakening of a Former White Nationalist.* Eli Saslow. Doubleday. 2018.

[28] *Narratives of Childhood Adversity and Adolescent Misconduct as Journal of Research in Crime and Delinquency Precursors to Violent Extremism: A Life-Course Criminological Approach.* Pete Simi, Karyn Sporer, and Bryan F. Bubolz. Published in *Journal of Research in Crime and Delinquency,* February 2, 2016.

[29] *FOURBEARS: The Myths of Forgiveness. Sammy Joe Rangle. Copyright 2011 by Sammy Rangle. La Prensa de LAH.*

[30] *Romantic Violence: Memoirs of an American Skinhead.* Christian Picciolini. Goldmill Group. 2015.

[31] *White American Youth: My Descent into America's Most Violent Hate Movement – and How I Got Out.* Christian Picciolini. Hachette Books. 2017.

[32] *Addicted to Hate: Identity Residual Among Former White Supremacists.* American Sociological Review. 2017. Pete Simi, Kathleen Blee, Matthew DeMichele, and Steven Windisch.

Part Two

[33] The Hate Crime Statistics Act, passed by Congress in 1990, required that the FBI gather data about crimes "that manifest prejudice based on certain group characteristics." The 1990 law allowed the government to count the incidence of hate crimes based on **religion, race, national origin,** and **sexual orientation.**

[34] The Church Arson Prevention Act made it a crime "to deface, damage, or destroy religious real property, or interfere with a person's religious practice, in situations affecting interstate commerce." The act barred defacing, damaging, or destroying religious property because of the perceived race, color, or ethnicity of persons associated with the property.

[35] While conducting cultural competency training at a Washington State Judicial Conference, the chair of the Diversity Committee overseeing all courts in the state, who was also a member of the State Supreme Court, told all trainers, "You cannot expect judges to know all the laws."

[36] Georgia's hate crime statute was struck down by the Georgia Supreme Court in 2004.

[37] *Beyond Hate: White Power and Popular Culture (The Cultural Politics of Media and Popular Culture).* C. Richard King and David J. Leonard. Ashgate Publishing, 2014.

[38] Sources: *The Secret Recipe for Funding Hate Groups: 5 Simple Facts About Chick-fil-A,* An article posted on HuffPost Gay Voices, August 10, 2010; *Chick-Fil-A Donated Nearly $2 Million To Anti-Gay Groups In 2010, posted on EqualityMatters July 2, 2012;* Not So Fast: Chick-fil-A Hasn't Ended All Questionable Giving, *posted on The Advocate, January, 28 2013; and others.*

[39] SPLC identified 20 CI Groups in 2017: America's Promise Ministries (Sandpoint, Idaho); Christian America Ministries (Greensburg, Louisiana); Christian Revival Center (Harrison,

Arkansas); Church of Israel (Schell City, Missouri); Covenant Nation Church of the Lord Jesus Christ (Center Point, Alabama); Covenant People's Ministry (Brooks, Georgia); Divine International Church of the Web (Morton, Illinois); Divine Truth Ministries (Statewide, Arkansas); Divine Truth Ministries * (Bainbridge, Ohio); Euro Folk Radio (Chicago, Illinois); Fellowship of God's Covenant People (Union, Kentucky); Kingdom Identity Ministries (Harrison, Arkansas); Mission to Israel (Scottsbluff, Nebraska); Non-Universal Teaching Ministries/Christogenea (Panama City, Florida); Our Place Fellowship (Colville, Washington); Sacred Truth Publishing & Ministries (Mountain City, Tennessee); Scriptures for America Worldwide Ministries (Laporte, Colorado); Truth in History (Owasso, Oklahoma); Yahushua Dual Seed Christian Identity Ministry (Livingston, Texas); Yahweh's Truth (Linwood, Michigan). The one group no longer listed by SPLC doesn't necessarily mean its former members have suddenly found compassion.

[40] As this book is being prepared for publication, the case of Jussie Smolette has been in news headlines. In January 2019, Smolett, a black, gay actor featured in the TV program *Empire*, reported to Chicago Police he was the victim of a hate crime in which he was beaten by two black men who, he said, also placed a noose around his neck. He was later arrested for allegedly staging the assault as a publicity stunt. Smolett has denied the allegations.

[41] The New Black Panther Party is not to be misconstrued as part of the now-defunct Black Panther Party, which despite violent gunfights ending in the death of BPP members in Los Angeles and Chicago, was never identified as a hate group. The BPP also gained a national reputation for creating localized community service programs, including health care clinics, free breakfasts for children, educational experiences, tuberculosis testing, legal aid, transportation assistance, ambulance service, and the manufacture and distribution of free shoes to poor people. BPP operatives also forged positive working relationships with elected officials, corporate leaders, and other community groups before the group disbanded in the late 1970s.

[42] Cracker is a colloquial term used indiscriminately and pejoratively in reference to white people.

[43] Slavery was implicitly permitted in the original Constitution through provisions such as Article I, Section 2, Clause 3, commonly known as the Three-Fifths Compromise, which detailed how each slave state's enslaved population would be factored into its total population count for the purposes of apportioning seats in the United States House of Representatives and direct taxes among the states. Though the Thirteenth Amendment formally abolished slavery throughout the United States, factors such as Black Codes, white supremacist violence, and selective enforcement of statutes continued to subject some black Americans to involuntary labor, particularly in the South.

[44] *The New Jim Crow: Mass Incarceration in the Age of Colorblindness.* The New Press. 2010, 2012.

Index

Page numbers with a *t* indicate a table; *n* indicates an endnote.

About the Author ,

Lonnie Lusardo, served as a reporter for a now-defunct metropolitan daily newspaper in Connecticut from 1973 to 1979. He became a freelance correspondent in 1979, writing for 35 local, regional, and national publications. His reporting on civil rights and human rights was nominated for journalistic excellence in 1985.

In 1991, after receiving a graduate degree in Education/Human Resources Development from Seattle University, Lonnie created The Diversity Collaborative, a veteran owned cultural competency and management training firm conducting diversity and inclusion training for government agencies and Fortune 500 companies. He became a popular keynote speaker and workshop presenter at regional and national conferences, colleges and universities, and for community groups experiencing white supremacist violence. Lonnie's newest workshop, The Truth About Hate Groups and Hate Crimes, is presented across the U.S. to consistently outstanding reviews.

Lonnie is known for personal candor and facilitating interactive learning experiences. A self-acknowledged "recovering racist," he developed a reengerized awareness and respect for ethnic and religious cultures during four years in the U.S. Navy and as a student at Boston University in the 1970s and through close personal relationships.

Lonnie started exploring the lives of white supremacists and other extremists after being profiled in the book *White Men Challenging Racism: 35 Personal Stories*, published by Duke University Press in 2003. Following dozens of interviews with former neo-Nazis and white supremacists, his research shifted from profiling people to examining the U.S. government's response to organized hate groups, leading to Part Two of this book.

Lonnie has also studied how other governments respond to cultural differences. In 1997-1998, Lonnie interviewed members of President Nelson Mandela's cabinet and leaders of community organizations in that country, to determine the effects of the move from apartheid to democracy. Lonnie conducted a similar project in Australia and New Zealand in 2012 to determine the extent to which indigenous populations have been regarded by historically white-led governments in those countries. He often incorporates that research into his training and presentations.

Made in the USA
Monee, IL
30 May 2024